PONTIAC
AND THE
INDIAN
UPRISING

GREAT LAKES BOOKS

A complete listing of the books in this series can be found at the back of this volume.

Philip P. Mason, Editor
Department of History, Wayne State University

Dr. Charles K. Hyde, Associate Editor
Department of History, Wayne State University

PONTIAC
AND THE
INDIAN
UPRISING

Howard H. Peckham

Foreword by John C. Dann

WAYNE STATE UNIVERSITY PRESS   DETROIT

Library of Congress Cataloging-in-Publication Data
Peckham, Howard Henry, 1910–
    Pontiac and the Indian Uprising / by Howard H. Peckham : foreword
by John C. Dann.
        p. cm.
    "Originally published in 1947 by Princeton University Press"—T.p.
verso.
    Includes bibliographical references and index.
    ISBN 0-8143-2469-X (pbk. : alk. paper)
    1. Pontiac's Conspiracy, 1763–1765.   2. Pontiac, Ottawa Chief,
d. 1769.   I. Title.
E83.76.P4   1994
973.2′7′092—dc20
[B]   93–36864

Affectionately Inscribed to
STEPHEN AND ANGELA,
my little savages

Contents

quesne. Ottawas at Braddock's defeat. Assist
Montcalm at Lake George. First reference
to Pontiac in a contemporary manuscript,
1757. Grant's defeat. Flight of the French.
Attempt to relieve Fort Niagara. Ottawas
counsel with Croghan at Fort Pitt. Pro-
English Ottawas move to Lake Erie. Pontiac's journey to Fort Pitt.

Rogers dispatched to Detroit. Meeting with
Ottawas on Lake Erie shore. Croghan paci-
fies Indians. Captain Campbell and life in
Detroit. Amherst's attitude toward Indians.
Senecas carry war belt to Lakes tribes.

Gladwin sent to Detroit, 1761. Angelique
Cuillerier appears. Johnson presides over
formal council. Reply of Ottawas. Trade
regulations and price list. Campbell's fears.
Garrisoning the other posts.

Detroit Indians discover real British policy.
Gladwin returns as commandant of fort.
Secret council at Ottawa village, 1762. Message of the Delaware Prophet. Grievances
of the Indians. International law at work.
Evidence of French instigation. Pontiac's
role.

Council on the Ecorse River. Pontiac's relation of the Delaware Prophet's gospel. Conference with Gladwin, May 1, 1763. Council
of war at Potawatomi village. Identity of
Gladwin's informant. Defense measures.

from Mackinac. Pontiac reproved at general
council. Attempt on the sloop *Michigan*.
Pontiac attends mass, issues bills of credit,
and wins help of young Frenchmen. Mc-
Dougall escapes. Wasson butchers Campbell. Pontiac's camp shelled. Potawatomies
make peace. Fire rafts tried against ships.
Replies from Illinois. Arrival of Dalyell.

Attempt to surprise Pontiac's camp. Am-
bush at Parent's Creek and costly retreat.
Meaning of victory for Pontiac. Progress
of Bouquet's expedition toward Fort Pitt.
Attack at Edge Hill. Indians of Western
Pennsylvania lose the offensive.

Raid along Dunning's Creek. Situation at
Carlisle. Murders up Juniata River. Shawnee raid on Greenbrier. Differences between
Virginia and Pennsylvania militias. Butchery at Wyoming. The Paxton Boys. Effect
of war on civilians.

Wreck of the *Michigan* and Montresor's
fortified camp. Massacre on the Niagara
portage. Johnson's failure. Amherst proposes use of smallpox against Indians. Gladwin's promotion.

Attack on the *Huron* repelled. Wabbicomigot talks peace with Gladwin. Chippewas
and an Ottawa faction follow suit. Pontiac's
last grand council. Messages from Illinois.
Pontiac's letter to Gladwin. Casualties of

the war. Wilkins' expedition battered by
storm. Amherst's departure.

Pontiac's new village on the Maumee.
Council at Fort de Chartres with De Villiers. Johnson's congress at Niagara. Bradstreet's punitive expedition. Pontiac meets
Morris up the Maumee. Delawares and
Shawnees deceive Bradstreet. Bouquet's expedition into Ohio.

Pontiac's plotting. Charlot Kaske's efforts
to obtain French support. Ross at Fort de
Chartres. Pontiac encounters Fraser. Coun-
cil at the fort. Pontiac ready for peace.
Sinnott's mission. Croghan's party attacked.
Pontiac submits to Croghan conditionally.
They go to Detroit.

Stabbing of an Illinois chief. Pontiac escorted to Fort Ontario. Council proceedings with Johnson. Jealousy of Pontiac.

Pontiac's new Anglophilism. He testifies in
Cuillerier murder case. Council proposed at
Lower Shawnee Town. Pontiac's exile from
his village.

Pontiac visits in St. Louis. Peoria council.
Assassination in Cahokia. Confusion over
burial place. Behavior of Peorias and of
Wilkins. Revenge for Pontiac's death. His
descendants.

CONTENTS

MAPS AND ILLUSTRATIONS

Foreword to the
Great Lakes Books Edition

THE PUBLICATION OF Howard H. Peckham's *Pontiac and the Indian Uprising* in 1947 was universally acclaimed by reviewers. Carl Bridenbaugh characterized the book as "definitive" in the *William and Mary Quarterly*. The description is just as appropriate today, almost fifty years later, as it was then.

Pontiac and the Indian Uprising was and is an exceptional book—the first modern scholarly biography of one of the towering figures in Native American history, all the more remarkable in that Pontiac himself left no written records in his own hand. What made the book a particularly daunting project was the fact that the subject had previously been exhaustively "done" with brilliant success and the complete satisfaction of readers and scholars alike by no less than Francis Parkman, who not only was a literary craftsman of the highest order, but a meticulous scholar. How could anyone improve upon the master of American colonial frontier history, or dare to do so?

Parkman's *History of the Conspiracy of Pontiac* (1851) and his entire series of volumes documenting the military conflicts of the seventeenth and eighteenth centuries was a bestseller when published, and remained basic historical reading well into the present century. Parkman wrote for a generation of Americans which was intrigued and mystified by the arrowheads and burial sites frequently unearthed on family farms, whose grandparents told bloodcurdling stories of Indian "savages" they had actually seen in their youth, and who grew up under the romantic spell of Cooper's Leather-Stocking Tales. The drama and mystery of Natty Bumppo, Chingachgook, and Uncas were more than equaled in Parkman's memorable descriptions of Indian leaders and frontier traders, of heroic and devious French and British military commanders as they fought an epic campaign for mastery of the American continent. Parkman's works, and the research of his contemporaries—George Bancroft, William Leete Stone, Lyman Draper, Henry R. Schoolcraft, Edmund B. O'Callaghan, and others—made the "Old Frontier" of the eastern half of the country the most exciting field of history for several generations of book collectors, readers, and writers of American history.

In a sense, the inspiration and research methods of these pioneering historians eventually consigned their published works to the top, unread shelf of the bookcase. Parkman and his contemporaries themselves had begun to tap source materials in European archives and American attics, but the process became far more widespread and systematic in the decades after their passing. Lyman Draper, as director of the Wisconsin Historical Society, assembled a remarkable collection of private papers documenting the eighteenth-century Allegheny and Ohio frontiers. Starting in the 1880s, the Public Archives of Canada began to systematically copy, calendar, and publish sources of the French and British colonial periods in European archives. This example was followed with increasingly professional editing and publishing by historical societies and archives in Wisconsin, Illinois, Michigan, Pennsylvania, and New York, making available crucial data on the 1760s—papers of Sir William Johnson, Henry Bouquet, Henry Gladwyn—sources largely unavailable to Parkman. In the 1920s, the Clements and Huntington libraries came into existence, providing scholars with unequaled resources on British military administration in eighteenth-century America in the papers of Abercromby, Loudoun, Gage, and Clinton. George Croghan's diary and papers were uncovered at the Historical Society of Pennsylvania in the late 1930s, and the vast correspondence of Jeffrey Amherst was made available on microfilm and indexed in the early 1940s.

Howard Peckham was at the right place at the right time to take full advantage of the situation. Following graduate work at the University of Michigan, and a brief newspaper career, he accepted and held the job as Curator of Manuscripts at the Clements Library from 1935 to 1945. In 1937, after the estate settlement of William L. Clements (1861–1934), the Gage Papers were delivered to the library Clements had founded fifteen years earlier, and Howard Peckham had the enviable task of cataloging and arranging them. The Gage Papers are a remarkable collection—the single most important documentary survival of the late American colonial period—and they include not only the general's papers themselves but several hundred letters and documents which General Amherst had turned over to Gage when he took command of the British Army on the American continent in 1763. They were full of crucial and previously inaccessible information on Pontiac and the ill-fated rebellion which bears his name.

In 1939, Clements Library director, Randolph G. Adams, created an exhibition on Pontiac, drawing upon a number of the exciting new finds which had surfaced in the Gage/Amherst Papers, and in an accompanying bulletin he invited scholars to make a new study of the Indian leader. Howard Peckham, encouraged by both Adams and Carl Van Doren (who was then in the process of completing his Pulitzer-Prize-winning *Secret History of the American Revolution* [1941] from new material in the Clinton Papers), accepted the challenge with enthusiasm. In addition to the Gage and Amherst manuscripts, the Clements Library also owned the Jehu Hay diary, letters of Lieutenant James MacDonald, and the James Stirling letterbook, invaluable sources on the siege of Detroit. Like most great historical works—especially for a scholar with family responsibilities, a full-time job, and a meticulous, judicious temperament—it was a long but rewarding project of six to seven years between commencement and completion.

The present-day reader must keep in mind the now distant era in which *Pontiac and the Indian Uprising* was written—during World War II and immediately thereafter. Native American people and those who write about them have developed strongly felt sensitivities to phrases used throughout the book: "redmen," "savages," "aboriginies," or pejorative descriptions of their culture as "inferior," their methods of warfare as "treacherous"—but these were commonplace among all American Indian scholars at the time. Our modern world has become far more conscious of the environmental devastation and inhumane aspects of Western culture to be as confident as we were in the 1940s that Pontiac's defeat was a victory for "civilization." But with *Pontiac and the Indian Uprising*, these criticisms are largely matters of semantics and appearances, not substance. The book, far from being a condemnation, is a highly respectful tribute to one of the great men of American history—a charismatic, visionary, pragmatic, and very human leader— just as fascinating but far more real than the mythic Pontiac of Parkman.

Scholarship and the discovery of new source materials in the five decades since Peckham's book came out have added significantly to our understanding of the frontier world in which Pontiac lived. (See bibliographical note) A few additional letters and documents relating to the Indian uprising and British military response have surfaced and been published: one more volume of William Johnson Papers was issued in 1957; additional Bouquet correspondence has been published by the Pennsylvania State Archives; and the orderly books and surveyors journal for the Bouquet Expedition (originals now at the Clements Library) have been edited with meticulous detail by Edward G. Williams. Nicholas Wainright's superb biography of George Croghan and John Shy's brilliant study of British Army policy help to illuminate some of the basic external causes of the rebellion. John Cuneo wrote a celebrated biography of Robert Rogers, not only a participant in the military campaign, but author of *Ponteach* (1766), a strange but interesting drama which made Pontiac its primary character.

A great deal of fine historical work has deepened all aspects of our understanding of Native American culture. Two recently published overviews provide insight and interpretation of the causes of Pontiac's actions within the larger context of Indian cultural changes. Gregory Dowd convincingly argues that both the Delaware prophet Neolin and war chief Pontiac were part of a nativist revival movement in which spiritual and secular elements coalesced and are impossible to separate or entirely understand today— lacking historical documentation of contacts and communication between Native American leaders themselves. Michael McConnell has shown that even at the height of Pontiac's rebellion, there was nothing approaching a unified Indian objective or strategy— each group of native participants reacted to its own particular grievances. There was a "rebellion," but it might be questionable to call it "Pontiac's" or to assume that it was carefully planned or organized in the modern sense.

Undoubtedly, a few more source materials on the Indian revolt of 1762–66 are yet to be uncovered. Future scholarship will certainly refine our understanding of the times, events, and personalities of this fascinating era of our history. But in the past five decades, no one has discovered any new fact of importance about Pontiac himself, or significantly altered the narrative of Pontiac's War so masterfully and engagingly written about by Howard Peckham in the present volume. The test of time, which has relegated many of the great historical works of the past to footnotes, has elevated *Pontiac and the Indian Uprising* to the ranks of a true and timeless classic of Native American historical literature.

John C. Dann
Director, Clements Library

Foreword

THE MOST FORMIDABLE Indian resistance that the English-speaking people ever faced was set in motion by an astute and purposeful Ottawa chief on the Detroit River. This was Pontiac. He epitomized the gathering resentment of the native to the invaders. With his defeat one era in Indian history ended and another began.

Who was Pontiac? is a fair question from an American today. After all, Pontiac has been dead for 178 years. The enemy he fought no longer controls the territory he tried to wrest from them. His French friends have been absorbed into Canadian or American nationality. His tribe has diminished and no longer inhabits the region it once knew intimately. The peculiar momentum of a superior culture, intensified by the attraction of the land's unbelievable resources, was irresistible. The savages were pushed aside or rolled over. And yet the problem Pontiac posed—or rather inflamed with his burning arrows—remains on our national conscience. True, it was erased by our application of force, but that victory was never a solution. We are not yet agreed on the centuries-old question of what to do about the Indian.

The right of conquest under international law did not dispose of the ethical problem, which cannot be dismissed, I think, merely because the Indians behaved at times like savages. The practice by white men of buying vast tracts of land for insignificant sums, of forcing removal of the Indians, of replacing intractable chiefs with compliant ones, of failing to keep their treaties, invited

⟨ xx ⟩

the reprisals that came. The French suffered least because
their policy was more one of infiltration and camaraderie,
than of extensive settlement and aloofness. The Indians
early recognized the difference in aim and temperament
between the French and British. Resistance to the latter
grew with every expansion westward. It reached its climax
early in 1763 when France surrendered Canada to the
British and Louisiana to the Spanish. Here was a moment
for the Indians to seize if they would turn the destiny
of a continent. One savage was alert to the grave opportunity.

What manner of man was it who dared oppose himself
to this fulfillment of progress and bring the whole
European imperialistic broil to a stop? How could he lead
four tribes to war and inspire the revolt of thrice that
number? Why was he able to capture nine British forts,
force the abandonment of a tenth, and besiege two more?
Who was this savage that defied a general who had just
won for his king a domain twelve times the size of
England? What local circumstances motivated and encouraged him? And finally, why did he fail?

Intrigued by the man and in search of the answers to
these questions, I undertook this investigation of the life
and times of Pontiac. The difficulties of writing his biography were threefold. First, Pontiac left no collection of
papers, for the very good reason that he could not write.
Nevertheless, his archives are not totally bare; we have a
few letters of his which he dictated, some land deeds
marked by him, and several of his speeches taken down by
his white listeners. Secondly, all of his contemporaries
who wrote about him were also his enemies, rendering it
impossible to obtain an objective or rounded picture of
the man. They were military officers who were fighting
him, Indian agents who opposed his policies, or traders
whose business was upset by his activities. Thirdly,

legends grew up about him even before he died and increased rapidly thereafter, making it necessary to weigh all evidence carefully.

Despite the scarcity and unsatisfactory nature of the material, the challenge of the man and of the fact that there is no adequate biography of him attracted me to undertake this life. I am not, however, the first to consider writing such a biography. Lewis Cass was planning in 1821 to write a life of Pontiac, but apparently did not proceed beyond the stage of gathering material. Nor must I omit Chief Tus-saw, a descendant of Pontiac, who was reported in 1825 to be dictating a biography of his forbear. It was never printed and probably was never finished.

Up to 1850 only brief sketches of Pontiac a page or two in length had appeared in the two books of Indian biography written by B. B. Thatcher and Samuel Gardner Drake. Francis Parkman's classic *History of the Conspiracy of Pontiac*, published in 1851, surpassed everything previously written on Pontiac's War in wealth of detail and readable style, yet in no sense is his monumental history a biography of Pontiac.

It is not necessary to mention the writers since 1851 who have produced sketches of Pontiac, because all of them have drawn their information from Parkman. The indefatigable Benson J. Lossing and Dr. Cyrus Thomas, however, did add details of birthplace, birth date, and parentage which Parkman apparently avoided. Randolph G. Adams culled the essential facts from these later writers for his brief sketch in the *Dictionary of American Biography*.

Important new source material on Pontiac has become available only in recent years. It enables us not only to understand the Ottawa chief better, but to trace his movements with some continuity. Fortunately, I have been able to examine all the written sources used by Parkman and to consult all the material since discovered. I have been helped as well by the progress made since 1851 by archaeologists, ethno-historians, and scholars of Great Lakes history.

In the work now offered to the reader, I have made a deliberate effort to print in full all of Pontiac's known letters and speeches, save for his lengthy discourse on the Delaware Prophet, since they are so few in number and so difficult to find. I have not attempted to "rewrite Parkman," to offer a history of the French and Indian War or of the Ottawa nation, or even to retell the story of the siege of Detroit, except from the Indians' point of view. I have tried to stick closely to my topic and avoid the omnipresent temptation to digress into tangent subjects on which material was more plentiful. Perhaps I should add that I have not made the familiar comparison of Pontiac with Tecumseh or with any other chief. Such comparisons seem pointless, particularly when Indians of different generations are weighed together. Moreover, for a comparative study of Pontiac and his contemporaries to have any value, I should have to make as thorough an investigation of the latter as I have made of the former.

No picture of Pontiac will be found in this book, because none made from life is known. Even verbal descriptions of the chief are disappointingly meager.

Explanation of certain small points of style may be owing the reader. I have called the French-speaking inhabitants of the Great Lakes region Frenchmen, rather than Canadians or Canadiens. In this century we usually think of Canada as limited to its present boundaries, and the term Canadian properly includes English-speaking people as well. I have also made a distinction between the British and the English colonists in America, reserving the former word for soldiers and government officials acting over here for the mother country, and using

English as a broader term in its linguistic sense to cover all English-speaking people in America. By this device I was freed of using the word American, with its attendant confusions before 1776.

The names of Indian tribes that I have used may not be the designations most familiar to all readers. My defense for my choices is that I have followed the form and spelling favored by the Smithsonian Institution's *Handbook of Indians North of Mexico*, edited by F. W. Hodge. Those forms are standard usage among archaeologists and anthropologists. I have, however, added s or es to make a plural of tribal names, contrary to Hodge's practice.

In the long course of preparing this volume several persons and institutions have laid me under deep gratitude for their expert counsel and generous service. Their names will be found in the section entitled Acknowledgments.

H. H. P.

——————— ⟨⟨⟨⟨◊⟩⟩⟩⟩ ———————

1

His Background

Down an unblazed trail, out of an unknown region came the Ottawa nation of Indians. By the time white men began to report on them, they had developed a distinctive character. Long before the birth of Pontiac they had achieved savage eminence and then had declined in prestige. The advent of the white man affected their way of life very early, but his continued contact hardly touched their character.

With the Chippewas and Potawatomies the Ottawas seem once to have lived as one nation along the northeastern Atlantic coast, although they must have reached that location from the far Northwest. They migrated westward toward Lake Huron, probably in search of fresh game regions. When Frenchmen first encountered them early in the seventeenth century, the original stem had split into three branches. The Chippewas were living around Lake Superior, the Potawatomies had moved into the lower peninsula of Michigan, and the Ottawas inhabited the islands in the northern curve of Lake Huron and the region around Lake Nipissing.

Although the Ottawas and Potawatomies still called the Chippewas "Elder Brothers," they maintained only the loosest kind of association, termed "the three fires." Each tribe practiced a different economy. The Chippewas were primarily a hunting people, and the Potawatomies were mainly agriculturists. The Ottawas hunted and raised a few crops, but for the most part preferred to act as traders, or middlemen, in imitation of their powerful southern neighbors, the Hurons. Indeed, circumstances allowed them to succeed the Hurons for a time.

Living around Georgian Bay, the Hurons supplied the French on the lower St. Lawrence River with the beaver skins and other pelts which the Europeans prized, in exchange for the manufactured trade goods that revolutionized the stone age culture of the Indians. Shrewd and wily, the Hurons had early set themselves up as middlemen, obtaining furs from the tribes to the north and west of them in return for their own corn and fish and some of the marvelous goods of the white man. Then they transported the furs down the Ottawa River in a brigade of pack-laden canoes each summer to sell for more goods to be taken back to Huronia. On the rim of this trade, the Ottawas hunted furs themselves and bought them from distant tribes to sell to the Hurons.

This pleasant economic circulation was congested, however, by the efforts of the Iroquois, in modern slang, to "muscle in" on the Huron "racket." The Iroquois had been supplying furs to the Dutch on the Hudson River. Unfortunately, the five nations of the Iroquois Confederation—Mohawks, Oneidas, Cayugas, Onondagas, and Senecas—occupied the relatively small territory between the Hudson and Niagara Rivers, which they soon denuded of beaver and other valuable fur-bearing animals. The tribes living to the east of them were trading directly with the British settlements in New England or with the French. The tribes to the west of them were satellites of the Hurons, revolving in their economic orbit. By 1640 the beaver supply for the Iroquois trade was exhausted, and unless they were willing to revert to the standard of living existing before the white man appeared, they had to obtain a new source of supply. The Northwest, monopolized by the Hurons, was their only hope.

The Iroquois eyed the Huron position enviously, de-

siring to play middleman too. Yet because the Hurons
were a much larger nation than all the Iroquois together,
the latter sought to obtain furs from them first by treaty.
The French, however, injected themselves into this diplomatic maneuvering to protect their own interests. They
did not want the Hurons to divert any of their furs to
the Iroquois and hence to the Dutch. The governors of
New France instructed the Jesuits and other missionaries
among the Hurons to prevent such a treaty, and the
patriotic fathers obliged, knowing that French missions
were served by French trade.

Failing of peaceful measures, the Iroquois next tried
"hijacking" the Huron canoe brigades as they descended
the Ottawa River loaded with furs. The Hurons retaliated
with bloody raids into the Iroquois country. As a result
the trade was so upset that the French called a peace
parley at Montreal in 1645. A commercial treaty was
patched up by which the Hurons and another northern
tribe were to sell some furs directly to the Iroquois. But
in 1646 the Hurons carried all their furs, the greatest cargo
yet obtained, directly to Montreal and ignored their
treaty commitments.

The Iroquois were not of a nature to suffer this insult
meekly. For two years they fumed and plotted and raided
and grew desperate. Then in 1648 a thousand of them
slipped away westward to attack the Hurons in their own
towns. In surprise assaults they sacked two villages and
started the Hurons on a flight of panic. The momentum
of their flight and the imminence of the Iroquois carried
the Ottawas and Potawatomies to the west side of Lake
Michigan. The long trek and a winter of famine proved
disastrous to the Hurons. One band of them, who found
refuge among the Eries on the south side of Lake Erie,
persuaded that nation to deliver a revengeful blow against
the enemy. The Iroquois, their bloodthirstiness aroused,

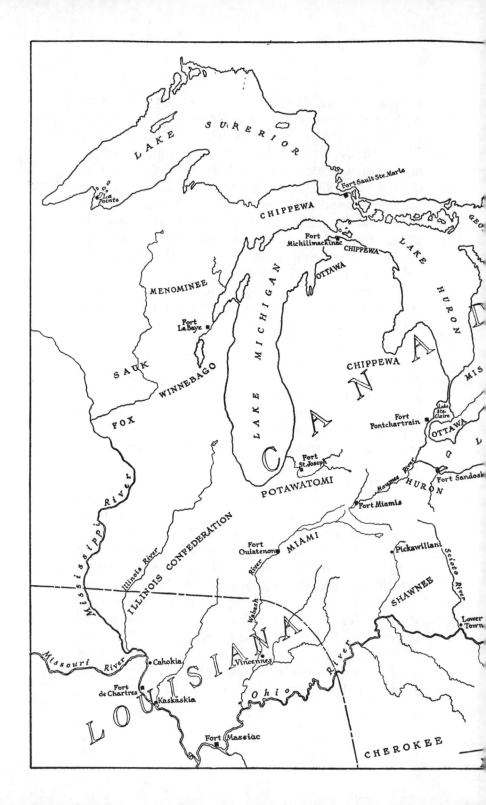

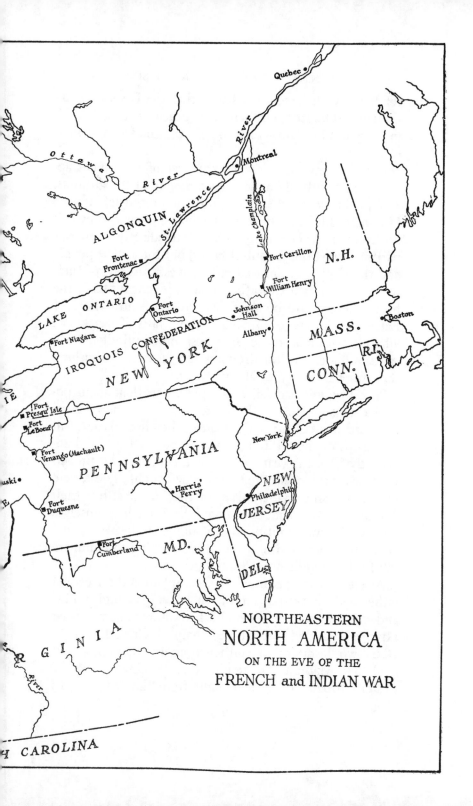

NORTHEASTERN
NORTH AMERICA
ON THE EVE OF THE
FRENCH and INDIAN WAR

retaliated with so severe a stroke that the Eries were annihilated. The Iroquois then made peace with the French in 1653 and looked forward to enjoying the fruits of their conquest.

Yet the very next year a great fleet of fur canoes appeared at Montreal—under the command of the Ottawas.

They had cannily stepped into the breach left by the Hurons and foiled the Iroquois, who were enraged by this unexpected development. They immediately sent war parties against the distant Ottawas, but those alert people and the Chippewas moved farther westward out of their reach. They migrated to the Mississippi, encountered the hostile Sioux, and bounced back to the south shore of Lake Superior and eventually to the Straits of Mackinac. The Ottawas held on to their position of middleman in the fur trade, and the Iroquois fell back to ambushing their fur fleets on the Ottawa River.

The Iroquois had failed completely in their main objective of supplanting the Hurons in the monopoly of the northwestern fur trade. Instead they had placed it in the hands of the Ottawas, who, in 1683 at least, and apparently for some years before that, supplied the French with two-thirds of all the beaver they bought. These were prosperous and mighty years for the Ottawas, but their dominance could not last long. The French themselves pushed westward and began obtaining the beaver at first hand from the hunting tribes, thus tending to eliminate the Indian middleman.

As early as 1615 Samuel de Champlain and a Recollet father had visited the Huron villages on Georgian Bay, and missions were soon established among them. Other explorers traveled through the chain of Great Lakes. In 1641 two Jesuit priests preached to the Chippewas at Sault Ste. Marie. Other Jesuits were working among the western tribes during their flight from the Iroquois. In

1665 Father Claude Allouez established a mission on Chequamegon Bay, Lake Superior. Three years later Father Jacques Marquette started a mission at Sault Ste. Marie, and in 1671 followed some remnant Hurons down to Mackinac Straits, where on the present site of St. Ignace, he began the mission of that name.

On the fourteenth of June, 1671, at the Sault occurred an ominous ceremony which the Indians who witnessed it did not comprehend. In the presence of three Jesuits, sixteen other Frenchmen, and several hundred Indians, the Sieur de St. Lusson solemnly took possession for France of Lakes Superior and Huron and "of all other countries, streams, lakes, and rivers contiguous and adjacent, as well discovered as to be discovered which are bounded on one side by the seas of the North and of the West, and on the other side by the South Sea [Pacific Ocean], and in all their length and breadth."[1]

This fabulous claim ignored, of course, the standing claims of Spain and Great Britain to this territory. And all three European powers ignored the fact that the Indians owned and occupied the region. A century later Pontiac was to deny that the French owned any of the Great Lakes region except the particular spots where they had settlements.

To strengthen the growing trading post and mission at St. Ignace, Fort de Buade was added there about 1690. France's new interest lay farther south, however. In 1691 Fort St. Joseph was established up the river of that name close to modern Niles, Michigan, in the heart of the Potawatomi and Miami country. The garrisons of both forts were withdrawn by royal orders before the end of the century.

The last commandant at Fort de Buade, Antoine de la

[1] Winsor, *The Pageant of Saint Lusson, Sault Ste. Marie, 1671*, pp. 24-26; *Dictionary of American History*, v, 35.

Mothe Cadillac, wanted to establish another settlement down on the Detroit River. He saw the riches to be gained by tapping the trade of the tribes living south of the Straits of Mackinac, and he was anxious to get away from the Jesuits, who bothered him, and get ahead of the English merchants who were looking across the mountains toward the western Great Lakes. With a large party he planted his settlement in 1701 and erected a stockaded fort and village called Fort Pontchartrain. Then he invited the Indians at Mackinac and to the west of him to settle around his new post, where they could trade their furs and be supplied with goods and weapons. Bands of Ottawas, Chippewas, and Hurons accepted his bidding and set up new villages along the Detroit River. A few Potawatomies and Miamies came over from the St. Joseph River. Some Foxes, with a few Sauks and Mascoutens, arrived from Green Bay.

The new settlement had administrative difficulties that need not concern us, and Indian troubles which foreshadowed coming events. The initial harmony among the surrounding bands was unstable at best. In 1706 the Ottawas attacked the Miamies and Hurons, after hearing that the latter intended to ambush them. This outbreak occurred during Cadillac's absence and resulted in considerable bloodshed, including the death of the Recollet missionary. On his return Cadillac made the mistake of promising the head of the Ottawa chief to the Miamies and then pardoning the Ottawas. In resentment the Miamies killed three Frenchmen, and Cadillac had to march against their principal village in 1708. Although they were forced to submit, their ill feeling toward the French increased until it gave serious trouble later. Shortly they removed to the headwaters of the Maumee River and settled on the portage of the Little Wabash. One band migrated far down the Wabash, near the Ohio River, and invited English traders to visit them.

⟨ 8 ⟩

The Foxes and their friends from Green Bay were not liked by the other tribes, and in the winter of 1711-1712 fighting broke out. The new commandant, who had just replaced Cadillac, favored the Ottawas and Hurons and permitted them to use Fort Pontchartrain for protection. The Foxes built a stockaded village a little distance to the northward and were subjected to a siege by their enemies. After nineteen days of fatal hunger and thirst, the surviving Foxes tried to escape by a sortie at night. They were overtaken and slaughtered. The remnants of this tribe, that had remained at Green Bay, blamed the French for this annihilation of their comrades and in future years they gave the French much trouble. Only four Indian villages remained along the Detroit River: Ottawa, Chippewa, Huron, and Potawatomi.

The Jesuits, who had been active at St. Ignace but were excluded by Cadillac from Detroit, had never forgiven him for enticing away their potential converts and wrecking the northern post. They were now soliciting the governor of Canada to reestablish a fort at the straits. There were economic and military arguments as well for maintaining a stronghold in that region. The Indians north of Lake Superior were carrying their furs to the British at Hudson Bay, and the whole region was losing its pro-French sympathies for want of a headquarters under the French flag. In 1715 Fort Michilimackinac was constructed on the south shore of the straits, at the northern tip of the lower peninsula of Michigan, the site of modern Mackinaw City. In 1717 a fort was erected at the south end of Green Bay and was commonly called Fort La Baye. The next year the post at Chequamegon Bay was reestablished on Madeline Island as Fort La Pointe.

With the Great Lakes securely under its control, France was not long in determining to connect its colony in Louisiana with Canada, thus fencing off the back country of the British colonies and limiting them to the

Atlantic seaboard. A chain of forts was gradually built from Detroit southwestward. A fort was raised among the Miamies at modern Fort Wayne, Indiana, before 1712, and in the next year La Salle's old Fort St. Louis on the Illinois River (near Utica) was repaired and re-garrisoned. Fort Ouiatenon was started on the Wabash, just below modern Lafayette, Indiana, about 1719. The next year saw Fort de Chartres completed on the Missis-sippi, between the mouths of the Missouri and Kaskaskia, near modern Prairie du Rocher, Illinois.

More forts were planned, but the situation as it was about 1720 is the object of our attention for the moment. At this date, then, French troops were garrisoned in nine posts in the Lakes country: Michilimackinac, La Baye, and La Pointe on the north; St. Joseph and Detroit op-posite each other in the lower Michigan peninsula; Miamis at the head of the Maumee and Ouiatenon on the Wabash, St. Louis on the Illinois and Chartres on the Mississippi. These were all extensions from France's settlements along the St. Lawrence and at Niagara.

The effect of these contacts upon the Indians was subtle and far-reaching. Aside from the new and engulfing market for furs created by the white man, his culture was so much richer than that of the red man, of course, that new appetites and demands were created among the Indians. Some of the elements of the Frenchman's ma-terial culture consisted simply of improvements over the Indian's. Thus the French had steel knives and axes while the Indians had stone; the former had brass kettles, the latter clay; the French had steel needles, the Indians used bone; the former had various and superior fabrics, and the savages had only furs and hides and rush mats. Even the French Catholic religion was understandable to the Indians, because they had their mysterious deities, made prayers, and believed in immortality. But the white men also introduced four novelties: guns, liquor, horses and several new communicable diseases.[2]

Muskets and powder at first appeared to be a marvelous gift to the Indians. Their hunting became more effective and less arduous than it had been with the bow and arrow. They acquired more furs, which they would trade for more manufactured goods and thus raise their standard of living. Guns also made them more formidable to their enemies who had not yet obtained this boon. Yet at the same time this new weapon rendered the red man more and more dependent on the white. The bow and arrow fell into disuse, and new generations lost their skill for lack of practice. The gun became the main support and protection of the household and of the village. But the Indians could not make a gun or perform even the simplest repair work; they could not mold lead or make powder. The gunsmiths at the forts were almost the most important white men in the wilderness. The Indians could never cut themselves off completely from contact with these artisans, no matter how much they might wish to be free of the white invader.

Liquor was never a boon to the Indians. It gave momentary pleasure, of course, by satisfying a taste which it had created. Like all uncivilized peoples, the Indians soon drank to excess. Brandy was the principal liquor traded by the French. It robbed the savages of their industry and endurance. It put them into a condition to be cheated by traders. To buy it the Indians sometimes traded their whole catch of furs, and after a drunken debauch had nothing to show for their winter's work. It caused them to commit crimes and outrages against the whites as well as their own people which they regretted in sober moments. The chiefs viewed it as a curse

[2] The white man's gifts to the Indians are discussed in detail in Wissler's *The American Indian.*

to their young braves and besought the traders and commandants to stop or limit the traffic. For short periods they were successful in limiting the sales, but they could never "stop up" the barrels. Responsible traders recognized the dangers of liquor, but as soon as they agreed among themselves to prohibit its sale, they shortly found themselves circumvented by unscrupulous traders who bootlegged liquor to the Indians and took their furs, which usually were owed to the more ethical traders for the past year's supplies.

The horse, though widely adopted by the plains Indians, was naturally less prized by the forest dwelling Algonquin and Iroquois of northeastern United States. On occasion a horse might be useful, or if stolen could be easily sold to another white man; but it was never utilized as a means of conveyance or as a draft animal. The Algonquins of the Lakes preferred their light, swift canoes.

The Indians were a comparatively healthy race before their contact with the white men. Presumably they had escaped the plagues and scourges that had swept over Europe every few centuries. Injuries were common, as also probably were disorders of the gastro-intestinal tract due to poor diet or improper preparation of food. Undernourishment and even famine were sometimes the lot of the Indians when bad weather or warfare disturbed their agriculture or their hunting. Mosquito-borne malaria was suffered, but the worst diseases were imported. Measles, smallpox, tuberculosis, and syphilis were "gifts" of the white man, dating from the arrival on the continent of the first sailors. Smallpox in particular, when once contracted, swept through villages leaving but few survivors. These diseases often spread far ahead of the white explorers and settlers, and became especially virulent among a race that had acquired no immunity to them. The Indians had their own "physicians" in the form of medicine men, who worked with incantations, hypnotic suggestion, and a few helpful herbs.[3]

By the end of the second decade of the eighteenth century the Ottawas had grown used to having Frenchmen among them seeking furs. Even the Iroquois wars belonged to the memories of their oldest men. The Ottawas had lost their position of minor-producing middlemen and now had to hunt beaver like the other tribes. As a result of their long contact with white men, they had also lost their old and cruder way of living. Imported goods had become a large part of their culture. For this reason the Frenchman was solidly planted in his strongholds and trading centers in the Great Lakes region, affecting the Indian way of life for better and for worse.

As a nation the Ottawas were not particularly liked by the French. Several of the early explorers despised them as brutal, cowardly, and unreliable. Pierre Radisson said, "They are the coursedest, unablest, the unfamous and cowar[d]liest people that I have seene amongst fower score nations that I have frequented."[4] La Potherie, writing in 1702, termed them fickle, unfriendly, and self-interested. On the other hand, Antoine Raudot, reporting in 1710, considered them brave warriors and mentioned that their contact with the French had subdued some of their savagery and given them better manners.[5] As late as the middle of the eighteenth century, however, they seemed to be characterized by a stubborn indifference to Christianity as taught by the French priests, by savage cruelty, and by childish changes of mood. No one denied that they were a clever people, shrewd and scheming for their own advantage.

[3] An article on the health of the Indians is found in Hodge's *Handbook of Indians North of Mexico.*

[4] Radisson, *Voyages,* p. 203.

[5] Kinietz, *The Indians of the Western Great Lakes,* pp. 233, 380.

Far to the east of the Great Lakes the representatives of another European country had entrenched themselves and were spreading westward toward inevitable conflict with the French. Ottawa life in Pontiac's time was to be complicated by the colonial rivalry of France and Great Britain.

2

His Early Life

IT IS AWKWARD, though not distressing, to be unable to set down in so many words the exact date and place of Pontiac's birth and the names of his parents, as the conventional biography demands. Unfortunately, there is no incontrovertible evidence on these points. There is, however, testimony and evidence as to the vicinity of Pontiac's birth, the decade in which he was born, and the tribal affiliations of his parents which must be considered.

No one has successfully questioned the fact that Pontiac belonged to the Ottawa nation by birth.[1] Dis-

[1] The Ottawa tradition of the nineteenth century gave Pontiac's mother as Ottawa, his father as Chippewa. Henry Conner, a United States Indian interpreter, declared that Pontiac's mother was a Chippewa. Henry R. Schoolcraft, the Indian agent, wrote in 1846: "Pontiac was an Ottawa, by a Chippewa mother." Peshewah, a half-breed Miami chief better known as Jean Baptiste Richardville (1761-1841), knew many Indians who had been associated with Pontiac. He is reported to have said that Pontiac's mother was a Miami. William Smith, the gossipy chief justice of New York, mentioned in a letter in 1763 that Pontiac was a Catawba captive who had managed to place himself at the head of his captors. Smith did not explain where he obtained this exclusive bit of information, and its truth is hardly admissible. Pierre Chouteau (1758-1849) of St. Louis told J. N. Nicollet he was of the opinion that Pontiac was a Nipissing, a small Algonquin tribe once located around Lake Nipissing in Ontario. Francis Baby, son of Jacques Duperon Baby who was active in Detroit in Pontiac's time, told Francis Parkman that he understood Pontiac belonged to a tribe living farther west and had been adopted into the Ottawa nation (Parkman Papers, 27d, p. 171). This evidence was only hearsay, and the sort of thing some Ottawas themselves might have perpetrated in a later effort to

agreement exists rather over which parent was the Ottawa. The other was variously reported as a Miami or a Chippewa. From these conflicting reports, we may conclude at least that Pontiac was not a full-blooded Ottawa. The Ottawas, Chippewas, and Miamies were friendly neighbors, and intermarriage was common. Tribal membership was inherited from either the father or the mother, depending on whether the husband had gone to live with his wife's people or the wife had joined her husband's village. It seems clear that Pontiac was born and raised in an Ottawa village, although we cannot be sure which parent was the Ottawa or name the tribal affiliation of the other parent.

At the time of Pontiac's birth the Ottawa nation was located at Michilimackinac, Saginaw Bay, and Detroit River, and Pontiac's first historical appearance at Detroit invites the reasoned conclusion that the great chief was probably born in the Ottawa village which in 1718 was still on the north side of the Detroit River, but which before 1732 was moved across to the site of modern Walkerville, Ontario.[2]

disown Pontiac. For instance, Andrew J. Blackbird, an Ottawa historian, called Pontiac a Chippewa with the same motive (*History of the Ottawa and Chippewa Indians in Michigan*, p. 7). Carver called Pontiac a chief of the Miamies (*Travels*, p. 153), and so did Heriot (*Travels Through Canada*, p. 179). The persons who actually knew Pontiac never referred to him otherwise than as an Ottawa.

[2] As for Pontiac's birthplace, Chief Richardville is the closest to a contemporary source we have. He was born near Fort Wayne, Indiana, and spent his life in that vicinity. He often asserted that Pontiac was born on the Maumee River at the mouth of the Auglaize. The city of Defiance, Ohio, now occupies this junction. Richardville was in a position to know and should have known, yet he may have been indulging the Indian predilection to claim close association with a famous chief for his tribe. There is no documentary evidence, nor as yet any archaeological evidence to indicate that an Ottawa band had settled along the Maumee

As for the date of Pontiac's birth, we can only guess at an approximate year by a process of induction. Since he was a respected chief in 1763 he was obviously a mature man; but as he was also an active warrior he was not yet beyond his prime. He indicated himself that he was a lead-

River in the first quarter of the eighteenth century. Although the Ottawas and Miamies had fought each other at Detroit in 1706, that quarrel appears to have been patched up by 1712. But not until 1748 is any mention made of Ottawas on the Maumee. A memoir on the western Indians dated 1736 implies, indeed, that the river valley was then uninhabited.

"Thirty miles up the river [from Lake Erie] is a place called La Glaise where Buffaloes are always to be found; they eat the clay and wallow in it. The Miamies are sixty leagues from Lake Erie, and number 400 . . ." (*Docs. Rel. Col. Hist. N.Y.*, ix, 891). In 1748 Kinousaki, an Ottawa chief, reported at Detroit that some Ottawas who were at Sandusky told him they wished to settle at the lower end of the Maumee (*ibid.*, p. 162). Yet in March 1750 a Miami reported to the French that "the Ottawa of Detroit were to make their village at La Roche de Bout [in the Maumee just above Waterville, Ohio] to be closer to the English of Great Miami River who have promised to sustain them and to supply all their needs. The English have been several times with forty or fifty horse loads of goods to the upper part of the river at Grand Glaize, where the greater part of the tribes have wintered." (*Ill. Hist. Coll.*, xxix, 168). Here are two more implications: that as yet there were no Ottawas living on the Maumee, and that the Glaize region in particular was a hunting ground not continuously inhabited.

The foregoing argument is not intended to refute Richard-ville's testimony, but only to open it to question. It is easy to understand how Richardville might have been mistaken. From hearing stories that Pontiac lived on the Maumee (which is true enough later on), he might have incorrectly concluded that Pontiac was also born there.

If Pontiac was not born in the Maumee Valley, where did he first come into the world? Benson J. Lossing, without citing any authority, says he was born on the Ottawa River. He even neglects to identify which Ottawa River. The Auglaize was once known as the Ottawa, and a tributary of it bears that name today. Presumably, Lossing meant the great Ottawa River which divides Ontario from Quebec in Canada. Yet again we must

ing warrior in 1746. Francis Parkman believed he was about fifty in 1763, but such an age was rather old for so active an Indian.[3] B. J. Lossing stated flatly that he was born in 1720, and Dr. Cyrus Thomas concurred in that belief when preparing his sketch of Pontiac for the Smithsonian Institution's *Handbook of Indians North of Mexico*. Certainly the year 1720 is more probable than 1713, and indeed Pontiac may have been born as late as 1725.

As no incidents of his childhood or early manhood have been preserved, we can only assume that his youth was passed in typical Ottawa fashion. The first ceremony in which he would be concerned was that of receiving a name. This did not occur until the Ottawa baby was a few months old and was construed to terminate its infancy. The parents then gave a feast to which a number of friends were invited. During the meal the parents kept recommending the baby to a god that would be recognized as his guardian spirit throughout life. The name selected was rarely an original one, but was more likely to be a name borne formerly in the family. At about this age also the baby had its ear lobes perforated for beads

question whether there were any Ottawas settled along that river in the first part of the eighteenth century. The river received its name in the seventeenth century because it was a highway to the Ottawa country and because the Ottawas used it when bringing their fur fleets down to Montreal.

[3] Parkman heard from Pierre Chouteau in St. Louis that Pontiac was between fifty and sixty years when he was killed in 1769 (Parkman Papers, 27a, pp. 215-41). C. E. Slocum, who wrote a history of the Maumee Valley in 1905, offered 1712 as the date of Pontiac's birth, possibly utilizing Parkman's estimate for arriving at such a year. Richardville, Conner, Schoolcraft, Lewis Cass, B. B. Thatcher, and S. G. Goodrich, all of whom discussed Pontiac, left no opinion as to his birth date. Lossing gave no authority for his pronouncement of 1720, but he visited Detroit in 1860 and may then have picked up this information.

and its nasal septum pierced to receive an ornamental stone as a protection against spells that enemies might try to cast on him.

The precise meaning of the name Pontiac has never been determined. The Ottawa tradition of the nineteenth century referred to him as *Obwandiyag* (the prefix O-being a pronoun in Ottawa), and Andrew J. Blackbird said the name was pronounced in the Ottawa language *Bwon-diac*. Bon or Bwon means "stopping," and Obwon would mean "his stopping" or "stopping it" or "stopping him." But no meaning has been discovered for "diyag" or "diac."[4] Both the French and the English, of course, spelled the name as it sounded to them; the former writing it *Pondiac* or *Pondiag*, the latter making it *Pontiac* or *Pontiack*. The substitution of *p* for *b* and *d* for *t* has no significance, as in the Ottawa language these consonants are considered identical. In careless pronunciation of the name the prefix O- would be dropped first, and doubtless that is what happened among the French. And their phonetic spelling of the rest of the name completed its perversion: In this book the familiar English spelling has been followed.

As a baby no doubt Pontiac was swaddled onto a small cradleboard having a small footrest and packed with down to make a bed. Indoors this was set up against the wall of the cabin. With the aid of a headband the mother could carry her child on her back in this cradleboard. Or she might carry the baby without the board inside her own robe. The child was not weaned until he was about three years old, and his first solid foods were fed him after they had been masticated by the mother. As a small boy Pontiac probably wore nothing in the summer time, and in the winter some brief garment for protection against

[4] Wood, *Historic Mackinac*, ii, 634; *Mich. Hist. Mag.*, iii (1919), 416; Baraga, *A Dictionary of the Otchipwe Language*.

the cold, plus moccasins. Children had no particular chores or duties to perform. Even obedience was rarely expected from them. They were given small bows and arrows with which to practice, and spears for fishing. Otherwise, they played games with one another and probably with the village dogs.

A typical Ottawa cabin was actually a story-and-a-half dormitory. It was constructed of long poles driven into the ground and curved together at the top and tied. Cross pieces were intertwined among the large poles as braces. Over this frame was laid fir and cedar bark, except at the ridge, where an open strip was left for smoke to escape. The general shape of these cabins, or arbors, resembled that of a loaf of bread. They ranged from 100 to 130 feet in length, by 24 feet wide and 20 feet high. Several families occupied one such cabin. Sleeping accommodations were built along each side like a string of double-deck bunks. At each end was a door. These cabins were set in fairly regular streets, and the villages fortified by a stockade of stakes. The old triple ring of pickets had given way to a single row of posts, particularly where the Indian village was near a fort.

When out hunting or traveling, the Ottawas utilized a simpler shelter—the tepee. It was made of poles cut on the spot; these were set up in a circle, their tops leaning inward in cone shape. Over them the Indians spread rush mats made in sections about five by fifteen feet which they carried along. The occupants usually slept in a curved position as there was seldom room to stretch out.

The Ottawa boy was taught woodcraft and all the nature lore necessary for him not only to maintain himself in the forest, but also to become a successful hunter and family provider. Life in the open was for the Indian a constant struggle to obtain even a bare comfort. Cultivated crops were crudely cared for and were at the mercy of the weather. Game might be plentiful one year and scarce the next, and hunting became more arduous the nearer the white man approached. Edible wild plants had to be learned and searched for. The Indians preserved only a few items of food, and those for only a few months ahead. Even warfare was conditioned by food supply, and long sieges were no part of savage strategy simply because the warriors had to take time off to provide food for themselves and their families.

At the same time that the boy was becoming an expert woodsman, he was learning to use the white man's weapons and tools: the gun, the steel ax and hunting knife, traps, and fishing nets. These were available from the French traders in Detroit and were so far superior to native weapons that they had largely replaced them.

The Indian youth was also taught the social traditions and customs by which the tribe preserved itself. First of all, he learned how to fight and make war, from the preliminary rallies in which the warriors worked up their enthusiasm for battle to the finalities of torturing prisoners. He received his initiation into battle by accompanying a war party on a raid, probably against a traditional enemy like the Indians living below the Ohio River. He was instructed also in the proper feasts and ceremonies that must be observed, the gods to be consulted or appeased, the ritual of speaking to another tribe or to white men, the kind of justice dealt out to criminals, the authority of the village chiefs, the powers of the medicine man, the meanings of dreams, the way to obtain a wife, and the care to be shown the dead.

Without textbooks or writing or schools of instruction, the education of the Ottawa youth was a family concern, carried on by oral direction and demonstration. A great deal was learned by trial and error, and the emphasis, of course, was on practical, useful knowledge. Hero worship played its part as an incentive, as well as the desire to excel and be admired by one's fellows. Rewards for aptness and hard work were certain and obvious. The expert hunter lived more comfortably than the poor one; the careless canoe maker might sink in a rapids. The ablest warrior was made the leader of a war party. The most effective speaker was listened to in council, and as he was deferred to his power grew.

The political organization of the Ottawas was loose, simple, and rather fluid. There was no chief over all the Ottawas. Each village had its chiefs—not one, but several —and the office had no particular tenure; neither was it necessarily hereditary. The son of a chief succeeded his father only if the village elders considered him capable. Any warrior could become a chief on his own abilities and if he persuaded other braves to follow his suggestions and directions. Especially was this true of war chiefs, who attained to leadership because they were hard fighters and superior tacticians. They maintained their position as war chiefs as long as they were successful in battle. A defeat or two would cause their followers to lose faith in their ability and to elect to follow another warrior who promised victory. A famous war chief might influence the braves of another village to combine under his general-ship, as Pontiac did.

Civil chiefs presided at local or intertribal councils and made broad decisions of peace or war, to move the village or not to move it, to admit white traders or exclude them, etc. As would be expected, the civil chiefs were older than the war chiefs and participated less in warfare. Probably they had been war chiefs in their younger days. They tried to control the war chiefs, but were not always successful in stopping them from committing hostilities. During a long war, indeed, the war chiefs might over-shadow the civil chiefs in all decisions. One civil chief's wisdom might be respected above that of all others, and he would act as a kind of chairman in village councils. Consequently he would be regarded as the head chief of the region. Chiefs of neighboring villages might even defer to his judgment at times, and thus he would give white men the false impression of being the ruler of the entire nation.

Chieftainship was further complicated by the interference of white men. If they found a village ruled by chiefs hostile to their advance, they attempted to entice a few villagers to friendship. Then the white men would decorate them with medals or gorgets and declare them to be chiefs in the eyes of the great white father across the Atlantic. The proud puppets would return to their village and attempt to supplant the other chiefs or at least divide the town so as to obtain a following and reduce the strength of the opposition. This king-making was an old game in European diplomacy which is still played around the globe. It usually worked among the Indians and produced a crop of what were contemptuously called "medal chiefs."

The shaman, or medicine man, among the Ottawas was not a powerful figure except in his own field of duty: presiding at *midewiwins*, or religious gatherings, chanting prayers on proper occasions, prophesying, blessing, working helpful magic, preserving rites and rituals, and recalling tribal history. He was the village priest, physician, archivist, and historian.

It might clarify understanding of the kind of life Pontiac led to reconstruct a typical year's events in an Ottawa village near the middle of the eighteenth century —when Pontiac was growing in strength and knowledge and was beginning to take a young man's part. Let us begin with the autumn season. The fields of maize and the garden patches, which had been tended all summer by the squaws, were harvested of their crops. Food that was to be kept through the winter underwent preservation. Corn was ground into flour, beans and peas were shelled, berries were dried, squash and pumpkins were cut into sections and strung up to dry. As colder weather came on, ducks and geese were shot as they flew south.

The village broke up as winter approached, families going out together to hunt, fish, and trap. Only the oldest persons and the sick were left behind. The family hunting parties might go in any direction, although the rich Ohio Valley attracted many of the Detroit Indians. The winter season was passed in hard work and sometimes in privation, for not only must life be sustained, but furs must be accumulated for trade in the spring. They hunted and trapped deer, bear, buffalo, beaver, otter, fox, raccoon, marten, and various birds. Venison was jerked for preservation, and bear fat was fried down into oil and poured into deerskin bags. Pelts were cleaned, stretched, and salted.

With the return of spring, the sap run lured the Ottawas to the "sugar bushes"—or stands of maple trees. The trees were tapped, the sap gathered in birch bark pails and boiled down into maple sugar. After a heavy meat diet all winter, the Ottawas consumed unbelievable quantities of sugar while in camp and carried many cakes of it back to their village. Hominy was made of corn and beans and eaten with bear oil and syrup poured over it.

If the village was near a fort, the Indians were greatly convenienced. If not, they visited the fort first and traded their winter's catch of furs for ammunition, gun repairs, household utensils, blankets, clothes, brandy, trinkets, etc. A charge account or deferred payment plan usually operated, however. That is, the winter's catch of furs often paid for supplies advanced the Indians the previous autumn before they set out on their hunt. Extra furs bought brandy for immediate consumption by way of celebrating the return from hunting. The more expert hunter or prudent provider might have furs left to trade for goods he wanted to use during the coming summer. The more frequent practice, however, was for the Indians to be totally out of necessary supplies by autumn and to purchase on credit the items needed to see them through the following winter.

After trading their furs the Ottawas returned to their village. The squaws began planting the fields with corn, squash, peas, beans, melons, and pumpkins. Canoes and clothes were repaired or made anew. The men and boys hunted small game and fished. Sometimes hunting parties went great distances. A rewarding spot for fishing was the shallow waters of Lake Ste. Claire's outlet into the Detroit River. Isle aux Pêches (horribly corrupted into Peach Island today) stood at this outlet and reportedly was a favorite summer haunt of Pontiac.

Summer was the season for making war. Grievances were revenged in force, or young men were detached to gain fighting experience. The southern tribes were always fair prey for the Ottawas and other northern tribes, so there was no lack of an enemy. Still, Ottawa life in the summer revolved around the village. Besides the confinement imposed by agriculture, there were celebrations and ceremonies to be observed while the inhabitants were all together. Recreations were not ignored. The game which the French named lacrosse was popular among the Ottawas, and matches were played between villages. Individuals played a game with straws and a dice game, betting on their skill. Foot races and canoe races among themselves or against the French were not uncommon. At night there were long and tiring dances. A contemporary Frenchman described a typical village dance of this period: "In the evening the women and the girls dance. They adorn themselves liberally, grease their hair, put on white chemises, and paint their faces with vermillion, also putting on all the porcelain beads they possess, so that after their fashion they look very well dressed. They dance to the sound of the drum and of the rattle, which is a sort of gourd with pellets of lead inside. There are four or five young men who sing, and keep time by beating the drum and the rattle, while the women dance to the rhythm and do not miss a step. This is a very pretty sight. And it lasts almost all night."[5]

When the supply of liquor permitted, there were orgies of drinking. Brawls and fatal fights among neighbors often resulted. The drunken murderer was usually excused because he was not responsible while drunk and apparently not to be blamed for drinking.

Courtship likewise took place while the village was inhabited, and the manner in which Pontiac probably found a wife may be recounted. Pontiac would be ready to marry when between twenty and twenty-five years old. Ottawa youths were allowed great freedom in their courtships. They made their own selections for mating, although the young man, after winning his sweetheart's consent, formally purchased her by giving lavish presents to her parents. Cadillac offers the best description of courtship among the Great Lakes tribes as it was practiced early in the century:

"You must know that lovers go courting there, as elsewhere, talk amorous nonsense and give one another tokens of respect and affection. The girls have this advantage, that they are allowed to take their pleasure and try experiments with marriage [i.e. at other times than during the meetings described below], as long as they like and with as many bachelors as they please, and no one finds

[5] Kinietz, op. cit., quoting Sabrevois, p. 270.

any fault with them, nor does it prevent them from finding a husband, when they are in a humor to do so.

"Their love affairs are carried on in this way. The young men have strips of bark rolled up in the form of a torch; at night they light them at one end and go through all the huts, if they please. The girls are lying down on the side of the walk, and when their beloved passes they stop him by a corner of his robe. The moment the gallant perceives this signal he stoops down, and then his mistress takes his roll of bark and puts it out, and makes the young man lie down beside her, and he tells her his love; with all this familiarity and complete liberty, it is not often that anything takes place but what is quite seemly and respectful, so true it is that one thinks less of what is permitted than of what is forbidden. For it is evident that, on these occasions, it is in the power of the two lovers to indulge their passion; yet they generally do nothing of the kind, especially if they intend to marry one another. Finally, when the fair one grows tired and wants to sleep, she tells her lover, who retires as soon as she bids him. That is called among them, 'running the light.' "[6]

Despite this unhampered method of finding a mate the Ottawas were not universally monogamists. Two or more wives were permitted if the husband so desired and if he could support them. The economic factor was usually the chief determinant. Formal divorce was unknown. The dissatisfied husband or wife simply cast off his partner and sought another. However, if the couple had children, separation rarely occurred; relatives exerted influence to persuade the husband and wife to stay together. Infidelity, on the other hand, was a disgraceful and punishable offense.

The identity of Pontiac's first wife is not known, nor

[6] *ibid.*, quoting Cadillac, p. 272.

the year of his marriage. Later on, after his prestige and affluence increased, he seems to have accumulated additional or successive wives. In 1768 he implied in a letter that he had a wife from one of the Illinois tribes. One of his alleged widows was living in 1807 in the Ottawa village at the mouth of the Maumee.[7] Her name was Kantuckeegun. Of course, she must have been much younger than her illustrious husband.

At maturity Pontiac was not attractive in appearance by the beauty standards of the white race. A fairly reliable source testifies that he was a tall man and not handsome, yet another reporter calls him "a remarkably well-looking man; nice in his person, and full of taste in his dress, and in the arrangement of his exterior ornaments."[8] He was physically strong, as would be expected of a good warrior, and his frame was solidly filled out. Of course, his hair was black and straight, and his face was free of beard. His skin was said to be lighter than average and probably was shiny from frequent oiling with bear fat. His body must have been considerably tattooed in conformity with custom. On ceremonial occasions he also painted his face according to his own design. His hair was worn in a narrow, short pompadour, diminishing from front to back. The Ottawas told Cadillac it gave their enemies less to take hold of. Besides the beads in his ears, the stone in his nose, and silver bracelets on his arms, Pontiac may have worn a collar of white plumes or beads around his neck and a few feathers tied in his short hair.

[7] Lossing, *Field Book of the War of 1812*, p. 490. Pontiac reportedly had a grown son in 1764. *Pa. Gazette*, Dec. 13, 1764.

[8] Nicollet, *Report*, p. 82. In 1845 John R. Williams of Detroit told Parkman he had heard from persons who had known Pontiac that he "was a man of medium stature, very well formed and strong." Francis Baby, whose father was familiar with the chief, said that Pontiac was "a tall man, not handsome." Parkman Papers, 27d, pp. 146, 170.

His dress was scanty, but showed the white man's influence. The seasons affected costume greatly. In winter Pontiac probably wore moccasins, deerskin leggings up to his thighs, a breechcloth, a loud calico shirt purchased from a trader, and possibly a coat of white manufacture, and a French stroud, or blanket, belted around him. Fur wraps were worn in extreme cold. In the hot summer, Pontiac doubtless peeled down to a shirt and breechcloth, or perhaps to but one of these. The Indian had not adopted the white man's dress yet; he simply added whatever caught his eye to his native foundation garments. The result was usually grotesque.

As for Pontiac's expression and manner, each of the three persons who mention them testifies that he had the air of a commander of men. His "manner" was "absolute and peremptory"; his "bearing" was "commanding and imperious"; he was "a proud, vindictive, war-like and easily offended man."[9] It is significant that this impression of the man's personality was more clearly remembered than his physical appearance.

[9] John R. Williams also told Parkman that Pontiac's manner was "absolute and peremptory, but he was greatly respected by his people. His authority was great." Later he added how haughty and commanding Pontiac was. Francis Baby testified that the chief was "of a very commanding and imperious bearing." Robert Navarre, a contemporary of Pontiac and keeper of a diary, wrote that he was "a proud, vindictive, war-like and easily offended man."

3

His First Activity

HAVING brought Pontiac up to manhood and having assumed that he was married, it is time to survey again the progress made by the French in developing their hold on the back country between Lake Erie and the Mississippi. They forged another link in their chain of forts connecting Canada with Louisiana by erecting another stronghold on the Wabash in 1731. The new post, named in honor of the builder and first commandant, was called Vincennes, and the city of that name today spreads over its site.

Detroit was growing, of course. In 1740 there were about one hundred resident families inside and outside the fort. They were traders, artisans, and small farmers. The garrison numbered seventeen soldiers in 1736. A census of Indian warriors made in the same year reveals that clustered around the fort were 200 Ottawas (meaning 800 to 1000 people altogether), 200 Hurons, and 100 Potawatomi braves. At Lake Ste. Claire were 60 Mississaugi-Chippewa fighting men, and at Saginaw Bay 80 more Ottawas. At the head of the Maumee River were 200 Miamies, while along the St. Joseph River were 100 Potawatomies, 10 Miamies and 8 Kaskaskias. To the north were 180 Ottawa warriors at Michilimackinac who moved to L'Arbre Croche (Cross Village, Michigan) in 1742. At St. Mary's Falls were 30 Chippewas, and over at Chequamegon Bay, Lake Superior, 150 of their braves.

This distribution of Indians was immediately changed by an incident at Detroit. A band of Hurons, having grown fearful of the Ottawas and Chippewas and dissatisfied with their treatment by the French, moved their village down to Sandusky Bay in 1738 under their chief Orontony, or Nicolas. There the English traders had little difficulty in reaching them, and at last the Indians of the western Great Lakes were released from a monopolized trade and began to discover that English goods were cheaper. Some of the Miamies on the Wabash, who had not forgotten their earlier chastisement by Cadillac, had been secretly trading with adventurous English merchants for several years.

As if to invite competition, the French inaugurated a policy of "farming out" the posts in 1742. That is, in order to raise revenue the government leased the fur trade of a western post to the highest bidder. The successful bidder in turn was given a free hand to exploit his monopoly, by which he was to make up the cost of his fee and to profit on his goods, if not to acquire a fortune for the rest of his life. Profits could be made most easily, of course, by lowering the price paid the Indians for furs and raising the price of manufactured articles sold to them. The license holder might allow other traders to share his monopoly at the cost of a stiff fee, and the commandant of the fort usually shared in the graft in return for not enforcing regulations too strictly. Traders from the English colonies, drawing on a more highly developed manufacturing country for their wares and paying no license fees, could undersell the French merchants.

The beginning of commercial competition in the Lakes region between France and Great Britain was suddenly intensified by the outbreak of war between the two countries in 1744. This was the first war affecting America to occur in Pontiac's lifetime. It is known in American history as King George's War, while in Europe it is called the War of the Austrian Succession. Although its cause was strictly a European quarrel, once England and France found themselves ranged on opposite sides, fighting broke out between their colonies in North America for supremacy on this continent. The theater of war in America was confined to the Northeast. The western Great Lakes were so deep within French territory—so far behind the lines, in a sense—that the war barely touched the French and Indians living in that region. Nevertheless, the English attempted to exploit the contact they had made at Sandusky and on the Wabash with the French-dominated Indians.

In this war both the French and the English found that the Indians could be useful allies or dangerous enemies. In 1745 the Hurons at Sandusky permitted the English traders to build a strong-house in their town on the north side of Sandusky Bay. Later the village was visited by Iroquois, instigated by the English, bearing war belts to persuade the Hurons to take up the hatchet against the French. Nicolas was swayed and laid plans to enlist other tribes and capture Detroit. Prematurely, however, a party of Hurons intercepted five French traders returning to Detroit in June 1747 and killed them. This hostile act, plus information volunteered by a squaw, revealed to Longueuil, commandant at Detroit, the intentions of Nicolas. Immediately Longueuil called the nearby settlers into the fort for protection and then sent for the neighboring chiefs to tell them he knew of their murderous scheme. The Ottawas, Potawatomies, and the Hurons not associated with Nicolas were quick to deny that they had any part in the conspiracy. Nevertheless, more French traders were killed or plundered during the summer.

Similar hostility developed at Michilimackinac. The Ottawas and Chippewas there (who seldom were of the same mind as their brethren around Detroit) were likewise inflamed by war belts from the pro-English Iroquois and possibly from Nicolas. They killed several French traders around the straits. The fort was also threatened, but Noyelle, acting commandant, did not hesitate to demand surrender of the murderers from the Indians. The war spirit calmed during the summer, and reinforcements to the fort found the crisis passed.

Later in the year 1747 Nicolas visited Detroit and sued for peace. Longueuil demanded first that he surrender the warriors who had killed the French traders, but later withdrew this condition. Nicolas returned to Sandusky and spent the winter there, not free from suspicion of continued hostility, inasmuch as Longueuil learned that some English traders visited him twice.

Early in the spring of 1748 Chief Mackinac of the friendly Ottawas gathered his warriors and aided by some Chippewas and Potawatomies resolved to visit Nicolas and demand that he either observe his pledge of friendship to the French or fight these allied nations. This threat, seconded by another French demand that he break off relations with the English, prompted the stubborn Nicolas to burn his village early in April and move most of his followers south to the Cuyahoga River, a tributary of the Wabash. The English traders were forced to vacate Sandusky Bay.

Longueuil held an Indian conference on April 28 at which the tribes swore renewed fidelity and obedience to the French. At Michilimackinac a similar peace council was held, and the Indians offered to surrender those warriors guilty of attacking the French. These, together with some remorseful Hurons from Sandusky, were dispatched to Quebec to make formal peace with the governor. Thus ended the English-instigated uprising in Michigan against the French.

Pontiac appears to have remained loyal to the French throughout this warfare. War parties of Ottawas from Detroit aided the French by taking part in raids into New York. As Pontiac aspired to be a war chief, probably he took part in some of these expeditions. With but one event in this period is his name associated. Indeed, it is the first act of his career on record, but the record is his own word. During a speech in 1763 urging the French of Detroit to help him drive out the British, Pontiac reminded them of an obligation they owed him. He is reported to have said:

"As a proof that I do not desire it [i.e. any harm to befall the *habitants*] just call to mind the war with the Foxes, and the way I behaved as regards you seventeen years ago. Now when the Chippewas and Ottawas of Michilimackinac, and all the northern nations, came with the Sacs and Foxes to destroy you, who was it that defended you? Was it not I and my men?

"When Mackinaw, the great chief of all these nations, said in his council that he would carry the head of your commander to his village, and devour his heart, and drink his blood, did I not take up your cause, and go to his village, and tell him that if he wanted to kill the French he would have to begin first with me and my men? Did I not help you rid yourselves of them and drive them away? How does it come then, my brothers, that you would think me today ready to turn my weapons against you? No, my brothers, I am the same French Pontiac who helped you seventeen years ago."[1]

Seventeen years before 1763 brings us to 1746. The Foxes and Sauks, or Sacs, had been giving the French trouble intermittently since 1712, but had been at peace since 1740. As for the threat against Detroit, this incident is difficult to verify.[2] Pontiac's story may or may not be

[1] Navarre, *Journal*, p. 124.
[2] Lyman C. Draper remarked in 1867: "If such a war occurred at that period, we have no particulars of it. It is possible

true. It is possible that Pontiac may have mistaken his date and referred to Nicolas' conspiracy of 1747, which was aimed at Detroit. The Foxes, Sauks, and northern Ottawas and Chippewas were solicited to join it. The Ottawa village at Detroit remained steadfastly loyal to the French. At the very least Pontiac's words must be allowed to indicate that in 1746 or 1747 he was a mature warrior greatly attached to the French around Detroit and perhaps already evincing qualities of leadership in his own tribe.

Just as peace was secured in Michigan, the pro-English Miamies of the Wabash boldly left that country to set up a village easier of access by the English traders. Under their chief La Demoiselle (who soon won the nickname of "Old Britain") they established a town in 1748 on the upper reaches of the Great Miami River called Picka-

that Pontiac may have erred as to the date, and may have personated himself, as Indians frequently do, as simply representing his nation. But it is quite probable, however, that he referred to a real outbreak at the time he mentioned." (*Wis. Hist. Coll.,* v, 103).

A search among the available French sources for information on this attack produced only a vague circumstantial mention. Chief Mackinac was suspected in July 1747 by the commandant of Detroit of being ready to join Nicolas' conspiracy against the fort. Yet this storm cloud blew over, and by the next spring Mackinac was ardently pro-French and opposed to Nicolas. Letters from Michilimackinac written in the summer of 1747 mention that the new commandant, on his arrival there, "has found that post very quiet; the Ottawas are beginning to be sorry for *what occurred last year.*" (Italics mine.) This tantalizing shred of evidence might refer to an attack on Detroit, or it might refer to many another incident. Nothing is said of Detroit's menace in the Canadian governor's journal of occurrences for 1746.

Mention of the attack on Detroit in Burton's *The City of Detroit,* II, 871, would seem to substantiate it, but I am reliably informed that Burton did not write the chapter containing this story; it was prepared by some hired hackwriter.

willany, the site of modern Piqua, Ohio. Thus when King George's War ended that year, the French had not been wholly successful in retaining the allegiance of the tribes inhabiting the dominions they claimed. Farther east they had won over temporarily one new ally from the English —the Shawnees.

Disgusted with unscrupulous English traders and a Pennsylvania government indifferent to their appeals for justice, the Shawnees (Chartier's band) swerved to French allegiance in 1745 and moved out of western Pennsylvania into Ohio. The less bold Delawares remained, although disliking the English. To prevent further alienation, some Iroquois moved down among the Delawares. The Iroquois still hated the French and were bound to the English by ties of trade; moreover, they did not want their gateway to the rich Ohio Valley hunting grounds blocked by Francophile Indians or by actual French settlements.

New York was the first British colony to awaken to the importance of maintaining and cultivating friendly relations with the Indians on its western border, both for the sake of peaceful trade and to thwart French influence. It was fortunate to have living in the Mohawk Valley an Irish landed proprietor and trader by the name of William Johnson, who had a way with Indians. The governor of New York put him in charge of Indian affairs in 1746, and the continued attachment of the Iroquois to British interests was largely his achievement.

Pennsylvania and Virginia now began to show an interest in Indian problems, and with the help of another Irish trader, George Croghan, set about improving relations with the Delawares and the Iroquois. Cheaper goods than the French could offer proved to be a solid attraction; the problem was to control trade practices and settlers as well as to combat French interference. A few Shawnees

⟨ 36 ⟩

returned to the English fold, and some Hurons, possibly from Nicolas' band, moved into western Pennsylvania. The distant Miamies then made overtures to the English, and all these nations were invited to a conference at Lancaster, Pennsylvania, in 1748. The resulting treaty promised that English traders would be sent among the Shawnees and Miamies provided that they would be protected.

Following the close of the war the French made vigorous efforts to combat the growing English influence and to confine the English settlements to the eastern side of the Appalachians. Pierre Joseph Céloron made a swift trip down the Allegheny and Ohio Rivers in 1749. He had a triple mission: to expel the English traders, awe the wavering Indians, and nail up lead plates warning Englishmen of the borders of French Canada. Instead, Céloron was received coolly by the Indians and could do no more than warn the English traders that they were trespassing and bury his famous lead plates. Nevertheless, the governor of Canada was determined to control the great Ohio waterway. In 1750 he asked permission of the tribes to build a fort at the Ohio forks, where Pittsburgh now stands. This was refused, for the Delawares and Iroquois preferred to have the English erect a post there.[3] Failing in that direction, the governor turned his attention to Detroit and urged the Paris government to send more emigrants. But a crop failure and an epidemic of smallpox there in 1751 discouraged the growth of Detroit. Pontiac must have followed these failures of his white brothers with uneasiness.

The French built a fort on Sandusky Bay, however, to thwart English encroachment around the end of Lake Erie a second time. In reprisal for a visit paid by George

[3] Downes, *Council Fires on the Upper Ohio*, pp. 20, 43-44, 53, 58.

Croghan with gifts to La Demoiselle's town of Picka-willany, the French struck decisively the next year. They commissioned a half-breed at Michilimackinac by the name of Charles Michel de Langlade to sack the town. He raised a force of 240 Frenchmen and Ottawas and swept down on Pickawillany in June 1752. The village was burned, many Miamies killed, five English traders taken prisoner and their goods seized, and La Demoiselle was reputedly boiled and eaten. The remaining Miamies returned to their nation at the head of the Maumee, convinced that the French were supreme. Forthright action of this kind was more to Pontiac's liking.

Growing bolder, the French occupied Presqu'Isle (Erie, Pennsylvania) in 1753 and began erecting Fort Ma-chault on the Allegheny River (Franklin, Pennsylvania). Their intent was clear and at last alarming to the English. Belatedly Virginia, which also claimed the upper Ohio River region in conflict with Pennsylvania, took the initiative which her neighbor had refused. She asked the French to withdraw from what she called British territory. Of course, the French refused. The Iroquois, Delawares, and local Shawnees fumed at the lateness and feebleness of all the English efforts; they were ready to act vigorously against the French intruders, but could not obtain leadership or even support from either Pennsylvania or Virginia.[4]

At length, early in 1754, Virginia began the construction of a fort at the forks—the point where the Allegheny and Monongahela Rivers meet to form the Ohio. A French force captured it easily in April, before it was finished, and completed the post, calling it Fort Du-quesne. English trade with the Indians of western Pennsylvania came to a standstill. Virginia sent an inadequate force under young George Washington to retake

[4] ibid., pp. 60-74.

the fort, but it was compelled to surrender and return home. The Indians were disgusted by this futile effort, and many of the Iroquois migrated back to their stronghold in central New York. Those remaining became known as Mingoes.

The band of Iroquois in western Pennsylvania had acted as overlords of the Delawares, Shawnees, and Hurons in that area and had determined the policy of aiding the English to repulse the French. The parent stock in New York now overruled this Iroquois branch and advised the tribes of western Pennsylvania to stay neutral. With amazing perception the New York Iroquois reasoned that the Indians always suffered when they took part in a white man's war, but by staying neutral they would not be punished by the victor. Moreover, they believed that the English, when sufficiently aroused, could defeat the French without Indian help.

The Iroquois advice was followed by the Delawares and Shawnees at first. In 1755, when the British government sent two regiments of regular troops to Virginia to recapture Fort Duquesne, the English force could obtain the services of but a few Indians. Similarly, the French who awaited the attack could not enlist enough local Indians and found it necessary to import allies from the Great Lakes.

Thus it was that Pontiac's tribe, owing to circumstances far beyond its control, became embroiled at last in the Anglo-French border dispute in Pennsylvania and took an active part in the new war that was beginning— the dark and bloody French and Indian War.

4

The Ottawas in the
French and Indian War

THE FRENCH AND INDIAN WAR was the final contest
between Great Britain and France for supremacy on the
American continent. It was inevitable because the previous war had settled nothing. The peace of 1748 was no
more than a truce, to last only until one country or the
other felt strong enough to resume the struggle. War in
Europe between these two powers did not break out
until 1756 and then it involved other nations because of
Europe's traditional alliances and jealousies. Lord Macaulay blamed Frederick the Great and summarized the
extent of the war in his caustic observation: "In order
that he might rob a neighbour whom he had promised
to defend, black men fought on the coast of Coromandel
and red men scalped each other by the great lakes of
North America."

After preliminary diplomatic maneuvering by France
and Britain to enlist allies, the two sides lined up: France,
Austria, Russia, Saxony, Poland, and Sweden against
Britain, Prussia, and Hanover. Important battles were
fought in Europe, where the struggle was known as the
Seven Years' War, and in Africa and India, but we shall
confine ourselves to certain battles in North America,
which was the theater of virtually a separate war.

The Canadian governor's completion of Fort Duquesne (Pittsburgh, Pennsylvania) in 1754 was an asser-
tion of dominion over land claimed as part of Pennsylvania and Virginia. Britain had no mind to let her ancient
rival thus set the western boundary of English colonies.

The challenge was accepted by the sending of two regiments of regulars to Virginia for the express purpose of seizing Fort Duquesne and driving the French "invaders" back to Lake Erie at least. The regiments were under the command of Maj. Gen. Edward Braddock, who was reckoned a good if somewhat coarse and unimaginative officer. He was also to command the militia raised by the colonies to augment the regulars. He arrived in Virginia early in 1755, but was unable to assemble his forces and begin his westward march until June. His expedition consisted of about 2,500 men.[1]

Against so formidable an army, the French garrison of Fort Duquesne made what preparations it could, but without much hope of holding out. The fort was strengthened, but the garrison was not reinforced owing to the complacency of the Canadian governor. When Braddock approached the vicinity of the fort, it held probably less than 300 French regulars and Canadian militia, although encamped around the stronghold were 800 to 1,000 Indians—mainly Ottawas, Chippewas, and Potawatomies from the Great Lakes, Abenakies and Caughnawagas from the St. Lawrence, Hurons from Lorette, and a few Delawares and Shawnees from the upper Ohio.[2]

The commandant, Capt. Pierre de Contrecoeur, apparently did not intend to face a siege and even entertained thoughts of an honorable capitulation. His junior, Capt. Daniel de Beaujeu, was of a different stamp, however, and proposed to attack Braddock's advance column

[1] Pargellis, "Braddock's Defeat" in *Amer. Hist. Rev.*, XLI (1936), 253-269. This study has been utilized further in this chapter.

[2] Sargent, *The History of an Expedition Against Fort DuQuesne, in 1755*, p. 222. One rumor mentioned that 500 Chippewas served at Fort Duquesne, but Ottawas and Potawatomies must have been lumped with them in this total. This number was told to Conrad Weiser, Pennsylvania Indian agent. *Pa. Col. Rec.*, VI, 615.

⟨ 41 ⟩

when it forded the Monongahela River. Braddock had divided his expedition in half, leaving his heavy baggage with the rear unit and himself pushing on with 1,300 men to attack the fort before the French should reinforce it and before summer rains should increase the difficulty of cutting a road through the wilderness. Beaujeu believed that a sudden attack might at least check the advance for a time. Contrecoeur gave him a detachment of regulars and allowed him to solicit the help of their Indian allies. Beaujeu rallied a force of more than 900, of which 600 were Indians, and on the evening of July 8, 1755, set out to meet the enemy.[3]

The French came in sight of the British about midday on July 9 and found to their dismay that Braddock had already completed his crossing of the river. The van was just coming up a slope, between a small hill on one side and a ravine on the other. After the first exchange of shots, the French and Indians fanned out in a U-shaped formation, taking cover on the hill and in the ravine. Braddock's advance guard under Lieut. Col. Thomas Gage fell back before this unexpected resistance, while the main body was ordered ahead before the nature of the attack had been ascertained. As there was not sufficient distance between the advance and the main body, the disorganized retreat of the one collided with the unorganized advance of the other, and everyone was thrown into confusion. Eighteenth century British tactics called for musket fire in volleys by platoons on visible enemies likewise bunched together (in the hope that some of the balls in this broadside would inflict damage). But here the soldiers became separated from their companies and were obliged to fire individually at enemies they could not see.

[3] *Docs. Rel. Col. Hist. N.Y.*, x, 303-304.

The Indians and French were now stationed along three sides of Braddock's confused column and were firing from good cover. After three hours of vainly trying to stand their ground, the English recrossed the river and began their retreat, carrying the mortally wounded Braddock with them. On the field were left 456 killed and some of the 421 wounded—casualties totalling two-thirds of the detachment. Among the wounded officers who retreated and survived were Lieut. Col. Gage, Lieut. Henry Gladwin, and Lieut. John Montresor, men we shall meet again. The flight of the survivors struck panic into the rear contingent with the heavy baggage. All the stores were destroyed, and the entire expedition turned back to Virginia. The accepted explanation for this disgrace to British arms has been the bad conduct of the private soldiers, but a recent study makes clear that incompetent generalship was entirely to blame.[4]

On the unexpectedly victorious side the loss was slight: three officers killed, including Captain de Beaujeu, and two wounded; twenty-seven soldiers and Indians killed, and about as many more wounded. The French and Indians might have killed many more of Braddock's men had not the immense amount of baggage and stores left on the field proved so attractive as loot that the fleeing Englishmen were allowed to escape. Cannon, powder, balls, muskets, wagons, horses, cattle, flour, clothing, utensils, liquor, the expedition's money chest, and Braddock's papers comprised the plunder. Scalps, arms, colorful pieces of clothing, and liquor were the booty most prized by the Indians.

Ottawas from the Detroit River participated in this initial, decisive victory over the English. Probably Pontiac was among them; but no evidence has been found by

[4] Pargellis, *op. cit.*

which we can say positively that he was there, either as a warrior or as the leader of a war party.[5]

With more certainty we can mention another colorful Great Lakes inhabitant who helped defeat Braddock. That person was Charles Michel de Langlade, the half-French, half-Ottawa trader of Michilimackinac who had led the assault on Pickawillany in 1752. His grandson and two British officers testify that he led the Ottawas and Chippewas of the North, and possibly the Ottawas of Detroit as well, to Fort Duquesne and that, further, he urged on Beaujeu the plan of attack which was followed so successfully.[6]

The French reported that twenty men and women were taken prisoners by the Indians. Another report set the number at thirty. A dozen of the men were disposed of that evening in grisly savage fashion. Their faces and bodies blackened, they were tied to stakes on the shore of Allegheny River opposite the fort. The Indians gathered around yelling and dancing in the firelight. After the prisoners had been tortured with firebrands and hot irons sufficiently to satisfy the savage appetite for that kind of spectacle, they were burned to death. The French probably could not have stopped this traditional victory ceremony even if they had wanted to. As for what happened to the women prisoners, we know only that one was kept by the commandant at the fort, and two were taken off by the Indians. The fate of another, perhaps one of the two just mentioned, will be related shortly.

[5] Parkman put the matter gingerly in 1851 by writing that the Ottawas were "led on, it is said, by" Pontiac. Who supplied Parkman with this information he does not say, and his papers do not reveal; nor have I been able to find anything in writing before 1851 relative to Pontiac's presence at Fort Duquesne.

[6] Wis. Hist. Coll., III, 213; Anburey, Travels, I, 315; Burgoyne, State of the Expedition, p. 10; DePeyster, Miscellanies, p. 17.

Sauuage de La f. 10. Nation

outaouaks.

Pipe

Jae apeclun

An Ottawa at the end of the seventeenth century,
drawn from life

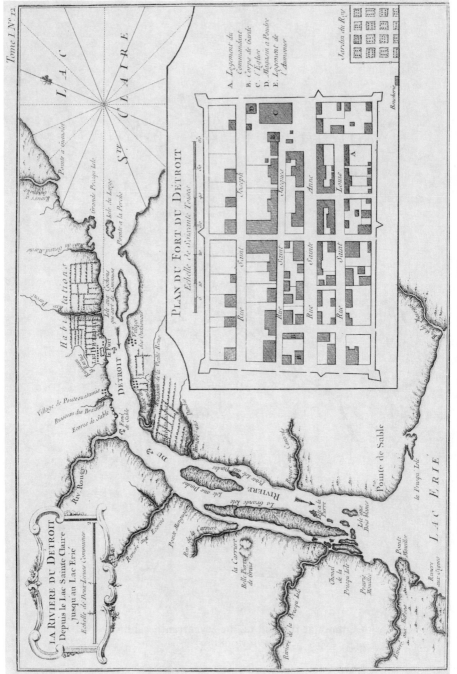

Bellin map "La Rivière du Detroit" with inset "Plan du Fort du Detroit."

The number of prisoners was soon augmented by frontier raids which Braddock's defeat encouraged the Indians gathered at Fort Duquesne to undertake. Lonely houses of pioneer settlers were burned, and the occupants slaughtered or carried off. After the surrender of Canada in 1760, the English recovered several hundred captives taken during the war. One Charles Stuart, who was seized on the frontier of Pennsylvania by a party of Delawares late in October 1755, was given to some Hurons and taken by them back to their village on the Detroit River. Two years later he was returned to New York, where he dictated a narrative of his experiences. He has left us brief mention of Pontiac's village. What follows is dated about November 1755:

"About two miles above the Wyandot [Huron] town stands the Ottawa town. Between these two towns live three French families. There are also three plantations in this distance belonging to three French merchants who live in Fort Detroit. The Ottawa town contains about 90 houses or Indian cabins, but no church, for the Ottawas are a heathen nation and not proselyted to the Roman Catholic religion. They are a barbarous, savage nation and very wicked. Soon after Braddock's battle they ripped up the belly of an English woman taken at the battle who was big with child, and took out the child and boiled and ate it, and cut the woman all to pieces. They also killed two prisoners of Braddock's men in a most inhuman manner, cutting off their legs, scalping them, dividing the skull, etc. The Ottawa warriors are not numerous, having lost many in the wars, they having been very much concerned in the incursions and attacks made on the English of Pennsylvania, Virginia, etc. I saw two companies of them going to war against the English, one of about 25 warriors and the other of about 35 warriors. . . . When

⟨ 45 ⟩

the French send out the Indians to war they give them a shirt and a steel, but give no rewards for scalps."[7]

The indifference of the Ottawas to Christianity, their love of warfare, and their loyalty to the French are marked here as characteristics most obvious to a newcomer. Stuart and his wife remained prisoners in the Huron town until April 1757, but he relates nothing more about the activities of the Ottawas except to say that they had standing or "constant orders" to make war on the English and "kill, burn, and destroy all, save none unless it be for their own use." He also reported that "the French oblige their Indians to go to war against the English by threatening the nations that refuse with bringing another Indian nation to cut them off."

In 1756 there were reported to be 300 Indians from Detroit and 700 from Michilimackinac assisting the French at Fort Duquesne. They did scouting duty and made frontier raids. The following year, Langlade and a number of Ottawas joined the army of General Montcalm at Montreal and moved up Lake Champlain with him. He sent them to scout Lake George in July where they discovered a force of 350 English soldiers in twenty-two barges near Sabbath-Day Point. After lying in ambush for them, the Ottawas fell on the detachment viciously, and only two barges escaped. Six were taken by the savages, the others sunk. One hundred sixty Englishmen were "killed, drowned or put to the torture"; 151 were carried prisoner back to the French camp. The skirmish unbelievably cost the Ottawas one brave, slightly wounded!

Montcalm managed to make the Ottawas surrender their prisoners, who were sent back to Montreal, and to press on against his objective, Fort William Henry at the

[7] James Smith's Account in Loudon, *Selection of Narratives*, 1, 152.

head of Lake George. He had a force of 6,200 regulars and Canadian militia and about 1,800 Indians of several nations. The official return of his army showed 337 Ottawas, of whom 30 were from Pontiac's village at Detroit. This expedition laid siege to the fort on August 3, 1757, and it surrendered on the 9th. The English garrison of 2,200 was allowed to return home on condition that the men would not serve against France during the next year and a half.

The Indians were disappointed by this capitulation; they were interested in revenge, scalps, and loot. On August 10 the English prisoners set out, escorted by some French regulars. Half a league down the road, however, the column was attacked by the Indians. About fifty English men and women were killed, and several hundred snatched away as captives. One French soldier was killed and three others were wounded in trying to stop this massacre. Montcalm and his officers rushed to the scene and succeeded in breaking up the Indian assault. He recovered some of the English seized by the savages, but about 200 were carried off to Montreal, where the Canadian governor ransomed and released them. Montcalm was disgusted by this outrage and regretted that he could not control the Indians.

In this same year of 1757 is dated the first contemporary document mentioning Pontiac by name. Among the papers of Sir William Johnson was a copy in French of a speech made by "Pontiague, Outava chief," at Fort Duquesne. Pontiac reported that George Croghan had tried to lure the western tribes away from the French by a false story that Quebec had fallen to the English. Pontiac went on to boast that he could not be influenced by such evil suggestions, but he did remind the commandant that the French had promised the Indians great advantage from allying themselves with the French.

Probably this last remark was the purport of the speech, and Pontiac wanted something like powder, blankets, or liquor as evidence of his ally's promised advantage.

The speech cannot be reproduced because the manuscript was burned and all that remains is the brief description of it indicated above.[8] Tantalizing as this fragment is by its brevity and vagueness, it does permit certain inferences. Obviously it shows that Pontiac had journeyed to Fort Duquesne and delivered a speech protesting his loyalty to the French and hinting at his wish for some tangible expressions of their gratitude. The manuscript also calls Pontiac an Ottawa chief, undoubtedly a war chief. It may mean that Pontiac had exposed the propaganda spread by George Croghan and therefore was becoming a man of influence in his region. Its lack of a specific date, however, does not permit us to say whether the visit to Fort Duquesne occurred at such a time as to preclude Pontiac's being with Montcalm at Lake George. He may, of course, have been at both places during the year.

In the spring of 1758 the British again determined to wrest Fort Duquesne from the hands of the French. Brig. Gen. John Forbes was ordered to lead an expedition from Philadelphia against the western post. News of the intended stroke reached Detroit in May, and the French commandant immediately dispatched runners to the surrounding tribes to send their warriors to Detroit, whence

[8] Day, *Calendar of the Sir William Johnson Manuscripts,* p. 92. Two years after the calendar was published many of the Johnson papers were burned up, including this particular document, in the fire that consumed the library wing of the New York State capitol. Dr. Day assigned this speech the date of 1757 only. As Fort Duquesne was taken by the British the next year and renamed, it could not be later than 1758, or earlier than 1755, when war was begun. No doubt Dr. Day had other evidence for his date. I was unable to find another copy of the speech.

they would proceed to the defense of Fort Duquesne. The fighting men of the Ottawas, Chippewas, Potawatomies, and Hurons assembled at Detroit in July and set out. "The common report was that they would serve him [General Forbes] as they did General Braddock, and obtain much plunder."[9]

The Lakes Indians arrived at Fort Duquesne in plenty of time. The advance troops of the British under Col. Henry Bouquet, a Swiss mercenary of considerable ability, were slowly cutting a new road through the mountainous wilderness which became known as Forbes' Road. Forbes was in no hurry, for he knew that the longer he delayed the more impatient grew the Indians collected by the French and the more pressing was the necessity for them to return home and hunt for food and furs. The possibility that Fort Duquesne might be reinforced by French regulars was slight. France had just lost the fortress of Louisburg on Cape Breton Island and Fort Ticonderoga on Lake Champlain; she dared not weaken her forces on the St. Lawrence or at Niagara.

The impatience of their Indian allies was a sore problem for the French, who tried to persuade them to take the offensive and attack the slowly advancing enemy. Before such a tactic materialized, a detachment of the enemy obligingly approached the fort. Major James Grant had persuaded Colonel Bouquet to let him move ahead against the Indian encampments around Duquesne. With a force of 842 officers and men, he marched to within sight of the fort without being detected. Then on the morning of September 14, 1758, discarding his splendid surprise, with drums beating and bagpipes blowing, he started his Highland regulars and provincials down the hill known today as Grant's Hill in Pittsburgh.

The French and Indians rallied at the noise and spread

[9] James Smith, op. cit., p. 240.

out in ambush. The English were surprised again and overwhelmed. Grant lost 270 killed, 42 wounded, 100 taken prisoner, including Grant himself. The Detroit Indians were at last rewarded for their long idleness. They also considered their service finished and immediately returned to their towns.

This initial defeat of an incautious advance detachment, however, was no check to the main body of Forbes' expedition, which pushed along the new road. On November 24, 1758, Captain de Lignery burned Fort Duquesne and fled with his garrison up the Allegheny River to Fort Machault, or Venango (Franklin, Pennsylvania). The English took possession of the site that same evening, and for the first time were formally established on the western side of the mountains. Almost their first act was to rechristen the settlement "Pittsburg," and the new fort they built was called Fort Pitt, in honor of the British prime minister.

The Indians of Detroit were disappointed by this weakness and flight of the French, but were told, of course, that the retreat was only temporary. The forks of the Ohio would be seized again and the British driven back across the mountains—with Indian help. During the winter of 1759 the Ottawas and other Lakes tribes were alerted for a summer offensive against Fort Pitt. The rendezvous was at Kuskuski, a Delaware town on the Beaver River, near modern New Castle, Pennsylvania. From this base of supplies, war parties were sent out to harass the frontier. Twice the settlers around Pittsburgh were called into the fort in anticipation of an attack. Captain de Lignery was not quite ready, however. By summer he had rounded up 400 French and 1,000 Indians, and his chances of reoccupying the fort were excellent. Possibly all that saved it was his receipt of orders on July 12 to rush reinforcements in the opposite direction to Fort Niagara.

A large force of British regulars and colonials, supported by 900 Iroquois under Sir William Johnson, laid siege to Fort Niagara on July 7. With less than 500 soldiers in the garrison, the French commandant, Capt. François Pouchot, sent out his distress call and prepared to hold out until the reinforcements arrived. The British proceeded methodically, but on July 20 their commander was killed by an accidental explosion, and Johnson assumed command.

Johnson was forty-four years old and growing rapidly in prestige. Great Britain at last had recognized the value of treating diplomatically with the Indians and had seen the dangers of leaving the business to the separate colonies. In 1756 two departments of Indian affairs, northern and southern, had been set up, each with a superintendent acting directly under the Crown and in cooperation with the military commander-in-chief in America. Johnson's success as New York's Indian agent caused his appointment as His Majesty's Superintendent in the Northern Department. His jurisdiction extended from the Potomac and Ohio Rivers northward, and westward ultimately to the Mississippi. He was especially influential over the Iroquois, among whom he lived on the Mohawk River. After his first wife died he lived successively with two Mohawk women as wives. His liking for the Indians was genuine, and they trusted him. He had been knighted in 1758 for defeating a French force on Lake George.

Meanwhile, De Lignery had been joined by reinforcements from Detroit and the far Illinois country. The combined force of about 2,300 French and Indians started for the relief of sorely pressed Niagara. Johnson got news of their approach on July 23 and moved a detachment around to the portage road which circled the falls.

About three miles above the fort he prepared an ambush. The next day the French and Indians, who should have landed on the west side of Niagara River as Pouchot had suggested, disembarked on the east side and marched down the portage road straight into the trap.

They were taken completely by surprise. While the English fired into their front, the war-loving Iroquois assaulted their extended flank. De Lignery was killed along with several other French officers. After sustaining heavy losses (one report says 500 killed and 120 captured), the rest of the column was put to wild flight and pursued for five miles. The Detroit Indians fled in their canoes across Lake Erie to their villages. The annihilation of his expected relief gave Captain Pouchot no choice but to surrender. It was assumed by the French that Johnson would move next on to Fort Pontchartrain at Detroit.

As to whether Pontiac himself took part in the summer raids out of Kuskuski and in the disastrous battle of July 24, again there is no evidence. Not all of the Indians who had gathered at Machault had gone to Niagara with De Lignery. Some stayed behind, and when news reached them of the fall of Fort Niagara, a delegation of Ottawas, Chippewas, and Hurons went down to Fort Pitt to confer with the Delawares and Shawnees, now friends again of the English.[10]

It was ever an Indian characteristic to favor the side that was successful. In the early part of the war the French had been victorious, and so the Indians they had persuaded to join them were faithful allies. But the fall of Fort Duquesne, Ticonderoga, and now Fort Niagara stirred doubts in the minds of the pro-French Indians about the ability of their friends to make war. If the English should prove able to vanquish the French, then

[10] George Croghan's ms. diary in the Cadwalader Papers, Pennsylvania Historical Society.

the Indians reasoned it was high time that they made up to them.

Such reasoning does not indicate a lack of principle so much as it reveals the logic of necessity on the part of a weaker third party. If the Indians, particularly those living near the boundary of English and French possessions, were to survive, they simply must be on the winning side when peace was made. Only a few of the older men were wise enough to perceive that even this effort was bound to be fruitless in the end. They realized dimly that there could be no victorious side for the Indian, since the French and English surely were not fighting over land which they intended to hand over to the Indians allied with the victor.

George Croghan invited this delegation from the three western tribes to a conference on August 7, 1759. Johnson had appointed him his deputy superintendent for the western nations, which Croghan had come to know so well as a trader and as an agent for the Pennsylvania government. Like Johnson, Croghan understood the red man's temperament and often sympathized with his point of view, yet he used his talents not to promote the Indian's welfare but to get around the savage's objections to British policy. Since the capture of Fort Duquesne he had worked hard to placate the tribes and swing more of them to English interest. He was now building near Pittsburgh a house called Croghan Hall for his headquarters.

Two "principal" Ottawas, out of the delegation of 24 that accepted Croghan's invitation, are identified by name: Messeaghage, who was apparently a civil chief, and Oulamy, a war chief. The absence of Pontiac's name is significant, as will be shown presently. At Croghan's instigation, the Delawares and Shawnees recalled the hatchet they had sent their western cousins and buried it under a large pine tree that it "may never be found more." The Ottawas and other western nations professed to be relieved by this symbolic act and promised not to let their warriors fight the English again.[11]

A month later Croghan held another conference with some Ottawas and Miamies. This time the Ottawas were represented by Oulamy and Mehemah. The latter endeavored to explain his tribe's attitude by saying: "Some years ago the French got the better of our understanding and by the assistance of the Evil Spirit put the hatchet into our hands, which we were foolish enough to make use of against our brothers, the English." Now, however, they were ready to take "fast hold of the new chain of friendship." The pipe of peace was smoked and passed around. Then Oulamy, "the chief warrior of the Ottawas," spoke: "It was we, the warriors, that carried on the war against you." He promised on their behalf never to use the hatchet against the English again.

Meanwhile at Detroit the loss of Niagara had two effects. The fort was enlarged and strengthened against the day when it would be attacked. The other result was a cooling of fervor for the French cause among the surrounding Indians. An English prisoner who escaped to Fort Pitt[12] said that they had even refused to accept the hatchet proffered by the French for attacking the English convoys along the road to Pittsburgh. The refusal was general, this informant said, except "for one small tribe" who resolved to stick with the French. This group more probably was a band or faction within a village, and one wonders whether it could have consisted of Pontiac and his followers. This division of allegiance among the Ottawas is made clear by the fact that some Ottawas from

[11] Minutes of conference in *Bouquet Papers*, Series 21655, pp. 70-75.
[12] The prisoner is quoted in Croghan's ms. diary, Oct. 10, 1759.

Detroit told Croghan in November 1759 that their tribe was divided. Those who no longer favored the French planned to move to "this side of the lake" (that is, to the south shore of Lake Erie) in the spring. The emigration actually took place that very winter, as Croghan was visited in February 1760 by some pro-English Ottawas who were newly settled at "Giahaga," or Guyahauga Creek, or Cuyahoga River as we know it today. The city of Cleveland extends across its mouth.

After the loss of Fort Niagara, Pontiac probably took no further part in the battles between the French and English. No doubt the commandant at Detroit was glad to have him remain in the vicinity to rally the Ottawas in case of an English attack.

The expected move against Detroit never materialized. The English were busy in the East striking more significant blows which, if successful, would give them Detroit without the least exertion in that direction. Niagara, Ticonderoga, and Quebec were in their hands by the end of 1759, added to their victories at Duquesne, Frontenac, and Louisburg the year before. The campaign of 1760 was aimed at Montreal, the new capital of Canada. Nevertheless, Detroit made ready and in the spring of 1760 counted a fighting strength of 45 regulars, 655 colonials (the "debris of their defeat at Niagara"), 150 more Frenchmen recently arrived from the Mississippi with provisions, and 600 *habitants* of the vicinity—a total of 1,450 men able to bear arms. In addition, surrounding the fort were 150 Hurons, 200 Ottawas, 100 Potawatomies, and 100 Chippewas, or 550 warriors in all.[13] This was the most respectable force French Detroit ever rallied, yet it never had a chance to fight.

George Croghan was busy in 1760 preparing the Indian

[13] Sergt. Coope or Cope was the reporter, *Mass. Hist. Coll.*, 4th Series, ix, 295.

mind for the British victory he was confident was coming. He gave generous presents to the savages who visited Fort Pitt to demonstrate the wealth of the English and the value they set on Indian friendship. If the story two Frenchmen related in 1764 may be believed, Pontiac himself and some other chiefs from Detroit made the journey to Fort Pitt to inquire into the kind of treatment they might expect from the English in case they were victorious. The chiefs were assured, probably by Croghan, that the rivers would run with rum and that trade goods would be so plentiful and so cheap that two beavers or four raccoons would buy them a blanket. Delighted, the chiefs returned to Detroit and spread this news with much insolence.

Croghan accompanied Colonel Bouquet northward when that officer established British posts at Venango and Presqu'Isle. Encountering in that neighborhood some Detroit Indians, possibly Pontiac and his delegation, he invited them all to a conference at Fort Pitt in August. This congress was a huge good-will assembly attended by a thousand Indians from the West: Delawares, Shawnees, Mingoes, Ottawas, Chippewas, Potawatomies, Hurons, Miamies, and Kickapoos. A message from General Amherst was read which promised restoration of the disrupted trade and assured the Indians that the British had no designs on their land. Even then Amherst's armies were closing in on Montreal.

5

The British Occupy Detroit

SIR JEFFERY AMHERST, commander-in-chief of His Majesty's Forces in North America, was doing what General Braddock and his two successors had failed to do: defeating the French in Canada and their Indian allies.

He was sent to this continent in 1758, and by his capacity for careful organization and his determination he had pushed the British troops from one victory to another. He was detailed in his orders to the point of "fussiness," and he kept a finger on every department and almost every company. His lack of imagination was no handicap in fighting this war, although it became a fatal weakness in the task of pacifying the French-allied Indians. He never learned to understand them and he would not listen to the advice of his able subordinates. He was a soldier of the king, direct, thorough, grave, and competent in the field. When the governor of Canada capitulated to him at Montreal on Septmber 8, 1760, Amherst had won for his royal master a domain twelve times the size of England.

Included in the surrender of the province were forts among the western Great Lakes which had never seen a British soldier except as a prisoner. General Amherst lost no time, therefore, in detaching a proper force to take over those posts and raise the British flag. The very next day he selected Maj. Robert Rogers to lead two companies of his Rangers on this delicate and dangerous mission.

Major Rogers was a 29-year-old native of New Hampshire of great talent in one line. He had trained a battalion of provincials to be expert riflemen and woodsmen, and with them he had carried out several dangerous scouting and raiding expeditions against French and Indians alike. Rogers' Rangers, indeed, outwitted and outfought the Indians at every engagement and struck respectful fear in the hearts of French regulars and militia. Given an objective to capture, an enemy force to be scouted, or a mission to perform, Rogers let no obstacle of nature or man distract him. He was at this time at the height of his remarkable, though later unfortunate, career.[1]

General Amherst's orders to Rogers were dated September 12, 1760, and the two hundred Rangers set off the next day from Montreal in fifteen whale boats. On his way Rogers was to report to Brig. Gen. Robert Monckton at Fort Pitt and pick up a company of regulars to garrison Detroit, since Rogers was ordered to return to headquarters after he had received the surrender. At Presqu'-Isle, therefore, the Rangers halted while supplies were collected, and Rogers hurried down to Pittsburgh. General Monckton ordered Capt. Donald Campbell and a company of Royal Americans (60th Regiment) to accompany Rogers and remain at Detroit. George Croghan was also sent along to confer with the Indians and win them over to British allegiance. He immediately dispatched Indian messengers ahead to inform the Detroit savages in advance that the British were coming.

[1] In 1766 Major Rogers obtained for himself the command of Fort Michilimackinac, where he showed himself careless, if not scheming, in a peacetime administrative position. He was removed from command, tried for treason, and acquitted. His career during the Revolution was shady, and he emigrated to England where he died in 1795. Allan Nevins' introduction to the Caxton Club's edition of *Ponteach, A Tragedy* contains the best biography of Rogers. New light on his career is available in the Gage and Clinton Papers in the Clements Library. Kenneth Roberts' account of him in *Northwest Passage* must be read with great caution.

The enlarged expedition left Presqu'Isle on November 4, heading into a cold west wind. At the mouth of Wajea Sipery (believed to be Ashtabula Creek) next afternoon the flotilla halted to speak to a group of about thirty Ottawas who had an English flag. They were part of the pro-English band who had removed from the Detroit River the previous winter. They were gratified to hear of the surrender of Canada and the imminent occupation of Detroit, saying they were glad to exchange "their fathers, the French, for their brethren, the English, who they were assured were much better able to supply them with all necessaries."

The chief, or "principle man of the Ottawas," said he had not long to live and recommended to Croghan's attention Oulamy and Mehemah, who had confirmed the peace treaty at Fort Pitt the previous year, as spokesmen for all business of the tribe.[2]

Bad weather held the expedition at the creek for several days, and the voyage was resumed on November 12. A day's rowing carried them to the mouth of the Cuyahoga River, where Croghan met some more of the Ottawas he knew. Neither he nor Rogers had yet been approached by Pontiac, although Rogers published in 1765 an elaborate and incongruous account of such a meeting which has been accepted as truthful by too many historical investigators from Lewis Cass to the present.[3]

[2] Croghan's journal is printed in Thwaites' *Early Western Travels*, vol. I, and in the *Mass. Hist. Coll.*, 4th Series, IX, 362-379. Although he does not mention Oulamy and Mehemah by name, they are easily identified by reference to Croghan's ms. diary in the Cadwalader Papers for Aug. 7 and Sept. 3, 1759, and Nov. 6, 1760.

[3] Rogers' journal of this voyage is in the Chalmers Papers at the New York Public Library; it was edited by V. H. Paltsits in the library's *Bulletin*, Apr. 1933. Rogers published it with very few changes in his *Journals*, London, 1765. In his account of meeting the Ottawas he does not mention Pontiac. But in his *Concise*

If Pontiac accosted Rogers at all during this journey, the meeting took place at the mouth of the Detroit River on November 27 in company with a number of other chiefs. They composed an official welcoming party of Ottawas, Hurons, and Potawatomies. Probably Pontiac was among this group. His attitude at this time toward

Account of North America, published later in the year Rogers offered a new version of the meeting as follows:

"The Indians on the lakes are generally at peace with one another, having a wide extended and fruitful country in their possession. They are formed into a sort of empire, and the Emperor is elected from the eldest tribe, which is the Ottawas, some of whom inhabit near our fort at Detroit, but are mostly further westward towards the Mississippi. Ponteack is their present King or Emperor, who has certainly the largest empire and greatest authority of any Indian Chief that has appeared on the continent since our acquaintance with it. He puts on an air of majesty and princely grandeur, and is greatly honoured and revered by his subjects. He not long since formed a design of uniting all the Indians nations together under his authority but miscarried in the attempt.

"In the year 1760, when I commanded and marched the first detachment into this country that was ever sent by the English, I was met in my way by an embassy from him, of some of his warriors, and some of the chiefs of the tribes that are under him; the purport of which was, to let me know, that Ponteack was at a small distance, coming peaceably, and that he desired me to halt my detachment till such time as he could see me with his own eyes. His ambassadors had also orders to inform me, that he was Ponteack, the King and Lord of the country I was in.

"At first salutation when we met, he demanded my business into his country, and how it happened that I dared to enter it without his leave? When I informed him that it was not with any design against the Indians that I came, but to remove the French out of his country, who had been an obstacle in our way to mutual peace and commerce, and acquainted him with my instructions for that purpose. I at the same time delivered him several friendly messages, or belts of wampum, which he received, but gave me no other answer, than that he stood in the path I travelled in till next morning, giving me a small string of wampum, as much as to say, I must not march further without his leave. When he departed for the night, he enquired whether

Major Henry Gladwin, in later life

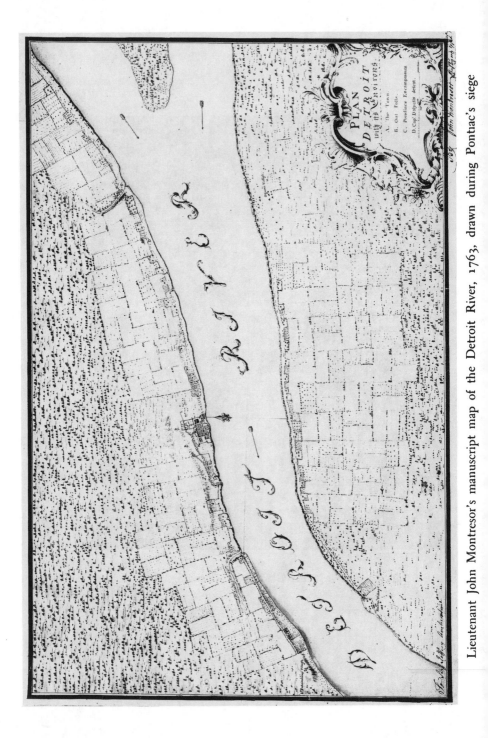

PLAN
of
DETROIT
with its Environs

A. The Town.
B. Out Posts.
C. Pontiacs Encampments.
D. Cap. D'Abyette defeat.

Lieutenant John Montresor's manuscript map of the Detroit River, 1763, drawn during Pontiac's siege

his recent enemies was reported to have been friendly. Regardless of his sympathies, curiosity about the new-comers and the presents the Indians would certainly receive would have brought Pontiac out to meet the British.

All the rest of the Indians around Detroit displayed

I wanted any thing that his country afforded, and he would send his warrior to fetch it? I assured him that any provisions they brought should be paid for; and the next day we were supplied by them with several bags of parched corn, and some other necessaries. At our second meeting he gave me the pipe of peace, and both of us by turns smoaked with it, and he assured me he had made peace with me and my detachment; that I might pass thro' his country unmolested, and relieve the French garrison; and that he would protect me and my party from any insults that might be offered or intended by the Indians; and, as an earnest of his friendship, he sent 100 warriors to protect and assist us in driving 100 fat cattle, which we had brought for the use of the detachment from Pittsburg, by the way of Presque Isle. He likewise sent to the several Indian towns on the south-side and west-end of Lake Erie, to inform them that I had his consent to come into the country. He attended me constantly after this interview till I arrived at Detroit, and while I remained in the country, and was the means of preserving the detachment from the fury of the Indians, who had assembled at the mouth of the strait with an intent to cut us off.

"I had several conferences with him, in which he discovered great strength of judgment, and a thirst after knowledge. He endeavoured to inform himself of our military order and discipline. He often intimated to me, that he could be content to reign in his country in subordination to the King of Great Britain, and was willing to pay him such annual acknowledgment as he was able in furs, and to call him his uncle. He was curious to know our methods of manufacturing cloth, iron, &c. and expressed a great desire to see England, and offered me a part of his country if I would conduct him there. He assured me, that he was inclined to live peaceably with the English while they used him as he deserved, and to encourage their settling in his country; but intimated, that, if they treated him with neglect, he should shut up the way, and exclude them from it; in short, his whole conversation sufficiently indicated that he was far from considering himself as a conquered Prince, and that he expected to be treated

a ready willingness to have the fort transferred from French to British hands. Characteristically, they had quickly abandoned the defeated side and prepared to make friends with the victor. In this instance they were influenced also by the promises made them that the English would open ample trading facilities for them at lower prices, in contrast to the restricted trade available from the French during the war. After all, it did not appear to the Indians of vital importance who controlled the little square of ground on which Fort Detroit stood, as the white men, with their gunsmiths, powder, lead, blankets, kettles, knives, axes, trinkets, and liquor were a convenience, if not a downright necessity. Had they fully understood the meaning of France's surrender of Canada to Britain, or comprehended that these Englishmen now regarded the Indians as living on *their* land, they would have acted differently.

Six miles up the Detroit River, Rogers was met by a French officer from the fort bearing a flag. He explained that the commandant, Capt. François de Bellestre, wished

---

with the respect and honour due to a King or Emperor, by all who came into his country, or treated with him." (pp. 239-243.)

This second version of the story was accepted by Parkman, and consequently by numerous other writers, except Thwaites, without reference to Rogers' strange inconsistency. Parkman wrote that this date marked "the first time that this remarkable man [Pontiac] stands forth distinctly on the page of history," and he adopted Rogers' characterization of the chief as authentic. The recent discovery of George Croghan's diary, in which the chiefs they met are named, destroys any defense of Rogers' inconsistency on the ground that he simply didn't bother to identify Pontiac by name in his *Journals*. The testimony of two Frenchmen, in the Gladwin manuscripts, does not bear out the attitude of Pontiac toward Rogers' coming as depicted by Rogers. Moreover, Rogers' background information about Pontiac is not correct: such as the Lakes tribes being formed into an empire with Pontiac elected emperor over all, his desire to go to England, and his willingness to pay tribute to King George.

to see a copy of the capitulation and the Canadian governor's letter to him ordering his surrender. This request was but a silly bid for time; Bellestre had known since September of the fall of Canada and had realized he must give up Detroit. In fact he had reduced his garrison by illegally sending off to New Orleans a detachment of regulars and militia under Captain La Chapelle. Nevertheless, Captain Campbell advanced to the fort with the documents Bellestre wanted to see. Rogers moved a little farther up the river and encamped for the night at an Indian village, probably the Huron town. Campbell reported to him there the news that Bellestre would be pleased to surrender the fort on the morrow.

At noon on November 29, 1760, Rogers and his party of about 275 troops landed just below the fort and drew up in ranks on the plain. The two hundred Rangers were dressed in their proud green buckskins and green Scotch caps, a uniform that struck more respect in the eyes of the audience of Indians than the more familiar red coats and blue trousers of the company of Royal Americans. Some of the French residents gathered sorrowfully at a distance to watch the ceremony of surrender, but the Indians had arrived in a mob, numbering 700 according to Rogers.

The sloping stockade of Fort Pontchartrain loomed just in front of the Englishmen. Some roof tops and the steeple of a church showed above the wall. Campbell and Croghan agreed that the fort was the finest they had seen. Rogers said the pickets stood 25 feet high and the fort measured 1,200 yards in circumference. Other estimates gave the pickets a height of 12 to 15 feet, which is no doubt much nearer the truth. Campbell said the fort was "very large," but gave no dimensions. It had, indeed, been enlarged three times during the 1750's and earth banked against the inside of the stockade to a height of seven feet.

〈 63 〉

"There are two bastions towards the water," Campbell wrote, "and a large flat bastion towards the land. In the point of the bastion is a cavalier of wood on which there are mounted three three-pounders and three small mortars, or coehorns. The palisades are in good order. There is a scaffolding round the whole which is only floored towards the land for want of plank. It is by way of a banket. There are seventy or eighty houses in the fort laid out in regular streets. The river is here about nine hundred yards over and very deep."[4]

The Detroit River flowed from east-northeast to west-southwest past the fort, and the structure stood on the north shore. One side of it paralleled the river bank, and a "water gate" opened directly on to the river, but without a wharf. There were three gates altogether, one on each side except the north. Presently the west gate opened and a French officer strode out alone bearing Captain Bellestre's compliments to Major Rogers. There was an exchange of military courtesies, then Rogers ordered two officers and 36 soldiers of the Royal Americans to enter. They marched in as if on dress parade to the beating of drums. They found an orderly though crowded interior. Besides houses and shops within the fort, there was a barracks and Ste. Anne's Church. Everyone was outside to see, if not welcome, the strangers. The French-built dwellings had sharply sloping roofs, dormer windows, and board siding, sometimes whitewashed, over the hewn logs. The commandant's house stood on a stone foundation measuring 43 by 32 feet, and all the rooms were plastered. The houses were crowded close together on narrow streets, four of which ran parallel to the river. None of the buildings was set up next to the palisades, and this open lane extending around inside of the stockade was called the *chemin du ronde*.

[4] *Bouquet Papers*, Series 21645, p. 224.

The most remarkable fact about the fort, however, was its situation on a slope running up from the edge of the water. It appeared to rest on a tilted plane. The bank of the river rose thirty feet a short distance back; consequently the pickets on two sides of the fort ran up hill. Each of the first two or three streets was successively higher than the preceding one. Cadillac's desire to have a water gate produced this sloping fort, which was to prove of military disadvantage, for a person standing across the river could look over into the fort. Nor was it a healthy post, as the drainage kept the lower south side muddy. The surrounding region was marshy and full of mosquitoes, and the stockade shut out the healthful western breeze.

The Royal Americans marched to the center parade, where the small French garrison was drawn up. The French arms were surrendered, the flag hauled down, and the British colors hoisted. The concourse of Indians outside the fort gave a shout on seeing this significant change of colors. The Rangers echoed their yell with cries of their own. The oath of allegiance was then administered en masse to the gathered French inhabitants, and they were asked to surrender their arms. Detroit had ended its long existence as a French settlement.

Within a few days Captain Bellestre and his garrison were sent under escort of some Rangers to Fort Pitt as prisoners to be exchanged. With them Croghan sent fifteen English captives, civilians and soldiers, whom he had recovered from the Indians. Although the winter season was almost upon him, Rogers made strenuous efforts to take possession of the other forts among the western Great Lakes. He sent a party of Rangers to occupy Fort Miamis at the head of the Maumee River and to secure Fort Ouiatenon on the Wabash. He himself attempted to lead a party up the lakes to Fort Michilimackinac, but was turned back by the ice. He left Detroit on December 23 and marched overland to Fort Pitt, which he reached on January 23, 1761. His tour of duty was finished, although he was destined to return to Detroit in less than three years and fight for his life.

Meanwhile, George Croghan had been holding a succession of conferences with the separate tribes. He emphasized that the French inhabitants of Detroit were now British subjects and he promised the Indians a free and open trade with the English. He asked that they deliver up their prisoners as proof of the sincerity of their friendship.

The chiefs blandly replied that they would give up those prisoners who chose not to stay with them. They asked that the prices of trade goods be settled and made lower than French prices, as had been promised earlier. Then they reminded the British that they had said, "This country was given by God to the Indians and that you would preserve it for our joint use."[5] This remark was indicative of an attitude to which the British gave little heed. The Indians also requested that a gunsmith and physician be kept at the fort for service to them. Dr. George Christian Anthon had accompanied the troops to Detroit, but a gunsmith was not made available to the savages for another year.

Croghan obtained the release of 42 more English captives. This total of 57 prisoners (and there were others not surrendered) is evidence of the active part taken by these Indians in the war. The conference ended in good harmony. The Detroit Indians invited their recent enemies, the Iroquois, some of whom were along with Croghan, to a conference in the spring to settle differences growing out of the battle at Niagara. Croghan left Detroit on December 11 and returned to Pittsburgh.

[5] Croghan's journal in *Mass. Hist. Coll.*, 4th Series, IX, 375.

Left in temporary command of Fort Detroit (the name Pontchartrain was dropped, of course) was Capt. Donald Campbell, a Scotsman who had come to America with the army in 1756. He was called "fat and unwieldy" by one of his fellow officers and he was known to be very nearsighted, but he was an alert and competent commander. As he could speak their language and participated in their social activities, he won the friendship of the French inhabitants. He also was respected and trusted by the Indians, and by Pontiac in particular. Unfortunately for his own safety, Campbell trusted Pontiac as well.

Distant as Detroit was from populated regions either English or French, it was by no means an uncivilized outpost. George Croghan said that the "country is fertile and level and capable of being made as fine a settlement as any I have seen in America." He added that the militia, made up of civilians, numbered about 800, although the total white population was about 500 seven years earlier and only 678, exclusive of the garrison, in 1768. The men farmed and fished, hunted and traded. Formerly they had managed a comfortable livelihood, but the last year of the war had almost exhausted their supplies. Accordingly, prices were high.

The country was inhabited for ten miles up and down the river on either side, but there was no depth to the settlement. The early French settlers were gregarious and had valued a water frontage more than large acreage conveniently laid out. So the grants of land took the form of long narrow strips, or ribbons, 400 to 800 feet wide and running back from the river two to three miles! The *habitant* built his house on the shore and thereby had easy access to water both for drinking and as a means of transportation. Moreover, his land holding was so narrow that his neighbors' houses on either side were in close sight. The rear acreage was never put under cultivation and seldom visited. The French had not come to farm anyway: they were traders and artisans with extensive gardens. The front yard was likely to be enclosed by a picket fence to keep out hogs, dogs, and drunken Indians, but not to discourage friendly intercourse. The loneliness of the American pioneer on his quarter-section a half-century later was unknown to the Frenchman, just as the Frenchman's house and furniture were superior to the cabin of the isolated American two generations later.

The *habitants* of the Detroit River were a convivial lot. Life was hard, but the people were robust and vivacious. Practically every adult could dance and play cards. Everybody could talk and did: they "have no talent for silence," as one observer noted; it was both a cause and an effect of their warm hospitality. To Croghan's surprise, they could all talk some Indian language. They played the Indian game which today is called lacrosse. They held foot races and canoe races. Their church was close to them; Sundays were days for dressing up and the numerous saints' days were occasions for celebrations.

Campbell found the French agreeable and ready to furnish the garrison with everything he asked of them. The British soldiers gave no offense to the *habitants*; Campbell explained: "No rum, that is the reason." The French were able to supply him with flour, Indian corn, and peas. Some cattle and barrels of salt pork were sent from Niagara. To supplement the meat provision, the Indians brought in plenty of venison.

Early in the spring of 1761 Campbell wrote to his superior, Col. Henry Bouquet, at Fort Pitt: "As for what concerns us in particular, we have passed a tolerable good winter. The women surpass our expectations, like the rest of America; the men very indifferent. There is a gathering every Sunday night in the home of the commandant [his own house], where there are to be found about twenty persons of both sexes. You have no such doings at Fort Pitt." To this description, Lieut. James MacDonald added: "I assure you they make a handsome appearance at the commandant's every Sunday night where they come to play at cards and continue till twelve o'clock at night."[6]

Campbell ingratiated himself with the Indians, although their demands worried him. He wrote to Colonel Bouquet in December, 1761, that he anticipated a great deal of trouble with them. "The French have a different manner of treating them from us. The four nations that live in the environs of Detroit are as much under the commandant as the inhabitants and come [to him] for everything they want. I have told my situation to General Monckton. I have nothing to give them, and the French left us very little in their stores, only mere trifles. Indeed they left us five hundred weight of good powder, which was more than I expected. You should encourage traders from Pittsburgh as much as possible this winter. We cannot prevail on the people to go there with their horses; they are only acquainted with traveling in canoes."[7]

Circumstanced as he was, Captain Campbell did well to keep the Indians' friendship. As a matter of policy the French had been in the habit of giving the Indians presents and of supplying them readily with ammunition for hunting and making war on the southern tribes. Naturally the Indians expected the British to continue this treatment; but the British were not inclined to maintain this expensive method of keeping savage allies. Their shortsighted policy was especially unfortunate because the Detroit Indians considered themselves peculiarly entitled to generous treatment for their recent display of allegiance to the English. Luckily for everyone concerned, British policy had not yet been crystallized into definite orders,

[6] *Bouquet Papers,* Series 21646, pp. 62-63.
[7] *ibid.,* Series 21645, p. 224.

and the clear-thinking Captain Campbell distributed ammunition as freely as he could on his own responsibility.
By this gesture he showed the Indians that the English appreciated them as much as the French, and by his speeches
he assured them that the English would do more for
them.

Early in the spring of 1761 English traders began to
arrive, affording the Indians an opportunity to dispose of
their winter's catch of furs and to purchase the many articles they needed or wanted. Unfortunately, the traders
came equipped mainly with goods the French would buy,
not the savages. Moreover, the Indians complained of the
prices charged. Impatiently, Campbell requested and
waited for official regulations to govern the trade: regulations that would fix prices, define the movements of
traders, clarify the credit system, provide for a supervisor
over the traders, and limit the quantity of rum per sale.
Campbell was not allowing any rum to be sold, although
some of the Indians went as far as Niagara and brought
it back.

General Amherst and Sir William Johnson were not
ignoring the western Indians, although they were slow in
deciding how the trade among them should be managed
and how the commandant at Detroit should treat them.
On receipt of Croghan's report of conditions at Detroit,
Johnson sent his recommendations to Amherst. Keeping
the Indians friendly, he emphasized, would depend largely
on the behavior of the commanding officer. "Next to that
there's nothing can more effectually establish and preserve a good understanding between us and them than a
free and open trade to be carried on with them under
proper regulations and restrictions . . . it is very necessary,
and will always be expected by the Indians, that the commanding officer of every post have it in his power to supply them in case of necessity with a little clothing, some

arms and ammunition to hunt with; also some provisions on their journey homewards, as well as a smith to repair their arms and working utensils, etc."[8]

Johnson suggested that since the traders at Oswego, on Lake Ontario, made a 50 per cent profit, which he thought reasonable for the expense and risk of transporting goods there, the traders in Detroit ought to be allowed somewhat more in proportion to the greater distance. He also sent to Amherst a list of merchandise usually wanted by the Indians. It is illuminating of their needs and tastes:

Strouds (coarse blankets) of blue, black, and scarlet; French and English blankets, the former being preferred; walsh cottons or pennistons for stockings; green napped frieze for stockings; worsted and yarn hose with clocks; flowered serges of lively colors; calicos and calimancos for gowns; ribbons of all sorts; linen for shirts and ready-made shirts; threads, needles, and awls; clasp knives and scalping knives; vermilion and verdigris for painting themselves; Jews harps and hawk bells; stone and plain rings; silver gorgets and trinkets; small beads, brass wire, horn combs, scissors, razors, and looking glasses; brass and tin kettles, large and small; tobacco and pipes and snuff boxes; tomahawks or small hatchets; black and white wampum; red leather trunks, pewter spoons, and gilt cups; flints, lead, duck shot; beaver and fox traps; iron fish spears; and rum.

In his reply Amherst assured Johnson that he intended to appoint to the command of Detroit an officer of strict integrity who would enforce the trade regulations on the traders and behave properly toward the Indians. "With regard to furnishing the latter with a little clothing, some arms and ammunition to hunt with, that is all very well in cases of necessity; but as, when the intended trade is once established they will be able to supply themselves

[8] *Johnson Papers*, III, 331, 334.

with these from the traders for their furs, I do not see why the Crown should be put to that expense. I am not either for giving them any provisions; when they find they can get it on asking for, they will grow remiss in their hunting, which must industriously be avoided; for so long as their minds are intent on business they will not have leisure to hatch mischief." He considered that Croghan had been too "bountiful" with the Indians at Fort Pitt. "Services must be rewarded; it has ever been a maxim with me. But as to purchasing the good behavior either of Indians or any others, [that] is what I do not understand. When men of whatsoever race behave ill, they must be punished but not bribed."[9]

Amherst's posture as a stern parent was ridiculous. It was the source of all the trouble that followed. At a time when the utmost tact and diplomacy were called for in order to cement the new friendship offered by the western Indians and to lead them permanently away from their old ties with the French, the commander-in-chief insisted on economy and discipline. He ignored the kind of treatment which the Indians had become accustomed to receive from the French and did not hesitate to inaugurate a contrasting policy. That the savages might come to look back upon the days of French supremacy as happier times apparently did not occur to him.

Moreover, he stupidly regarded the giving of presents as a kind of bribery, and he would have none of it. It was not bribery at all, but a technique of maintaining friendship—in the absence of other expressions of good will common among nations of white people—which the Indian could understand. He was accustomed to sharing food, clothing, and shelter with every visitor and stranger who came along. Therefore, it seemed to the Indian only

[9] *ibid.*, III, 345.

a mark of hospitality to be given food or clothing or ammunition by his host when he visited a fort.

The particular item of rum was a further irritation. While France controlled the Great Lakes, the British had encouraged English traders to go among the Indians and sell them all the rum they wanted. By this means the English obtained furs which the French wanted, won the friendship of the Indians, and hoped that drunkenness might provoke some trouble between the French and the savages. Now that the British had supplanted the French in the Great Lakes, the shoe was on the other foot. They wanted to keep liquor away from the Indians in order to avoid troubles growing out of drunkenness. To prevent unscrupulous traders from selling rum, it was necessary to confine the trade to the forts, where the traders could be watched and made accountable. The Indians disliked both this sudden stoppage of rum and the necessity of always bringing their furs into the fort in order to sell them. Formerly they had been able to sell to traders, or bush rangers, who followed them to their winter hunting camps.

The new régime of the British, therefore, was not what the Indians had been led to anticipate. No presents, no ammunition, no provisions were to be given them beyond a little clothing or powder in cases of necessity. No rum was to be sold them. Trade was to be confined to the forts. It is not surprising that the Indians found these measures harsh after the generosity and easy intercourse they had enjoyed with the French. Croghan and Johnson privately disapproved of Amherst's attitude and felt uneasy about the future.

The 1761 spring conference which the Detroit Indians planned with the Iroquois apparently never materialized. Nevertheless, two Seneca chiefs and a party of followers reached Detroit on June 14 with a message from the Iroquois council. The Senecas, living farthest west in New York province, had long been the least amenable (of that confederation) to English supervision. Since the fall of Fort Niagara in 1759 they had been harboring a private grudge because they had not been allowed to massacre the garrison. In 1760 their warriors had accompanied Amherst to Montreal, and again they had been restrained from scalping and plundering in revenge for injuries suffered by their ancestors at the hands of the French. Now, instead of being rewarded, they found that Amherst would give them no presents, nor allow them enough ammunition. He also restricted their movements and even now was giving away their lands.

This last charge was unfortunately as true as the others. Amherst had sought to reward some of his officers by allotting them land near Niagara. Not only did he exceed his authority, but he violated an old treaty between the Iroquois and the colony of New York. He was overruled in this measure as soon as news of it reached London. But for the moment the Senecas had very real grievances and they persuaded the Iroquois council to take action.

The message from the council to the western tribes was contained in a red wampum belt. It called for war against the English. The Senecas carried it to the Delawares and Shawnees in Ohio and to the Ottawas, Hurons, Chippewas, and Potawatomies of Detroit. They proposed nothing less than a simultaneous assault on the British posts at Detroit, Pittsburgh, Presqu'Isle, Venango, and Niagara. The ambitious attack was to be made about July 1.

Captain Campbell learned of the Senecas' proposal two days after they arrived at Detroit. He wrote immediately to the commandants at Fort Pitt, Presqu'Isle, and Niagara. He also sent boats to the Indian town of Sandusky to remove a large store of trader's goods which contained muskets, powder, lead, tomahawks, and knives. As the Senecas had invited the local tribes to a grand council in the vicinity of Sandusky, they might very well seize those trade goods as their first move. Campbell then sent for the chiefs of the four local tribes and told them he knew what the Senecas wanted.

Although these chiefs were disappointed by the British régime, they were not ready to make war. Besides, they had not yet forgiven the Iroquois for the attack on them at Niagara. Therefore, they said they would not go to Sandusky to the council. This demonstration of loyalty to the English, it should be noted, included Pontiac's village of Ottawas. The Senecas were forced to hold their council at the Huron town across the river on July 3.

Campbell employed a Frenchman to conceal himself and listen to the proceedings. The two Seneca chiefs, Kyashuta and Tahaiadoris by name, asked the western tribes to overlook the killings at Niagara and unite with the Iroquois to "cut off the English at Fort Detroit."[10] As was customary the local Indians did not return an answer until the following day, and then they insisted on making their reply at the fort in the presence of Captain Campbell. They told him what the Senecas had proposed and instead of accepting the war belt they turned it over to the commandant. The Senecas were abashed by this rebuff, but they stood up and recited their grievances against the English. Campbell advised them to return home and give up their hostile intentions. They said they would follow his advice and then departed.

The alarm was over, but it was a portent of what was rising in the wind.

[10] *Bouquet Papers*, Series 21646, pp. 210, 217, 230; Series 21655, pp. 123-124.

6

Peacemaking at Detroit

GEORGE CROGHAN had gone to New York in May 1761 to confer with Sir William Johnson about Indian affairs in the West. Although they had not yet learned of the two Senecas' mission to Detroit, Johnson realized that something ill was brewing. From Croghan's report he saw that peace in the West could not be insured unless a better understanding was reached. The change from French to English dominion must be made as smooth as possible. He conferred with General Amherst at Albany, and two decisions were reached: Johnson and Croghan would go to Detroit and hold a grand council with the Indians; and Amherst would send a large detachment of soldiers to complete the occupation of the western posts of Michilimackinac, Green Bay, St. Joseph, and a new fort at Sandusky, and to relieve the Rangers at Miamis and Ouiatenon.

The command of this expedition was entrusted to Maj. Henry Gladwin.

This was the same Henry Gladwin who as a lieutenant was wounded at Braddock's defeat in 1755. He had come to America under Braddock as an officer in the 48th Regiment. In December 1757 he was promoted to a captaincy, and early the next year he transferred to the 80th Regiment of Light Armed Foot, a new regiment raised by Col. Thomas Gage for wilderness fighting. His abilities were appreciated by Gage, and in the summer of 1759 Gladwin was left in command of the 80th with the temporary rank of major, during Gage's absence. Amherst made him a temporary major three times before the rank was confirmed in December 1760.

Gladwin had been with the rear guard in Amherst's advance on Montreal that summer and he was placed in command of the captured Fort de Levis, which was promptly renamed Fort William Augustus. It was situated on an island in the St. Lawrence River now called Chimney Island, about three miles above modern Ogdensburg, New York. Gladwin's colonel, now Brigadier General Gage, was made governor of Montreal.

As a post commandant Gladwin continued in the high esteem he had early won from Amherst. He was properly subordinate and careful in obeying orders, dodged no responsibility, and earned the reputation of being a ready and competent officer. Moreover, although he seems to have enjoyed the patronage of the Duke of Richmond, Gladwin was not so ambitious for promotion that he sought advancement through friends in England behind his commander's back, as so many officers with noble connections did. Amherst considered his merits too long neglected by the War Office. Even so, Gladwin had not done badly for himself; he was thirty-two years old and a major. And he was destined for greater glory as Pontiac's principal antagonist.

Amherst's orders to him were dated June 22, 1761, and required him to explore the new posts and make a proper distribution of troops to maintain them. Johnson's intended Indian council was mentioned, and Gladwin was cautioned to obey any of the superintendent's suggestions touching Indian affairs or for giving him assistance.

Gladwin made his way up to Niagara in July with 300 men of his regiment in boats. His equipment was not carried up the steep portage road around the falls until August 12. He met Johnson at Niagara where he was holding a preliminary Indian conference and waiting for his boats.

Gladwin went on ahead of him, his detachment increased at Johnson's suggestion by 60 men and two officers from Fort Niagara, in order to reinforce Captain Campbell at Detroit.

Meanwhile, George Croghan, who had returned to Pittsburgh from Johnson's, set out for Detroit at the end of July. As he picked up some Delaware chiefs on the way and stopped at Sandusky, he did not arrive in Detroit until August 16. He was welcomed by the chiefs of the Ottawas, Hurons, and Potawatomies. While awaiting Johnson's arrival he prepared the way for the grand council by some preliminary speeches. His Delaware friends spoke to the tribes, complimenting them on their refusal of the war belt offered by the Senecas and bidding them continue at peace with the English. Croghan allowed each nation a keg of rum and sought in other ways to induce a friendly mood.

After a stormy passage across treacherous Lake Erie, a passage made worse by illness, Major Gladwin arrived on September 1 with his detachment and promptly went to bed. He had developed a severe fever, probably malaria. He was unable to carry out any of his duties, and the loss of a large part of his provisions required a change of plans. For the time being the whole force remained in Detroit.

Johnson, his secretary and assistants, his retinue of Iroquois chiefs and boatmen, all appeared on September 3. The arrival of so distinguished a Crown officer required proper social activities by way of recognizing his rank as well as his widely known tastes. He was entertained at dinner twice by Captain Campbell in company with the other principal officers, and on the 6th the captain held another of his Sunday soirées, this time a ball. Johnson wrote in his journal that the ladies "assembled at 8 o'clock at night, to the number of about twenty. I opened the ball with Mademoiselle Curie—a fine girl. We danced until five o'clock next morning."[1]

The young lady, whose name Johnson did not catch correctly, was Angélique Cuillerier dit Beaubien, the belle of Detroit. She was 26 years old and lived with her older brother and parents just east of the fort. Her three older sisters were married—and at an age Angélique had passed by several years. Why so popular a girl was still single remains a mystery. Perhaps she was fickle, or felt herself too good for the local swains, or had suffered a disappointment. Certainly her family was respectable. The recent French commandant, Captain Bellestre, was her father's half-brother, and through him she was related to Alphonse Tonti, an earlier commandant of Detroit and Cadillac's colleague in founding the post. Her family was more North American than French, as her grandparents were all born in Canada. Her father, a trader, could afford a handsome dowry. Eventually Angélique did marry, and Pontiac unwittingly played Cupid.

The grand council was opened out of doors on September 9, after some preliminary greetings had been disposed of. The ceremonies and formalities of such occasions deserve some explanation. The party calling the conference spoke first and said all he had to say without interruption. He stopped frequently to allow interpreters to restate his speech in the language or languages of his audience. In the absence of writing, the speaker emphasized his points by handing over to his audience a string of wampum or a belt of wampum, made of shell or glass beads. These strings and belts were fashioned in various colors and patterns, following in some instances conventional and meaningful designs. They became the only tangible record of a speech intelligible to the In-

[1] Stone, *Johnson*, II, 459.

dians. They were preserved as evidence of the speaker's sincerity and to help recall what he had said. Months later an Indian would reconstruct the principal import of a speech by studying the wampum.

Among Indians a speaker was rarely answered until the next day. When he finished, he might be followed by one of his assistants or allies who had something to add. After everybody on one side had finished, the conference broke up until the following day. The chiefs who were addressed retired and discussed what they had heard. They determined on their answer and selected one of their number to deliver it. Proper strings or belts of wampum to emphasize the message had to be made up, if available ones were not suitable. When the conference reconvened, the delegated chief replied for his colleagues and delivered the proper pieces of wampum. The first speaker might then rise and acknowledge the reply. The formal part of the council concluded, the party who had called it, particularly if he was a white man, passed out presents of clothing, ammunition, trinkets, and liquor.

The council at Detroit followed this traditional pattern. Johnson made the first speech. He complimented the tribes on their friendly behavior since the arrival of the English and said he had come to brighten the "chain of friendship" (a favorite metaphor) and to urge them to "hold fast" to it. Actually he was, as the king's representative, formally proclaiming peace between these Indians and the British. He expatiated on how attentive King George was to the welfare of all his subjects and assured them of his royal clemency and favor to all who were willing to enter into an alliance with the British Crown. He denied that the Indians would be deprived of any more land than was necessary for promoting an extensive commerce advantageous to them, or than that "to which they [the English] have lawful claim." He gently remonstrated with them for not having yet turned in all their captives and for stealing horses.

Despite its formal setting and its high-flown phrases, the speech was rather thin for Johnson to have traveled so far to deliver in person. It must have disappointed the assembled Indians, for it made no mention of the two factors most disturbing to them: the high prices of goods and the scarcity of ammunition. Johnson's intentions had been good, but he had had the meat taken out of his speech before he arrived. While on his way west he had received fresh instructions dated August 9 from Amherst, who ordered him to give up the practice of "purchasing the good behavior of the Indians by presents" and added that "keeping them scarce of ammunition is not less to be recommended." Amherst had written: "I think it much better to avoid all presents in the future, since that will oblige them to supply themselves by barter and of course keep them more constantly employed, by means of which they will have less time to concert, or carry into execution, any schemes prejudicial to His Majesty's interests," and as for ammunition, "nothing can be so impolitic as to furnish them with the means of accomplishing the evil which is so much dreaded."[2] This order was so dangerous that Johnson dared not even hint of the new policy to the Indians.

His speech was followed by echoes from one of his faithful Mohawks, who testified to the advantage of being allied to the English. (He did not know of Amherst's recent orders either.) He also warned the tribes to pay no attention to rumors carried by any other Iroquois tribe, such as the Senecas, since the Mohawks would be first to know the intentions of the English because they lived closest to them.

The next day the Detroit tribes made their reply. A

[2] *Johnson Papers*, III, 515.

Huron chief, Anaiasa, spoke first, expressing gratification that their conduct had merited the approval of Johnson and General Amherst and pledging his nation to be henceforth faithful allies of the English. He admitted some horse stealing, but said it had been done by "some of our idle young men, who you know are very difficult to restrain." He said that the last English prisoners among the Hurons had just been delivered up to Croghan. Then he urged Johnson to make good his promises of an extensive trade, because so far the Indians had found goods expensive and ammunition very scarce, which latter restriction seriously affected their hunting. Having given Johnson a belt of wampum for each point in his speech, Anaiasa sat down.

The speaker for the Ottawas then rose. It was not Pontiac, but another chief named Macatepilesis. No mention of Pontiac's presence at the council is found. Yet it is difficult to believe that he would have missed so signal an event. No doubt he was there, but his earlier cordiality or at least toleration for the English was fast disappearing. He was skeptical of their promises; their stinginess and high prices were the realities he encountered. Whether or not Johnson's smooth tongue mollified him for the moment, the effect did not last.

The choice of Macatepilesis for speaker reflects one of two possibilities: either Pontiac was passed over because he was not in sympathy with his village's ready acceptance of Johnson's speech, or simply it was the right and duty of an older civil chief to speak in such a council, and Pontiac was a war chief. Macatepilesis spoke for the "Ottawa confederation," as Johnson termed it. This does not mean a confederation of the Ottawas, Chippewas, and Potawatomies, as some historians have thought, but the association of four bands which composed the nation called Ottawa. These four were the Kiskakons, Sinagoes, Sables, and the Nassauaketons.

After exchanging preliminary courtesies, Macatepilesis continued, addressing Johnson as "Brother Warraghiyagey":

"We were called to Fort Duquesne at the time of the war between you and the French [1759]. We immediately attended your summons, where we found Mr. Croghan, who spoke to us by order of the general, that we might acquaint the nations of his intentions to live at peace with them, and to require them to do the same and act as friends and allies to the English; since which time we have begun to look upon you as friends and not in the light in which you had been represented to us by the French."

Here he handed over a belt of wampum and proceeded:

"Brother, I speak on the part of all our confederacy here present, who are charmed with the speech which you made to them yesterday, and determined to act for the future agreeable thereto, and to make all nations of Indians acquainted therewith, even to the setting sun, and with the great work which you have now executed, whereby you have established tranquility throughout the land and made the roads and the waters of our lakes smooth and passable which were before rough and dangerous."

He gave another belt.

"Brother, you have wisely recommended to us to pay no regard for the future to any evil reports which may be spread, and you desire to know the people who sent the bad bird lately amongst us to stir us up against our brethren. It is certain such bad birds have been amongst us, but we should look upon ourselves as a very unhappy people if we paid any attention to such disturbers of peace whom we shall always despise for attempting to put such evil thoughts into our ears, who are all determined as one man to hold fast by the covenant chain for ever."[3]

He offered another belt and turned to the Mohawks, assuring them that the Ottawas no longer bore them any ill will. He gave them a bunch of black and white wampum and sat down.

A Chippewa chief also spoke, and then Johnson concluded the meeting. On the following day he distributed the presents he had brought along and ordered an ox roasted for a general feast. He dared not hint that these presents were not a sample of English generosity, but rather the last gifts the Indians might receive.

On September 14 and 15 Johnson returned the civilities he had received by entertaining the principal inhabitants at dinner the first night and by giving a ball the second. "In the evening," he wrote in his journal, "the ladies and gentlemen assembled at my quarters [the house of the late French commandant], danced the whole night until 7 o'clock in the morning, when all parted very much pleased and happy. I promised to write Mademoiselle Curie as soon as possible my sentiments; there never was so brilliant an assembly here before."[4]

Whatever Sir William's sentiments regarding the fascinating Angélique Cuillerier may have been, he apparently did not set them down on paper. But the young lady was not destined to pass into obscurity. She was yet to play a dramatic and romantic role in Detroit.

Johnson remained in Detroit until September 17, holding private conferences with particular chiefs and drawing up regulations for trade and instructions to the commanding officers of the western posts. At least he could do that much.

Johnson's price list for Detroit is not available, but the

[3] *ibid.*, III, 487-488.
[4] Stone, *Johnson*, II, 462-463.

exchanges can be easily estimated from his list for Fort Miamis as compared with that for Fort Pitt and Croghan's list for Sandusky issued the previous winter. Not only was the cost of trade goods in pelts important to the Indians, but the relative value of particular kinds of fur as well. Prices were quoted in terms of beavers or buckskins, from which latter we derive our slang expression of "bucks" for dollars. Johnson's ratio of exchange in furs was the same for Pittsburgh and Miamis, and therefore must have been no different for Detroit. He decreed that one beaver was worth one good buckskin or one small buckskin and one doeskin. Two beavers were worth three buckskins, and three beavers, four buckskins. One small beaver was worth one marten—or two raccoons; and apparently it required four or five raccoons to equal one good beaver. However, Croghan had listed six raccoons for one beaver at Sandusky in February 1761.

In terms of trade goods, one stroud (the great common denominator of trade) cost three beavers, or four bucks, at Miamis and Sandusky and doubtless at Detroit. The price was lower at Pittsburgh, being two beavers. A man's large blanket cost three beavers at Detroit, while a single striped one cost two beavers. Gunpowder was one beaver per pound. Four bars of lead likewise cost one beaver. A man's shirt cost one beaver, while a ruffled shirt was twice as much. These are samples from a long list.[5]

Johnson's instructions to commanding officers advised them "to keep up a good understanding with all Indians" who lived near their post, to keep in touch with other commandants so that they could act uniformly, to employ an interpreter, to see that the traders complied with the regulations, and to allow the Indians to have their arms

[5] *Johnson Papers*, III, 531-535; *Bouquet Papers*, Series 21646, p. 26.

repaired by a smith at Crown expense. No mention was made about giving presents or distributing powder.

On his departure Johnson stopped at the Huron town across the river and held another meeting. There Anaiasa asked that the English traders advance the Indians goods on credit, after the custom of the French traders. He also requested that their guns and hatchets be repaired free of charge and that some hoes be sent them for cultivation of their cornfields. These requests really were urgent. The Indians had allowed their domestic economy to decline during the war by not replacing goods that were used up, by neglecting their planting, and by exhausting their ammunition. Moreover, many of their best hunters had been killed in the war. Johnson promised to send a gunsmith and a couple of hundred hoes to Detroit (both of which he did), but he explained that as each English trader was free to offer credit or not, he could not compel them to do so.

Johnson arrived at his home the last of October and reported optimistically to Amherst that he had left "the western nations extremely well disposed towards the English; and I am of opinion that matters are settled on so stable a foundation there that unless greatly irritated thereto, they will never break the peace established with them."[6] The qualifying phrase was the important part of the statement. He forwarded some additional information he had picked up. He had learned that in all there were 1,180 fighting men among the savages of the Detroit River and Saginaw Bay, the Ottawas contributing upwards of 220 to that total. "They are all connected together in an offensive and defensive alliance with the Delawares, Shawnees, Miamies, Weas, Mascoutens, Kickapoos and all the nations of the North." In a broad hint to Amherst, he mentioned that under the French régime

[6] *Johnson Papers*, III, 559.

the Indians never showed any dislike of the garrisons maintained at the forts, but were suspicious if those garrisons were increased or if new forts were built.

Amherst got the hint. "With regard to their objection against our erecting a blockhouse at Sandusky," he replied, "that has no manner of weight with me. A post at that place is absolutely necessary, not only for the above purposes of keeping up the communication, but also to keep the Canadians in proper subjection; I must and will, therefore, say what they will, have one at that place."[7] Blandly he went on to say that "the disposition you left the western Indians in leaves me no doubt but that everything in those parts will remain quiet, as there can be no fear of their being irritated or provoked by any of His Majesty's subjects."

Peace, peace, all was serene. Yet already Pontiac was murmuring. He said the English were liars. Instead of selling blankets for two beavers, as promised him at Fort Pitt the year before, a blanket cost three beavers. He was correct, although he may have misunderstood; more likely he had been deceived. A blanket could be had for two beavers at Pittsburgh, but the price was higher at Detroit. Moreover, Pontiac complained that the British had told him last year that four raccoons would be accepted for one beaver, and now he said the English traders wanted six raccoons for one beaver. Indeed that was the exchange ratio fixed at Sandusky by Croghan, but Johnson had lowered it apparently to four or five raccoons per beaver. Possibly the traders were flouting the new regulation.

Pontiac also complained of the ban on sales of rum, which had been so plentiful during the war. He was disappointed at the failure to institute annual congresses of Indians and British where presents were heaped on the former. What should have been alarming to the English

[7] *ibid.*, III, 515-516, 570.

was that Pontiac was winning converts to his point of view.

Amherst's assumption that none of His Majesty's subjects would irritate the Indians was as absurd as his belief that he himself did not provoke them. He seemed to waver between regarding the Indians as self-dependent allies and as conquered subjects. Speaking of the Senecas' unsuccessful war mission to Detroit, he boasted that their machinations had never given him a moment's concern. "I had it in my power not only to frustrate them, but to punish the delinquents with entire destruction, which I am firmly resolved on whenever any of them give me cause."

After Captain Campbell learned privately from Johnson of Amherst's orders, he confided his apprehension to Bouquet at Fort Pitt. "Every thing is now quiet, tho I am certain if the Indians knew General Amherst's sentiments about keeping them short of powder it would be impossible to keep them in temper." And in a postscript he added: "If you could send us some ammunition it would be doing a good thing, tho it is against the general's orders."[8] Toward the end of November, Campbell wrote again. "All the Indian nations have gone to their hunting and by that means will be quiet here till spring. I hope the general will change his present way of thinking with regard to Indian affairs. As I am of the opinion if they were supplied with ammunition it would prevent their doing mischief."[9]

Campbell knew his Indians far better than the austere general did. Croghan and Johnson agreed privately with him, but did not dare confront Amherst and call him a fool. However, Johnson did write, early in December: "There is in my opinion a necessity for putting some

[8] *Bouquet Papers*, Series 21647, pp. 161-162.
[9] *ibid.*, Series 21647, p. 210.

clothing, ammunition, etc. into the hands of the commanding officers at Oswego, Niagara, and Detroit, etc. to be occasionally given to such Indians as are found deserving and serviceable, and as they have been used heretofore to receive presents in great abundance. I submit it to your Excellency whether it will be thought convenient to break off that expence all at once, until everything be entirely settled throughout the country."[10]

He was putting the matter as casually and delicately as he could. General Amherst replied that he did not think presents necessary. Fortunately for the British, they were safe from the effects of this policy until spring, when the Indians would come in from their winter's hunting. Possibly Amherst felt he was safe in the West by the new distribution of British troops, which had taken place in spite of Major Gladwin's illness. Capt. Henry Balfour had taken 120 men northward from Detroit on September 9. He arrived at Fort Michilimackinac on the 28th and posted Lieut. William Leslye and twenty-eight men to the garrison. It had been abandoned by the French commandant, Capt. Louis de Beaujeu, in the fall of 1760 in violation of the terms of Canada's surrender. Captain de Beaujeu took his garrison down to Fort de Chartres on the Mississippi, where he remained to make trouble.

Michilimackinac was on the sandy beach on the south side of the straits. The stockade of posts was roughly square and contained five long barracks for soldiers and traders, a few houses and storerooms, a church and priest's house, a powder magazine, guard house, and a few other buildings. Although much smaller than Fort Detroit, its interior was less crowded. The fort was the most important one north of Detroit, since it controlled the commerce on three lakes and served as a place of deposit for fur traders and as a place of resort for several Indian tribes.

[10] *Johnson Papers*, III, 582.

Chippewas inhabited the immediate vicinity, but a considerable village of Ottawas was located twenty miles southwest on Lake Michigan. The post had been occupied for a year by bush-ranging French traders, largely half-breeds. Nominal command had been left to Lieut. Charles de Langlade, the trader and partisan officer who had served in the late war. From him Captain Balfour received whatever forms remained of an official transfer of authority. A few hardy English traders had preceded their troops to the place in an effort to preempt some of the rich northern trade. Mercantile as well as imperial interests demanded the presence of British arms at these outposts of civilization.

Balfour next visited the fort of La Baye, at the head of Green Bay, which was likewise abandoned. He renamed it Fort Edward Augustus and placed Ensign James Gorrell in command on October 12 with seventeen men. This fort protected the main route from the Ottawa River and Lake Michigan to the Upper Mississippi via the Wisconsin River, and it drew on the trade of the Winnebagoes, Menominees, Sauks, and Foxes.

Returning to Lake Michigan, Balfour's expedition proceeded southward to the St. Joseph River and passed southeastward up that stream to Fort St. Joseph, whose French garrison long since had departed. In the heart of the Potawatomi country, this post guarded the route from the head of Lake Michigan to the French settlements on the middle Mississippi via the St. Joseph-Kankakee portage and the Illinois River. Ensign Francis Schlosser, a very young man too fond of liquor, was left in command on November 9 with fifteen men. With his remaining party Balfour returned to Detroit overland.

Meanwhile, in October Ensign Robert Holmes was dispatched from Detroit to Fort Miamis with fifteen men to relieve Lieutenant Butler of Rogers' Rangers. This fort commanded the portage between the Maumee and the Little Wabash, which rivers connected Lake Erie with the Ohio. On November 6, Lieut. Edward Jenkins and twenty men were sent to Fort Ouiatenon to relieve Ensign Wait of the Rangers. This Wabash River post guarded the southwestern extension of Canada, for below it the high land (Terre Haute) marked the boundary between Canada and Louisiana.

The rest of Gladwin's command had been returned to Niagara under Capt. Norman McLeod to forward provisions to Detroit. Gladwin himself did not recover sufficiently to travel until the middle of October, when he returned to Fort William Augustus in the St. Lawrence. His first visit to Detroit was not only inauspicious, it was disappointing on all sides.

The new blockhouse at Sandusky, on the south shore of the bay a dozen miles from its mouth, was finished late in November; and the builder, Lieut. Elias Meyer, remained to command it with fifteen men. The British flag seemed firmly planted among the western Great Lakes.

7

Origin of Pontiac's War

DURING 1762 the Detroit Indians gradually discovered what neither Campbell nor Johnson dared tell them: the real nature of British Indian policy as laid down by General Amherst.

That revelation came slowly, but it cracked the peace which Johnson thought he had cemented by his grand council. The Indians returned to their villages in the spring, bringing in the furs from the animals they had shot or trapped during the winter. Once more they found no rum to be had for celebration. What was more ominous to them, their ammunition was shot away and they could procure only a little more—hardly enough with which to supply their families with game during the summer.

The situation was somewhat relieved by the increased number of traders in Detroit with stocks of ammunition to sell, sometimes on credit. However, the Indians expected anything so vital to their welfare as powder to be a gift from the English, as it had been from the French, out of friendship and gratitude to an ally. It was the old Indian idea of sharing property as against the white man's concept of private property. Campbell smoothed over this dissatisfaction as best he could by diplomatic speeches, gifts of tobacco and rum and even a little powder. The gunsmith promised by Johnson was now in Detroit ready to repair Indian arms, and the two hundred hoes were distributed to the Hurons. Campbell believed the prohibition on rum was having a good effect, but he wrote to Bouquet on July 3:

"The general says the Crown is to be no longer at the expense of maintaining the Indians, that they may very well live by their hunting, and desires to keep them scarce of powder. I should be glad to know what you do in that respect. I am certain if the Indians in this country had the least hint that we intended to prevent them from the use of ammunition, it would be impossible to keep them quiet. I dare not trust even the interpreters with the secret. The Indians are a good deal elevated on the news of a Spanish war [Spain had joined France, and Britain had thereupon declared war on her January 2, 1762] and daily reports spread amongst them that the French and Spaniards are soon to retake Quebec, etc. This goes from one nation to another, and it is impossible to prevent it. I assure you they only want a good opportunity to fall upon us if they had encouragement from an enemy."[1]

The last sentence was prophetic. What Amherst never realized was that by his policy he was playing directly into the hands of the disaffected French. After all, France and Great Britain were still at war; the capitulation of Canada had been only one great victory. But Spain had just come into the war on the side of France, and France still held Louisiana, which province included the forts on the Mississippi and Vincennes on the Wabash. Loyal Frenchmen were still hopeful that from somewhere France might draw the strength to throw back the British and recover Canada. They were not averse to suggesting to the Indians that a new French expedition was on its way to recapture Quebec and Montreal. The Indians, knowing nothing of affairs in Europe, some of them hoping these rumors were true, often did believe them.

Moreover, the French told them that the English se-

[1] *Bouquet Papers*, Series 21648, p. 1.

cretly planned to wipe out the Indians. Their first step was to deprive the Indians of ammunition so they would be unable to defend themselves. Was it not so? The Indians could not deny that they were being kept short of powder. What if the explanation whispered by the French were correct?

Affairs within the fort went along much as usual in 1762. Campbell was kept busy trying to get enough provisions forwarded to Detroit and thence distributed to the dependent posts. Sir Robert Davers, one of those British tourists still to be found in odd corners of the earth, had spent the winter in Detroit learning the Indian languages and making himself an agreeable visitor. About the first of May he left for a tour of the Lakes. Thomas Hutchins, a young native of New Jersey who had studied surveying and cartography, arrived at Detroit toward the end of April bound on a mission for George Croghan to map the Great Lakes. Campbell gave him what assistance he could and saw him safely on his way northward.

On June 4, King George's birthday, Campbell gave a ball at which, he wrote to Johnson, "a certain acquaintance of yours appeared to great advantage. She never neglects an opportunity of asking about the general. What, says she, is there no Indian councils to be held here this summer? I think by her talk Sir William had promised to return to Detroit. She desired I would present you her best compliments."[2]

Angélique Cuillerier was hardly pining away, however. A young Irish trader named James Sterling had arrived in Detroit the year before and by his personal charm seems to have won acceptance among several French families. He was hard working, ambitious, and cultivated the friendship of the Indians, who were both his customers and his suppliers. Whenever he raised his eyes from busi-

[2] *Johnson Papers*, III, 759.

ness, they fastened agreeably upon Angélique, who found his interest pleasant.

Changes were in store for Detroit. General Amherst wanted Lake Superior explored this year and the French posts there garrisoned. The Canada he had conquered stretched clear to the upper Mississippi, and the British flag had not yet been carried beyond Green Bay. He decided to appoint Major Gladwin to the command of Detroit and move Captain Campbell up to the fort at St. Mary's River (Sault Ste. Marie), built in 1751, where he would have charge of the Lake Superior region. However, his instructions to Gladwin allowed that officer discretion in assigning Campbell.

Gladwin arrived in Detroit on August 23, 1762, bringing with him Capt. George Etherington, Lieuts. John Jamet and Jehu Hay, and another company of the Royal Americans. Learning that the Lake Superior posts were in ruins, he decided to keep Campbell at Detroit, as well as Lieutenant Hay, who earns our gratitude for having started the next year to keep a daily diary. Gladwin sent Captain Etherington to supersede Lieutenant Leslye at Fort Michilimackinac, and Lieutenant Jamet was to occupy the fort at St. Mary's. The latter assignment proved shortlived, for on December 10 the fort burned to the ground, and Jamet took his small garrison into Fort Michilimackinac for the winter. The only other change in command was the relief of Lieutenant Meyer at Fort Sandusky, who was succeeded by his second, Ensign Christopher Pauli.

The summer and fall passed without incident among the Indians, Gladwin thought, but of one significant occurrence he never learned. On the night of September 28 a Detroit Indian reached George Croghan's house on the edge of Pittsburgh and related a strange story. He said that a secret council had been held during the summer at the Ottawa village on the Detroit River. It was attended by civil and war chiefs of the Ottawas, Chippewas, Hurons, Potawatomies, and of the tribes around Lake Superior, which latter delegates were accompanied by two Frenchmen in Indian dress. The informer did not know what was discussed in the council, but he was sure they were plotting against the English. He did know that deputies were sent to carry the council's message to the tribes on the Wabash and to the Shawnees in the Ohio Valley; otherwise the council was kept secret even from the other Indians around Detroit.[3]

Croghan was disturbed, and two days later he related this news to three Iroquois he knew to be trustworthy and loyal. They replied that they had heard the same news from a Shawnee brave. Thereupon Croghan sent his intelligence to Johnson and Amherst. The general dismissed it with the comment that he could see nothing of consequence in it. Blindly he had just ordered a reduction in the expenses and personnel of the Indian department under Johnson, thus stopping the presents which Croghan had been giving the Indians because the fort commandants could not.

It is difficult to resist the temptation to see Pontiac's hand in this council. The Ottawas had always been most attached to the French and were least cordial to the English. Within a few short months he was to emerge as the leader of those Indians who hated the English and wanted to restore the French. He had been expressing his disgust with British rule since the previous autumn, although it does not follow that he called the conference. Much more probably the instigators of it were the two Frenchmen, who may have come from Illinois or have been acting on orders from there.

Croghan found support for his faith in the story from

[3] Croghan's ms. diary, Sept. 28, 1762.

⟨ 96 ⟩

the report of Thomas Hutchins, who returned at the end of September from his extensive mapping tour of the Great Lakes. "They were disappointed," said Hutchins of the northern Ottawas and Chippewas, "in their expectations of my having presents for them; and as the French have always accustomed themselves, both in time of peace and during the late war, to make these people great presents three or four times a year and always allowed them a sufficient quantity of ammunition at the posts, they think it very strange that this custom should be so immediately broke off by the English, and the traders not allowed even to take so much ammunition with them as to enable those Indians to kill game sufficient for the support of their families."[4]

In December 1762 another of Croghan's agents who had been several weeks among the Shawnees (decimated by a plague during the summer) returned and reported that they had received a war belt and hatchet from the Weas on the Wabash the previous spring, who had received it from the French in Illinois. Croghan was very pessimistic in his letter to Johnson. He warned that the western tribes believed now that the English were preparing them for annihilation and that the blow would fall as soon as all the white captives had been recovered from them.

"The Indians are a very jealous people," he reminded his superior, "and they had great expectations of being very generally supplied by us, and from their poverty and mercenary disposition they can't bear such a disappointment. Undoubtedly the general has his own reason for not allowing any present or ammunition to be given them, and I wish it may have its desired effect, but I take this opportunity to acquaint you that I dread the event

[4] Hutchins' report to Croghan, *Mich. Hist. Mag.*, x (1926), 372-373.

as I know Indians can't long persevere. They are a rash, inconsistent people and inclined to mischief and will never consider consequences, though it may end in their ruin. Their success the beginning of this war on our frontiers is too recent in their memory to suffer them to consider their present inability to make war with us, and if the Senecas, Delawares and Shawnees should break with us, it will end in a general war with all the western nations, though they at present seem jealous of each other."[5]

That jealousy—the inability to cooperate under a single leader—was all that saved the English from an Indian war, Croghan believed. But that leader was in the making. And the force that would modify intertribal jealousies and turn the nations against a common enemy was burgeoning in the Ohio Valley. It remained only for the coming leader to adopt this doctrine and preach it as a call to arms—then war would be inevitable.

Down in the Ohio Valley a psychopathic Delaware was having strange visions and exhorting his people to change their way of living. White men were slow to hear of him, and the few who did learn of his revolutionary doctrines did not know his name. He was called the Delaware Prophet, or the Impostor. John McCullough, who was captured on the frontier by the Delawares and taken to Mahoning on Beaver Creek, refers to him in 1762 as follows:

"My brother has gone to Tus-ca-la-ways [Tuscarawas, a Delaware town on the Tuscarawas River], about forty or fifty miles off, to see and hear a prophet that had just made his appearance amongst them. He was of the Delaware nation; I never saw nor heard him. It was said by those who went to see him, that he had certain hieroglyphics marked on a piece of parchment, denoting the probation that human beings were subjected to whilst

[5] *Johnson Papers*, III, 965.

they were living on earth, and also denoting something of a future state. They informed me that he was almost constantly crying whilst he was exhorting them. I saw a copy of his hieroglyphics, as numbers of them had got them copied and undertook to preach or instruct others. The first (or principle doctrine) they taught them was to purify themselves from sin, which they taught they could do by the use of emetics and abstainence from carnal knowledge of the different sexes; to quit the use of fire arms, and to live entirely in their original state that they were in before the white people found out their country; nay, they taught that the fire was not pure that was made by steel and flint, but that they should make it by rubbing two sticks together. . . . It was said that their prophet taught them, or made them believe, that he had his instructions immediately from Keesh-she-la-mil-lang-up, or a being that thought us into being, and that by following his instructions they should in a few years be able to drive the white people out of their country."[6]

The fact that the Prophet was "almost constantly crying whilst he was exhorting them" suggests his mental condition. His force as a prophet was increased by his visible sincerity and his heaven-declared authority. James Kenny, a young Quaker trader in Pittsburgh, describes him in more detail in his diary. Under date of October 15, 1762, he wrote:

"I think I have made mention before [he had not] of the Imposter which is raised amongst the Delawares, in order to show them the right way to Heaven. This plan is portrayed on a dressed leather skin and some[times] on paper; [it] fixes the earth at the bottom and heaven at the top, having a stright line from one to the other by which their forefathers used to ascend to happiness. About the middle is like a long square cutting their way

[6] McCullough's Narrative in Loudon, *Selections*, I, 321-322.

to happiness at right angles and stopping them, representing the white people. The outside is a long square-like black stroke circumscribing the whole within it, and joining on the left hand, issuing from the white people's place, is cut many strokes parallel to their square of situation. All these strokes represent all the sins and vices which the Indians have learned from the white people through which now they must go, the good road being stopped. Hell being fixed not far off, there they are led irrevocably. The doctrine issued on this and the way to help it is said to be to learn to live without any trade or connections with the white people, clothing and supporting themselves as their forefathers did; it's also said that the Imposter prognosticates that there will be two or three good talks [i.e. conferences] and then war. This gains amongst them so much that mostly they have quit hunting any more than to supply nature in that way."[7]

It seems clear from this account that the Prophet had learned a smattering of Christianity, which after meditation and self-induced visions he had adapted or misinterpreted for Indian consumption. Kenny also furnishes a clue as to where the Prophet obtained his idea of shaking off the white man's unhappy influence by going back to primitive living. In his diary for February 27, 1762, Kenny mentions that several years earlier some strange Indians from the West visited the Delaware towns. They told of their own people, who used only bows and arrows and had no dealings with the white men. The reason, of course, was that they lived beyond the reach of white traders. But the fact that there were tribes existing who could and did support themselves without firearms or other articles introduced by white men possibly impressed itself on the mind of the Prophet.

It should be noted that the Delaware Prophet was not

[7] Pa. Mag. of Hist. and Biog., xxxvii (1913), 170, 175.

a war chief who desired to lead a military expedition to drive out the English and restore French domination. He decried the baneful influence of all white men because it had brought the Indians to their present unhappy plight. He was an evangelist, a revivalist, preaching a new religion. He was trying to change the personal habits of the Indians in order to free them from imported vices and to make them entirely self-dependent. He gave his hearers faith and hope that they could live without the manufactures of the white man. He offered them salvation through hard work and steadfast purpose.

Reports of this doctrine spread among the Indian nations. Groups of Indians traveled far to hear the Delaware Prophet, and disciples took up his message and relayed it. From one of them, possibly from the master himself, Pontiac heard the narrative of the Prophet's vision. Whether or not he followed the interpretation to the conclusion of simple, resourceful living, he shrewdly recognized the power of the Prophet's argument. Here was an appeal that could unite the Indians in a common war effort!

The situation was indeed ripe for an explosion. The Indians' grievances against the English were solid and numerous. Foremost among them was the English refusal to supply them free ammunition for hunting. Unreasonable as such a grievance may appear today, the French had accustomed the Indians to this vital handout. When the English denied them, their refusal was akin to taking the bread from their mouths. That astute soldier of fortune, Col. Henry Bouquet, observed to General Gage as Pontiac's war was dying out: "And we have visibly brought upon us this Indian War by being too saving of a few presents to the savages which properly distributed would certainly have prevented it."[8] Secondly,

[8] *Bouquet Papers*, Series 21653, p. 334.

the prices of trade goods were not as low as the Indians had been led to anticipate. Thirdly, the English did not make them presents as often or as bountifully as the French had done, either as rent for the land or as gratitude for friendship. The English objected even to giving gifts when captives were returned. Fourthly, the Indians objected to the prohibition on liquor, even though the wiser chiefs regarded it as beneficial. The young braves resented it not alone because they liked to get drunk, but because as long as the French controlled the forts the English had been so generous in supplying rum. Now in control themselves, the English dropped the mask and showed their contempt for such Indian tastes.

Finally, the Indians were not slow to realize that actually the English had no liking for them. The arrogance, or reserve, toward native peoples which has usually characterized British colonial administrators was typified in Amherst. The Indians had been useful pawns during the war, and it was a stratagem of warfare to lure them away from the French. Now that Canada had surrendered and peace was in sight, the Indians had no further military value. They were not only to be dismissed, but insofar as possible ignored. Their "begging" was a nuisance and an expense, and Amherst thought he could humble them with discipline. That arrogance was further expressed in the orders forbidding the soldiers to mingle with the Indians. Neither were the savages welcomed in the forts. They were expected to state their business and get out. Gladwin himself was accused of showing contempt for Indian customs. Intermarriage was frowned upon. All this was in marked contrast to the camaraderie and friendliness of the French, many of whom had found the Indian maidens attractive enough to take as wives.

Farther east the Delawares and Iroquois had other grievances. They had been led to believe that the British were going to drive out the French and restore their invaded hunting grounds to the Indians. But after the British drove out the French, they stayed; and new settlers were moving into the Monongahela Valley, west of the mountains, and into the Susquehanna Valley, claimed by the Iroquois. Even the British military could not justify this westward expansion and did make efforts to eject the lawless squatters. The job was too big for the garrison at Fort Pitt, however, for the settlers continued to pour over the mountains. The Senecas also resented the demands of the English in criminal cases and were at the moment objecting to the surrender of the murderers of a white man for trial and punishment by Englishmen.

The Great Lakes tribes had not yet been crowded by farmer settlers, but they heard the complaints of the nations to the east of them and could see the danger ahead. The Lakes tribes had indicated their attitude toward the land to George Croghan in December 1760. They regarded it as theirs to hunt on, and the French as tenants who had been allowed a few acres here and there on which to establish trading posts and forts as much for the convenience of the Indians as for the profit of the French. The land was not theirs to transfer to the British, although they might assign them the forts agreeable to the Indian landlords. The English had to all appearances accepted this view by notifying the Indians of their intended occupation of the forts, by assuring them of generous treatment and advantageous trade (rent, in a sense), and by seeking their friendship. In other words, these savages believed that the British had succeeded the French at the western posts by permission of the Indians.

Logical as it was, this attitude was ignored by the British, who in common with other Europeans never recognized the Indian tribes as sovereign nations. They purchased land from the Indians as owners, but did so primarily as a means of avoiding expensive warfare, rather than of securing valid title. That body of usages called international law was not construed by European colonial powers as conferring any rights on savage or even unchristian nations. Such nations were not considered members of that vague entity called "the family of nations" who enjoyed the rights and were bound by the duties of international law.[9] The United States of America was in fact the first non-European country admitted to the family of nations.

This legal concept had been expressed as recently as 1758 in a famous treatise produced by the eminent Swiss jurist, Emer de Vattel. Ignoring ethical considerations, Vattel laid down the principle that the uncertain occupancy by wandering tribes of the vast regions of the New World "cannot be held as real and lawful taking possession; and when the Nations of Europe, which are too confined at home, come upon lands which the savages have no special need of and are making no present and continuous use of, they may lawfully take possession of them and establish colonies in them."[10] What Vattel failed to realize, of course, was that a hunting people could not settle down in one region and expect the game to remain there too. They "wandered" in search of food, and the land which the savages seemed to "have no special need of" was vital game cover which replenished itself while they hunted in a fresh region. White men not only

[9] Fenwick, *International Law*, p. 83.

[10] *ibid.*, p. 223. Vattel's reasoning was also in great vogue in the nineteenth century, when various European powers were seizing portions of Africa from savage and unchristian natives. Abyssinia is an example of a primitive country which successfully resisted European conquest and eventually achieved recognition as a member of the family of nations. The day passed when her territorial integrity had no meaning in international law, and consequently Mussolini's attempt in 1935 to annex the country as a colony was abhorred as a breach of international law.

killed off the game themselves, but by their settlements scared away the animals from formerly rich hunting areas.

Added to all these rankling thoughts in the Indian mind, plus the exhortation of the "divinely appointed" Prophet, were the intrigues of the French in Illinois urging revolt and promising aid. Possibly the Indians would have taken up the hatchet in time by themselves, although they would have been slower to act without the whispered assurances of the French. The role of the Illinois French in encouraging war was lawful prior to September 24, 1763, the date official news reached Illinois that France had signed the treaty of peace and thereby bound the Province of Louisiana to its observance. Before that date war was still in progress, and the undefeated French of Louisiana had every right to prosecute it by stirring up the Indians against the English. For the French of Canada to do so, however, was a violation of the terms of the capitulation of September 8, 1760, a point of honor in eighteenth century warfare.

The evidence of French instigation is indirect, yet fairly conclusive. We do not know it from French sources, but both the British and Indians blamed the French, and their accusations cannot be laid entirely to prejudice in the one case or the desire to exculpate themselves in the other. There is the fact of the two Frenchmen attending the secret council in the Ottawa village, probably to bring war belts. Then the Shawnees reported that the Weas had received a war belt from the French in Illinois. Similarly, the rumor among the Detroit Indians that a French and Spanish force was on its way to retake Quebec was obviously of French origin designed to hearten the Indians to strike a blow in the West.

Johnson, Croghan, and Gladwin, who were in the best position to judge of the origin of the war, all declared definitely that the French were at the bottom of it. Lieut.

Jehu Hay entered in his diary for January 14, 1764, that the Huron chiefs told the interpreter that the attack had its rise in the belts promising succour from Illinois which were circulated "two years ago"—that is, in 1762. Pontiac himself reminded his allies in May 1763 of the several belts he had received from the French urging him to make war.

Coincident with the French machinations in the West, the perennially dissatisfied Senecas in the East were promoting a definite conspiracy. Whether the Senecas were proceeding independently and on their own initiative remains in doubt. Johnson believed that the French had been tampering with them, and that the wampum belt calling for war sent out by the Senecas had been given them sometime earlier by the French. That the French at the head of the St. Lawrence were active is also suggested by the statement of Wabbicomigot, a Mississaugi-Chippewa chief, who related that St. Luc de La Corne had given him a war belt at Toronto which the chief refused.

The Senecas gave a war belt to their neighbors the Delawares with the injunction to pass it on westward. When it should reach the tribes around Fort Ouiatenon, all were to rise and put the British to death in their respective localities. The date on which the Senecas started this belt on its way is not certain, but it passed from the Delawares to the Shawnees and reached the Miamies at the head of the Wabash in March 1763. Ensign Holmes, the commandant of the fort there, then discovered it and persuaded the Miamies to deliver it to him. The Miamies related its provenance and destination and confessed having no desire to paiticipate in such a war. They said further that the Seneca chief who started it was "the one that is always doing mischief." Probably this was our old friend Kyashuta.[11]

[11] A. W. Patterson in his *History of the Backwoods*, published

The route of this war belt implies that it was not intended for the tribes in Michigan. However, they were not being ignored. Another belt was sent to them directly from the Senecas early in 1763, according to an Ottawa named Notawas. The Huron chief at Sandusky, called Big Jaw, evidently saw one of the belts, for he later blamed the Senecas for starting the war. Despite the belligerent and treacherous efforts of this Iroquois tribe, the plan for a united uprising (which strategy may well have been suggested by the French) did not materialize. Their one belt did not complete its course before being discovered; the other may have encouraged the Detroit Indians to action later, but it produced no allied cooperation nor did the recipients pursue the shrewd Seneca plan for a general and simultaneous revolt.

Detroit thus was assailed from both east and west with promptings to action, and the Indians there finally accepted the initiative. This resolution was due to Pontiac, who listened to these incendiary proposals with growing approval and enthusiasm. Convinced that the Indians could and should drive out the British, he agitated for war among the Ottawas and their neighbors. Because he was an accomplished war chief and an effective orator and because he had a program of positive action backed by French promises of aid to lay before the disgruntled tribes, he naturally acquired more and more influence. As he persuaded others to agree with him he rose to leadership, not only in his village but also in the vicinity embracing the Chippewa, Huron, and Potawatomi settlements.

Pontiac's role in the approaching war was that of commander over the three villages surrounding Fort Detroit and a chief-to-be-consulted over the Chippewas and Pota-

in 1843, called the Indian uprising the "Kiyasuta and Pontiac war. . . . This was the name this war bore among the former inhabitants, and continued to bear among the settlers." (p. 128)

watomies who came from a distance to join him. As for a general uprising of all the western tribes against all the British western posts, Pontiac may have thought of it, but his abilities were taxed in uniting his immediate neighbors and devising a surprise assault on one fort.[12]

[12] This interpretation is at variance with Parkman's thesis. Parkman believed that Pontiac was the initiator and strategist of the whole war, as he makes clear in this passage: "At the close of the year 1762, he sent out ambassadors to the different nations. They visited the country of the Ohio and its tributaries, passed northward to the region of the upper lakes, and the wild borders of the River Ottawa; and far southward towards the mouth of the Mississippi. (Ms. letter, D'Abbadie to Neyon, 1764.) Bearing with them the war-belt of wampum, broad and long, as the importance of the message demanded; and the tomahawk stained red, in token of war; they went from camp to camp, and village to village. Wherever they appeared, the sachems and old men assembled, to hear the words of the great Pontiac. Then the head chief of the embassy flung down the tomahawk on the ground before them, and holding the war-belt in his hand, delivered, with vehement gesture, word for word, the speech with which he was charged. It was heard every where with approbation; the belt was accepted, the hatchet snatched up, and the assembled chiefs stood pledged to take part in the war. The blow was to be struck at a certain time in the month of May following, to be indicated by the changes of the moon. The tribes were to rise together, each destroying the English garrison in its neighborhood, and then, with a general rush, the whole were to turn against the settlements on the frontier." (Chapter 8.)

What was Parkman's authority for this belief that Pontiac engineered a general and simultaneous uprising? The D'Abbadie letter of 1764 which he cites is presumably that of Jan. 30, which speaks of Pontiac's efforts to renew the war, but says nothing about the origin of it. Parkman's notes and correspondence make no mention of this point which is the central thesis of his book, as indicated by the title. His memorandum of a conversation with John R. Williams in Detroit in 1845 indicates that this version of the origin of the war was traditional in Detroit. Williams, it should be added, while native to Detroit was born in 1782 and knew the story of Pontiac's war only from others. Tradition may well perpetuate a truth, but it cannot be relied on as proof of a disputed fact. It is easy to understand how the prominence of Pontiac in the war may have led Detroiters to believe that he

Perhaps the French agents assured him that they would engineer simultaneous attacks on the other forts once he took the initiative. They understood Indians well enough to know that once Pontiac was successful in capturing

instigated the whole rebellion, and that the participation of the other tribes must have been owing to his invitation made in advance and his scheme for a simultaneous attack.

If all the forts had been attacked on the same day, or in the same week, that fact would have been clear evidence of a preconcerted conspiracy. But the attacks were not simultaneous. Pontiac struck first on May 8, and the last fort was attacked on June 22. There is indisputable evidence that detachments from Pontiac's forces at Detroit led the assaults on several of the other forts. Although this fact points to Pontiac's leadership in the war, it is not consistent with what Parkman wrote about ambassadors to other tribes, the acceptance of the war hatchet, and the plan for a united and simultaneous attack.

Certain other persons, however, uttered sentiments similar to Parkman's view. William Smith, purveying the news to his friend Horatio Gates in England on November 22, 1763, related the following about the western Indians: "The besiegers are led on by an enterprising fellow called Pondiac. He is a genius, for he possesses great bravery, art, & tho' a Catawba prisoner, has had the address to get himself not only at the head of his conquerors, but elected generalissimo of all the confederate forces now acting against us. Perhaps he may deserve to be called the Methridates of the West." Smith implies that there was a confederation of the tribes acting under the leadership of Pontiac. This is a half-truth demanding certain qualifications which will become clear later in this biography. Probably Smith is reflecting the attitude current in New York which by November had come to regard Pontiac as the leader of the war, since he had inspired or forced other tribes to take up arms.

A local historian writing in the *Michigan Pioneer and Historical Collections* of 1900 asserted that Pontiac visited the Ottawas along Grand River (near Grand Rapids, Michigan) in 1762 and enlisted them in his contemplated war. Inasmuch as no white man attended such a council, the evidence of it is only Indian tradition, which is seldom reliable. Moreover, as the author wrote after Parkman's book was popularized, his statement may be an assumption influenced by Parkman's passage.

Similarly, in the *Wisconsin Historical Collections* for 1879

Detroit, the other tribes, not to be outdone, would fall on
the forts in their vicinity in order to demonstrate equal
prowess. Or, another possibility is that Pontiac may have
privately considered moving on to another fort after

~~~~~~~~~~

Louis P. Porlier related what a Menominee told him in 1848.
The Indian, Shononee by name, was repeating what his ancestors had told him: namely, that Pontiac had visited the vicinity
of Milwaukee, allegedly in 1762 or early 1763, and had spoken
to the assembled tribes about united action against the British.
This incident has the additional authority of purporting to repeat
Pontiac's speech on that occasion. Therein lies its weakness, for
the speech does not have the ring of authenticity. In it he urged
war against all white men, not merely the British, a sentiment
quite foreign to what we know of his plans.

Beyond these doubtful statements, there appears to be no documentary evidence of a conspiracy headed by Pontiac. No contemporary British officer gave such an interpretation of the war.
There was a conspiracy among the three tribes at Detroit for surprising that fort, yes; but there is no mention of the "ambassadors" that Parkman said he sent to the other tribes in 1762. Intertribal jealousies were such as to have prevented unification of
all the western tribes, had Pontiac attempted it. Those jealousies
played into his hands, however, once he had initiated the attack
on Detroit. Then his action was advertised to encourage hesitant
tribes, both as an example to follow and as a challenge to be
equaled.

Working independently of Parkman, Col. Charles Whittlesey
(1808-1866), historian and archaeologist of Cleveland, reached
a similar conclusion regarding Pontiac's role in the war. In a
memorandum of 1844, Whittlesey wrote: "He [Pontiac] from
his central position in the south of Michigan secretly visited the
tribes of the Lakes and the Ohio representing to them that they
were strong and the English were weak. But that their soldiers
were continually arriving and in a few moons the Indians would
be weak and the white man strong. That the design of the whites
was now manifest—one nation had without their consent sold
them to another, and they might no one knew how soon be again
transferred like slaves to some other power. . . . Pontiac directed
a simultaneous attack upon every garrison west of Niagara. . . .
The time arrived in the fall of 1763 when the project was to be
carried into execution." (Whittlesey Papers, No. 4, 1844.)

Whittlesey has failed to distinguish the fact that Pontiac was

⟨ 110 ⟩

taking Detroit, mustering additional tribes or villages there under his leadership and destroying that new objective, then on to another, and eventually entering western New York, Pennsylvania, or Virginia at the head of an enormous horde of allied savages.

It was not the nature of the Indian mind to foresee all consequences or to prepare for all eventualities. Nor were the Indians, of course, acquainted with the diplomatic niceties observed by European governments which would prevent the French court from countenancing a savage uprising undertaken to restore French dominion while a defeated France was seeking peace with Britain.

Pontiac planned his coup against Detroit carefully and with admirable ingenuity, but probably had only vague hopes as to his next move should he be successful. He did not even wait for an answer from the Chippewas at Saginaw Bay before making his first attempt on the fort. There was no grand conspiracy or preconcerted plan on his part embracing all the western tribes, such as the Senecas had proposed. Pontiac once referred to it as "the beaver war." What it developed into, of course, was a war for Indian independence as modified by French economic penetration. In the beginning there was only a local conspiracy at Detroit directed by Pontiac, who, however, improvised a more general uprising after his initial tactics failed. And his second attempts almost succeeded in loosening the British hold.

It was Napoleon who said that generalship is the art of improvisation.

---

not fighting the white men as a race, but the British alone, and was willing to have the French remain. And his gross error in stating the time of the uprising leaves one wondering how close he was to the sources of this event. Probably he obtained his information from Detroiters, who repeated the tradition.

───────────── 〈〈〈〈◊〉〉〉〉 ─────────────

8

The Plot and its Discovery

As SOON AS THE INDIANS began returning to their villages after the winter of hunting and trapping, hostile schemes were hatched. Pelts could be traded for powder. The water highways and the forest trails were open for communication. A season of good weather stretched ahead. The time for action was near.

At Detroit, Major Gladwin anticipated no trouble. In February 1763 he had received news of the cessation of hostilities between France and Great Britain. The diplomats were now negotiating definitive peace terms. He announced the news to the French and Indians of his post, hoping the *habitants* would perceive the footlessness of encouraging discontent among the Indians. Gladwin told Amherst that the savages did not relish the war's end, but that if he could have 70 or 80 medals to bestow on their chiefs as rewards and distinctions they would be satisfied. In April he learned of the Seneca war belt discovered at Fort Miamis, but he was not alarmed. The time was not yet.

During that same April, Pontiac meditated on his plan for striking the English. He was impressed by the teachings of the Delaware Prophet, the boldness of the Senecas, the urgings and promises of the French. He looked across the river at the stockaded fort, the ships at anchor, and the uniformed figures going and coming. His own Ottawas would follow him for the most part, he was sure. Consulting his neighboring chiefs, he had no difficulty in securing the support of the Potawatomies under Ninivois for an assault on the fort. The Hurons, however, were divided into two factions under separate chiefs. One of them, Teata, whose band had been proselytized by the Jesuits, rejected Pontiac's proposal; the other, Také, fell in with it. Pontiac thereupon decided to proceed with the allies at hand, who totalled 460 fighting men, and called a general council for April 27 on the Ecorse River, about ten miles below the fort.

Despite the large number attending and although the fact of such a meeting was known at least to the French, the council's true purpose was not discovered by the British. Pontiac shrewdly opened the meeting by inspiring his followers with the story and message of the Delaware Prophet. Since that strange gospel has only been touched upon, Pontiac's colored version of the Prophet's experience is summarized here.[1]

This Delaware, who was eager to make the acquaintance of the Master of Life, resolved to undertake a secret journey to his dwelling place in Paradise. But as he did not know how to reach that place, he waited for a dream to guide him. In his dream he was advised simply to set out and he would be guided along his route. Accordingly he equipped himself for a long journey and started. For eight days he traveled without discouragement, until he came to a clearing into which three trails converged. He did not know which one to take, but finally chose the widest. After following it for half a day, he encountered a great fire coming out of the earth. As it appeared to spread toward him he retraced his steps and took another trail. This, too, led him to a pit of fire, and he returned and started down the last path. He followed it to its end at the foot of a gleaming white mountain. Puzzled, he looked around and perceived a beautiful woman, clothed

[1] Navarre, *Journal*, pp. 21-32; Schoolcraft, *Algic Researches*, I, 239-248.

in white, who addressed him in his own tongue. She knew the purpose of his journey and advised him that his way lay across the mountain; but to ascend it he must first undress, bathe, and leave his clothes behind.

The Indian did as he was told, and when he had climbed to the top of the mountain he saw three villages ahead of him. He walked toward the most attractive one and was met at the gate by a man in white. This stranger greeted him and led him in to meet the Master of Life. The Divine Being took him by the hand and gave him a fancy hat which he was to sit on. Then the Master addressed him:

"I am the Master of Life, and since I know what thou desirest to know, and to whom thou wishest to speak, listen well to what I am going to say to thee and to all the Indians:

"I am He who hath created the heavens and the earth, the trees, lakes, rivers, all men, and all that thou seest and hast seen upon the earth. Because I love you, ye must do what I say and love, and not do what I hate. I do not love that ye should drink to the point of madness, as ye do; and I do not like that ye should fight one another. Ye take two wives, or run after the wives of others; ye do not well, and I hate that. Ye ought to have but one wife, and keep her till death. When ye wish to go to war, ye conjure and resort to the medicine dance, believing that ye speak to me; ye are mistaken,—it is to Manitou that ye speak, an evil spirit who prompts you to nothing but wrong, and who listens to you out of ignorance of me.

"This land where ye dwell I have made for you and not for others. Whence comes it that ye permit the Whites upon your lands? Can ye not live without them? I know that those whom ye call the children of your Great Father supply your needs, but if ye were not evil, as ye are, ye could surely do without them. Ye could live as ye did live before knowing them,—before those whom ye call your brothers had come upon your lands. Did ye not live by the bow and arrow? Ye had no need of gun or powder, or anything else, and nevertheless ye caught animals to live upon and to dress yourselves with their skins. But when I saw that ye were given up to evil, I led the wild animals to the depths of the forests so that ye had to depend upon your brothers to feed and shelter you. Ye have only to become good again and do what I wish, and I will send back the animals for your food. I do not forbid you to permit among you the children of your Father; I love them. They know me and pray to me, and I supply their wants and all they give you. But as to those who come to trouble your lands,—drive them out, make war upon them. I do not like them at all; they know me not, and are my enemies, and the enemies of your brothers. Send them back to the lands which I have created for them and let them stay there. Here is a prayer which I give thee in writing to learn by heart and to teach to the Indians and their children."

The Delaware confessed that he could not read, so the Master told him to give the prayer to his chief when he returned to his village. In summary the Master of Life repeated his injunctions:

"Do not drink more than once, or at most twice, in a day; have only one wife and do not run after the wives of others nor after the girls; do not fight among yourselves; do not 'make medicine,' but pray, because in 'making medicine' one talks with the evil spirit; drive off your land those dogs clothed in red who will do you nothing but harm. And when ye shall have need of anything address yourselves to me; and as to your brothers, I shall give to you as to them; do not sell to your brothers what I put on earth for food. In short, become good and ye shall receive your needs. When ye meet one another exchange greetings and proffer the left hand, which is nearest the heart. In all things I command thee to repeat every morning and night the prayer which I have given thee."

The Delaware was then conducted out of the village and down to the foot of the mountain where he recovered his clothes and returned to his home. He called upon his chief first and delivered to him the prayer and the law of the Master of Life. News of the adventure soon spread, and neighboring Indians came to visit the Delaware and hear his gospel. Thus it was spread from village to village until Pontiac said he heard it and he declared that he believed it all.

If we may trust our two white reporters, quoted in the previous chapter, then it is apparent that Pontiac had altered the Prophet's message slightly to support his own ambitions. The Delaware had urged the eventual expulsion of all white men; Pontiac twisted his meaning to point it at the British and except the French. It was an ingenious trick, by which he gained divine sanction for his own scheme.

His recital deeply impressed the audience on the Ecorse, and had the effect of firmly uniting those Indians under Pontiac for the grim business ahead. They declared themselves ready to obey everything he asked of them. Pontiac then issued his first orders and revealed the first step in his stratagem. He asked the Potawatomies and Hurons to return to their villages and remain quiet, except to prepare their weapons for war. In four days he himself, with some of his young men, would go into the fort to dance the calumet, ostensibly to entertain the officers but actually to gain an opportunity for spying out the strength of the garrison, the number of traders, and the houses they occupied. This latter information was important for the sake of plundering the traders' goods, which was a powerful incentive for war.

Accordingly, on Sunday, May 1, in mid-afternoon Pontiac and forty or fifty of his picked warriors appeared at one of the fort's gates. One contemporary mentions that Major Gladwin, having got wind of some bad intentions among the Indians, had ordered the sentries not to let them enter. Pontiac complained to the interpreter, Pierre La Butte, at this unfriendly reception, and on the interpreter's plea Gladwin allowed them to come in. Gladwin himself and Lieutenant Hay, in their brief accounts of this visit, do not mention that there was any delay or objection.

Once inside most of the savages took their places for the ceremonial dance of the war pipe in front of Captain Campbell's house. It involved leaping, stamping, and whirling, beating a post stuck in the ground, and chanting accounts of their recent exploits in war. But ten of the warriors quietly melted away through the narrow streets and made careful observations. When they returned to Campbell's quarters, the dancing ended. Pontiac announced to Gladwin that he would return in a few days to pay him a formal visit with many of his people, explaining that as yet not all of them had returned from hunting. Whether or not this was true, the statement afforded a pretext for another visit in greater numbers. Pontiac then asked for a little bread, tobacco, and beer (rum being banned), and some was served out to them.

The delegation returned to the Ottawa village across the river and upstream. There each of the ten spies reported what he had seen. Pontiac sent a summary of these reports by messengers to the Potawatomies and Hurons. Macatepilesis, who had negotiated with Johnson in 1761, was one of the messengers, and he was now called "second chief of the Ottawas."

⟨ 117 ⟩

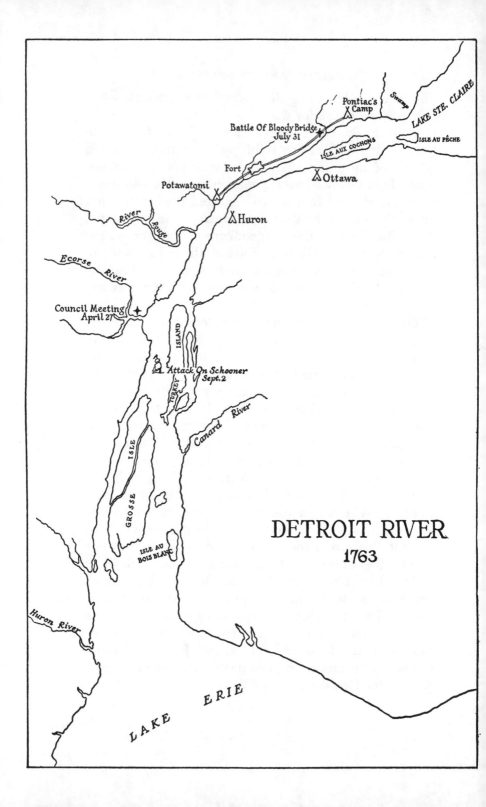

Battle Of Bloody Bridge
July 31

Pontiac's
Camp

Swamp

LAKE STE. CLAIRE

ISLE AU PÊCHE

ISLE AUX COCHONS

Fort

Ottawa

Potawatomi

River

Rouge

Huron

Ecorse River

Council Meeting
April 27

ISLAND

Attack On Schooner
Sept. 2

TURKEY

Canard River

ISLE

GROSSE

ISLE AU
BOIS BLANC

DETROIT RIVER
1763

Huron River

LAKE ERIE

Next day Pontiac sent runners to the two villages to notify them of a second war council to be held in the Potawatomi village at mid-day on Thursday, May 5. He specified that no woman should be allowed to attend or to remain in the town while the council was in session. Apparently he must also have sent messengers to the Chippewas of Saginaw Bay, informing them of his plans as so far developed and urging them to cast their lot with him by attacking a boatload of soldiers he had seen headed north. It is said that similar messages were dispatched to the Ottawas at L'Arbre Croche and to the Mississaugi-Chippewas on the Thames River in modern Ontario.

When the appointed day arrived, the Ottawas and the Huron band repaired to the Potawatomi village, which lay on the same side of the river as the fort and about two miles below it. The women had been sent away, and Pontiac ordered sentinels stationed around the town while the council met. After all the Indians had seated themselves, Pontiac opened the session with the following speech:

"It is important for us, my brothers, that we extermi-nate from our lands this nation which seeks only to destroy us. You see as well as I that we can no longer supply our needs, as we have done from our brothers, the French. The English sell us goods twice as dear as the French do, and their goods do not last. Scarcely have we bought a blanket or something else to cover ourselves with before we must think of getting another; and when we wish to set out for our winter camps they do not want to give us any credit as our brothers the French do.

"When I go to see the English commander and say to him that some of our comrades are dead, instead of be-wailing their death, as our French brothers do, he laughs at me and at you. If I ask anything for our sick, he re-fuses with the reply that he has no use for us. From all this you can well see that they are seeking our ruin. Therefore, my brothers, we must all swear their destruction and wait no longer. Nothing prevents us; they are few in numbers, and we can accomplish it.

"All the nations who are our brothers attack them—why should not we strike too? Are we not men like them? Have I not shown you the wampum belts which I received from our Great Father, the Frenchman? He tells us to strike them. Why do we not listen to his words? What do we fear? It is time. Do we fear that our brothers, the French, who are here among us will prevent us? They do not know our plans,[2] and they could not hinder anyway, if they would. You all know as well as I that when the English came upon our lands to drive out our father, Bellestre, they took away all the Frenchmen's guns and that they now have no arms to protect themselves with. Therefore, it is time for us to strike. If there are any French who side with them, let us strike them as well as the English. Remember what the Master of Life told our brother, the Delaware, to do. That concerns us all as well as others.

"I have sent wampum belts and messengers to our brothers, the Chippewas of Saginaw, and to our brothers, the Ottawas of Michilimackinac, and to those of the Thames River to join us. They will not be slow in coming, but while we wait let us strike anyway. There is no more time to lose. When the English are defeated we shall then see what there is left to do, and we shall stop up the ways hither so that they may never come again upon our lands."

The assembled Indians received the speech with full approval. They then proceeded to the business of plotting

[2] Our only authority for this speech is Navarre, who being French may have inserted this statement or twisted something Pontiac said in favor of the innocence of the *habitants*.

a surprise assault. Pontiac was to enter the fort on the second day following at the head of sixty selected warriors and ask Major Gladwin for a grand council. They would carry tomahawks, knives and sawed off muskets hidden under their blankets. The rest of the Ottawa adults, men and women together, were to follow into the fort, also with weapons hidden on them, and distribute themselves around the place while the council was taking place. At a given signal all were to fall on the luckless English.

The Hurons and Potawatomies were to divide forces: one band to surround the fort at a distance in order to seize those persons who might be working outside the stockade, the other to go down the Detroit River to cut off any English reinforcements or ships that might happen to be approaching.

The main flaw in this scheme of Pontiac's was his faith that it could be kept secret from the English and French for the two days before it was put in execution. The Indians were not of equal enthusiasm for the undertaking; some of them probably were more farsighted than Pontiac; and some of them had friends among the officers or traders in the fort, or false friends among the French who would in turn warn the English. Inevitably the secret leaked out. Gladwin was informed of the plot by the next night—the night before it was to be carried out.

More than one person has been identified as Gladwin's informant and has consequently been lauded as the savior of Detroit. No investigator has been able to determine the one entitled to the honor to the exclusion of all others. The multiplicity of claims suggests what is highly probable: namely, that more than one person brought the dread news into the fort. Gladwin reported to Amherst only that "I was luckily informed the night before" of

Pontiac's real intention.[3] He is said to have told the Indians that his informant was one of them, but possibly he made the accusation in order to create dissension among the savages.

The most persistent and popular of the informants in Detroit legend has been a squaw variously described as young and comely or old and homely, as a Potawatomi or a Chippewa. Usually she was called Catherine. Four contemporary writers declare that the Indians accused a squaw of revealing their plan to Gladwin, but they do not say she was actually guilty.[4] Three residents of Detroit related years later that a squaw named Catherine was the informant.[5] Henry Conner, Indian interpreter at Detroit early in the nineteenth century, was familiar with the story and said that he had been acquainted with Catherine. He added that she was young and in love with Gladwin and—startling detail—that long afterward she had perished by falling while drunk into a vat of boiling maple syrup.[6]

[3] Amherst Papers, vol. 2, Clements Library. Gladwin did not identify his informant then in order to protect him or her from Indian revenge.

[4] Porteous' ms. journal; Navarre, *Journal*, pp. 48-49; Lieut. James MacDonald's letter to Dr. Campbell, July 9, 1763, in Huntington Library; Rogers' *Journals* (Hough's ed.), p. 126; letter of an anonymous soldier in *New York Gazette*, Aug. 4, 1763. An excellent investigation of this mystery will be found in Helen Humphrey's article, "The Identity of Major Gladwin's Informant," *Miss. Val. Hist. Rev.*, xxi (1934), 147-162.

[5] Mrs. Meloche, Jacques Parent, and Mr. Peltier in *Mich. P. and H. Coll.*, viii, 341, 358, 359. Carver published this local tradition to the world in his *Travels*, 1778.

[6] Conner's version was related by Henry Schoolcraft to Parkman (Parkman Papers, 27a, pp. 199-200). It is printed in Schoolcraft, *Personal Memoirs*, p. 350. Thomas McKenney, Lewis Cass, and James H. Lanman repeated it in their writings during the next few years. By the time Parkman wrote, the tradition was firmly established and he elaborated it in graphic manner.

When Parkman visited Detroit in 1845, Francis Baby told him he knew nothing of Catherine. The story he had always heard was that when Gladwin agreed to admit all the warriors to the fort for a conference, the two interpreters advised him that they believed some treachery was planned and persuaded him to admit only the chiefs.[7] John R. Williams, another Detroiter, corroborated Baby and added that the interpreter, La Butte, was informed of the evil design by his daughter, who had overheard some savages speaking of it. Gabriel St. Aubin, however, testified in 1824 that it was his mother who had informed La Butte after seeing the Indians filing off their musket barrels so as to be able to conceal them under their blankets. Old Mr. Peltier of Detroit remembered that the savages borrowed files from the *habitants* for this work and refused to explain why they wanted the gun barrels shortened.

To add further confusion to this refutation of Catherine and the introduction of Mlle. La Butte (or Mme. St. Aubin), Ensign Price wrote to Colonel Bouquet on June 26, 1763, that Jacques Duperon Baby—Francis Baby's father—had disclosed the plot!

Robert Navarre, a French witness to the siege, ascribed in his contemporary narrative the revelation of the scheme to a disaffected Ottawa named Mahiganne, a story that gains credence from Gladwin's alleged accusation.

Charles Gouin related in 1824 that his father, Thomas Gouin, had learned of the plot from the Indians and had sent Jacques Chovin to warn Captain Campbell on the morning appointed for the council. This may be true, although, as we have seen, Gladwin was notified the night before.

[7] Parkman Papers, 27d, pp. 172 and 178. Francis Baby was the son of Gladwin's friend, Jacques Duperon Baby.

Tradition among the Tucker family in Macomb County, Michigan, credits William Tucker with informing Gladwin. William had been captured by Chippewas on the frontier of Virginia and carried off to Michigan, where he was adopted into a Chippewa family and grew up. His foster family was encamped near Detroit in the spring of 1763. Early in May he planned a trip into Ontario, but his foster sister, who was very fond of him, urged him privately not to go. William finally extracted from her the information that she feared he might be killed because an assault on Detroit was imminent. He went at once and told Gladwin.[8]

While visiting Detroit in 1845, Parkman was also told that "Mr. Askin has heard that a Pawnee slave conveyed the intelligence."

A curious bill has come to light recently presented by Caesar Cormick, or McCormick, Detroit merchant, to Gladwin on May 13, 1763. One item in the account rendered is "To paid a Person for privet Intelligence £6-17-6."[9] Cormick had paid the informant and was now seeking reimbursement, which he received. Clearly, therefore, the intelligence was of importance to the garrison. It may be argued that a sum this large would have been paid a white man rather than an Indian. The date suggests that the information may have dealt with Pontiac's secret design, but there is no way of proving it. It may have been information brought into the fort shortly after the siege began.

In 1773 Maj. Henry Basset, then commanding Detroit, wrote to Maj. General Haldimand: "I beg to recommend Mr. James Sterling, who is the first merchant at this place and a gentleman of good character; during the late war,

[8] Sheldon, *Early History of Michigan*, p. 342; letter of Robert F. Eldredge to me, June 22, 1938.
[9] Amherst Papers, vol. 7, Clements Library.

through a lady that he then courted, from whom he had the best information, [he] was in part a means to save this garrison. This gentleman is now married to that lady and is connected with the best part of this settlement."[10] In 1765 Sterling had married Angélique Cuillerier, the girl who had so impressed Sir William Johnson. She was the daughter of Antoine Cuillerier, a friend of Pontiac's whom the chief had determined to install as commandant of the fort after the British were wiped out. At least one council with Pontiac was held at Cuillerier's house. A romantic story can be reconstructed by assuming that Angélique learned of Pontiac's plot in her own house, that to protect the life of her lover she warned him of his danger, and that he thereupon informed Gladwin.

Such then is the roster of persons credited with saving Detroit. One of them undoubtedly is the person who "luckily informed" Gladwin "the night before," but the major never knew how much mystery was to be created by his taciturnity.

Aware of the treachery that was intended for him on the morrow, Gladwin was faced with the necessity of taking decisive counter-action. He has left us no explanation of the decision he made (which even Amherst questioned), and we can only surmise his reasoning. Obviously it must have occurred to him that he could simply refuse to let Pontiac enter the fort, and if the chief wanted to know why, he could make the accusation. However, Gladwin knew that Pontiac would promptly deny any evil design with great haughtiness. Doubtless he would stalk off and send complaints of his treatment to Johnson, who would hint to Amherst that his officer at Detroit should be more circumspect in his duty in order to promote the greatest harmony with the Indians etc., etc. Besides, Gladwin remembered, Lieutenant Robertson

[10] "Haldimand Papers" in *Mich. P. & H. Coll.*, xix, 310.

with a boat's crew and Sir Robert Davers were outside the fort, having gone up across Lake Ste. Claire a few days ago to take soundings. If Gladwin should make the rupture with Pontiac, the Indians in revenge might fall on this party. Moreover, Pontiac was sufficiently cunning so that after disavowing hostile intentions he would wait patiently until all suspicion was allayed and then try again.

Secondly, Gladwin possibly considered admitting the Ottawas and then seizing the chiefs or all the warriors. He would thus ruin the surprise they planned in the most humiliating manner, but he would only create fresh problems for himself. The Ottawa squaws would come begging for food and for the release of their men. He would have to feed and guard his horde of prisoners. In the end there would be no punishment, merely a long peace conference, and after suitable promises had been given the Indians would be released. Perhaps also his seizure of the Ottawas might stir the other tribes to action.

Thirdly, Gladwin could admit the Indians and face them down by demonstrating the readiness of the garrison. If this did not show Pontiac that his stratagem was discovered—implying that everything was known to the English—it would at least persuade him that the garrison was always on the alert and could not be taken by surprise.[11] Pontiac would have to retire, his plan foiled. Such a reception might disgrace him with his associated chiefs and end all this hostile plotting like pricking a bubble. The whole affair might then blow over without creating any great disturbance. Considering the Indian character, it seemed worth the chance.

Gladwin's resources for withstanding a full-dress Indian war were not encouraging. The stockade was fairly strong

[11] Porteous said that Gladwin despised the Indians so much he was willing to let them all come in. (Ms. journal in Burton Historical Collection.)

and high, but made of wood, of course. The danger of its being set on fire had been considerably reduced when the French banked earth against the cedar pickets on the inside to a height of several feet. Even so, all the buildings inside were exposed to fire arrows. Gladwin had three bastions, one at either corner next to the river and one in the north wall. They controlled the approaches on every side of the fort. Two small blockhouses, detached from the fort, stood five hundred feet to the north. However, he lacked sufficient cannon to arm each bastion; he had two six-pounders, both on the drill ground and therefore useless, one three-pounder mounted in the north bastion, and three mortars. On the water side he had the two-masted schooner *Huron* of six guns and the somewhat larger sloop *Michigan*. He anchored the *Huron* at the upper corner of the fort and the sloop at the lower end.

The size of the garrison under Major Gladwin is not known reliably. It consisted of two companies of Royal Americans and one company of Queen's Rangers and their respective officers, plus the ships' crews who had wintered in Detroit. An official return of the Rangers shows that this company numbered 22. A company of the 60th, or Royal Americans, when full, amounted to 78. Probably the two companies did not total 125. Moreover, a detachment of 18 soldiers and French oarsmen under Sergeant Shaw had been sent to Fort Michilimackinac in April, and a squad of six soldiers had gone with Lieutenant Robertson's party to take soundings. Detroit's available garrison, therefore, must have numbered about 120. Such a number was hardly sufficient to man the long stockade day and night. There was a score or more of English traders in the fort who could be counted on to help.[12]

[12] Navarre said the garrison numbered 130 soldiers and officers besides some 40 traders. Lieut. Jehu Hay reported 120 officers,

The most serious disadvantage at Detroit was lack of provisions. The merchant John Porteous said there was scarcely two weeks' supply on hand at the rate of a pound of flour and two ounces of pork a man per day. Food supplies were still shipped from England, and Fort Niagara was the distributing point for the West. Gladwin had not yet received his first spring shipment, and he was responsible for supplying five dependent posts. If he could delay hostilities a little while longer, he would be in a more comfortable position. However, he probably did not worry much at the start about provisions because he did not anticipate a siege.

Detroit's strongest resource was Gladwin himself. Pontiac knew him, but certainly underestimated his strength. The Ottawa chief probably had never met this kind of white man before. Gladwin was obviously unlike the convivial, friendly French; but neither was he a blustering Braddock, a brilliant Wolfe, a talkative Croghan, nor an easygoing Campbell. He was not unique among his countrymen even though he was new in western North America. He was a new type; his kind was

soldiers, and traders. Lieut. James MacDonald indicated that the garrison totalled about 100. John Porteous recorded a tally of 70 officers and soldiers and about 20 merchants. James Sterling agreed that the total number of soldiers, officers, merchants, and servants did not amount to 100. In his history of the Royal Americans, Butler (*Annals of the King's Royal Corps*) errs in saying (vol. 1, p. 128) that Gladwin had a company of the 80th and a company of the 60th Regiment at Detroit. Butler mentions (p. 130) the reduction of the 1st Battalion of the 60th to nine companies, totalling 500 men, or about 55 men to a company, but it appears not to have been enforced at Detroit before the siege began.

The day by day account of the first week of war is compiled from Jehu Hay's *Diary*, Robert Navarre's *Journal*, and John Porteous' ms. journal, the three great sources on the siege. Subsequent accounts of the siege are taken largely from these three records.

beginning to appear in Great Britain. Without being aware of it, he was a bull-headed Empire Builder.

Given a post to hold, Gladwin would hold it till the last man was killed, never doubting the right of his country to claim such a place nor the wisdom of his commander in ordering it held at all costs. This trait was neither super-patriotism nor conscious heroics. It was hard tenacity, untroubled by philosophic introspection or military imagination.

Pontiac had encountered a block of granite.

9

The First Blows

PONTIAC gathered his braves around him, ignorant that his intended treachery was discovered. Followed by the squaws of the village, the party confidently crossed the river and approached the east gate of Fort Detroit on Saturday morning, May 7, 1763. It was about ten o'clock and strangely enough not a Frenchman had entered the fort that morning, but many women and children who lived inside had gone out. This movement alone was sufficient indication that bloodshed was expected.

The Indians numbered about 300, and each wore a blanket thrown over his shoulders or strapped around him in order to conceal the weapons he carried. The fort's gates were open as usual, but the Indians must have been a little perturbed to find the number of sentinels doubled, each with his bayonet fixed. Nevertheless, the savages pushed past with their usual crowding and irregularity. Small groups broke away and with seeming carelessness posted themselves around the gates, the soldiers' barracks, and the merchants' shops.

Pontiac, with ten minor chiefs[1] and a number of warriors, moved on directly toward Captain Campbell's house where the conference was to be held. He must have grown more uneasy at every step. The merchants had locked their shops and were assembled at James Sterling's place.

―――――――――――――――――――――

[1] St. Aubin identifies four of them as Mukeeta, Pinaasee, Neewish, and Waubinema. *Mich. P. & H. Coll.*, VIII, 352. Four others may have been Macatepilesis, Chavinon, Breton, and Pontiac's unnamed nephew, as he included them in some of his later movements.

On the parade ground all the soldiers not on guard duty were drawn up under arms. Capt. Joseph Hopkins of the Queen's Rangers was in command of them. Waiting at the council house to hear the chiefs were only Major Gladwin and Captain Campbell, wearing their sidearms, and the interpreters. The other officers were among the men and near the gates. It was all too plain that the British expected trouble and were ready. There was muttering among the chiefs and they did not sit down to council at once. At length Pontiac addressed himself to the major.

"We are greatly surprised, brother, at this unusual step thou hast taken, to have all the soldiers under arms, and that thy young chiefs are not at council as formerly. We would be very glad to know the reason for this, for we imagine some bad bird has given thee ill news of us, which we advise thee not to believe, my brother, for there are bad birds who want to stir thee up against thy brothers, the Indians, who have been always in perfect friendship with their brothers, the English."[2]

Gladwin replied that some other nations were coming to see him and he intended to have the garrison under arms when they came. Fearing that these strangers might be affronted by such a reception, he had resolved to begin the custom with his greatest friends, the Ottawas, who he was sure would not take it amiss. This was a transparent lie which Pontiac must have recognized, yet he could not dispute the commandant. Holding up a belt of wampum, white on one side and reputedly green on the other, Pontiac displayed the white side and made a long speech about the death of six of their chiefs during the past winter. He hoped his brother would give them something to calm their minds and banish their sorrow. According to two contemporaries, the turning of this belt from the

[2] Porteous' ms. journal.

white to the green side was the signal for the massacre. A French writer asserted that a war whoop was to be the signal.[3] Whichever it was, Pontiac gave no sign.

Gladwin made the chiefs a present of six suits of clothes in memory of the departed chiefs and distributed a little bread and tobacco. The council broke up, and the chiefs retired in silent fury. The warriors around the town likewise slunk away visibly enraged and confused. They all embarked in their canoes and returned to the Ottawa village. Gladwin's estimate of their reaction to his alert had been correct—so far.

At the Ottawa village the braves met in council immediately, and Pontiac was upbraided for not having given the signal agreed upon for attack. He reminded them of the visible preparation of the garrison and assured them that they would have lost some warriors. The younger men declared they were willing to suffer casualties, so incensed were they against those "dogs." Pontiac promised he would secure them another opportunity to strike.

Discussion turned to the question of how the garrison had learned of the intended attack. For some reason suspicion centered on the squaw named Catherine, a Catholic convert. She was a Chippewa, but resident in the Potawatomi village. Pontiac sent four Indians after her. They crossed the river, seized the woman, and then took her into the fort! Gladwin heard their accusation and their request that he identify her as the "bad bird" who had attributed evil intentions to the Ottawas. Gladwin denied that she had ever come to him, but remarked that one of them, that is, an Indian, had warned him. Never-

[3] Porteous and Thomas Mante in his *History of the Late War* mention the turning of the belt as the signal. Navarre, p. 40, speaks of the war whoop.

theless, the warriors took Catherine over to Pontiac, at whose orders she received a flogging.

Whether or not Pontiac thought he had caught the informer who had ruined his surprise, he was under the necessity of plotting a new stratagem. He told his braves he had conceived another plan and that tomorrow he would return to the fort and assure the commandant that he had been deceived about the Ottawas. Then a fresh surprise would be possible.

On Sunday, May 8, Pontiac crossed the river again with three other Ottawa chiefs—Macatepilesis, Breton, and Chavinon—for the purpose of allaying the suspicions of the British. They were granted an interview with Gladwin and talked at length of his misunderstanding of the friendship of the Ottawas. Pontiac had with him a calumet, or pipe of peace, which he put into Gladwin's hands as a guarantee of good behavior. He added that he would bring his young warriors in tomorrow to smoke the peace pipe, shake hands with the commandant, and remove all suspicions from his mind. Gladwin accepted the calumet, but was not taken in by the chief's words. He replied that he could admit only chieftains to council and that the young braves had no reason to visit him. Pontiac withdrew, satisfied with his mission nevertheless. He did not know that Gladwin promptly increased the guard to a captain's, consisting of thirty men.

Back in his village again, Pontiac sent messengers to invite the Hurons, Potawatomies, and the French to come and play lacrosse with his warriors. He thought that this recreation would impress the garrison with the general peaceableness of the Indians. The games started late in the afternoon and continued until about seven o'clock. Pontiac then related to the Hurons and Potawatomies the substance of his council with Gladwin and told them he would return to the fort with many of his warriors on the morrow, when apparently he intended to carry out the treachery he had dared not execute the day before.

Monday, May 9, was the first of the three Rogation Days in the calendar of the Catholic Church, and Father Simple Bocquet led his flock in chanting procession from Ste. Anne's church outside the fort. The early morning passed as peacefully as the preceding day. Anticipating trouble, however, Gladwin set his men to work in defensive preparations. The bastions were put in order, and the cannon prepared for action. Families living outside the fort, particularly English residents, were offered sanctuary within the stockade. The movements of the savages were closely observed.

The warriors of the Ottawa town crossed the river in a flotilla of sixty-five canoes about eleven o'clock and began moving toward the fort in a body. Gladwin sent out his interpreters, St. Martin and La Butte, to inform Pontiac that only he and a few of his leading men could enter. The chief complained that all his people wanted to smell the smoke of the peace pipe, and that if they could not all come in to council none would come and they would throw away the belt of friendship which they had received from Sir William Johnson. When the interpreters delivered this answer to Gladwin, he relented somewhat and said that the Ottawas might enter in relays of small parties. Pontiac, enraged that his treachery could no longer be carried out, ordered his people back to the village.

There was no retreat, however, from his determination to let English blood. He had to think fast, moreover, to maintain his leadership. He could not afford to let his twice-disappointed warriors ask "What next?" without having a satisfactory answer. So he fatefully decided on action without the advantage of initial surprise.

On reentering his village he caught up a tomahawk and

began chanting the war song. He cried out that if he could not strike the English within the fort, he would attack those on the outside. He boasted that he would cut off the garrison and force them to surrender. All his people, men, women, and children, he ordered to abandon the village and set up a new camp across the river on the farm of Jean Baptiste Meloche. The site was two miles above the fort and protected on that side by a small stream called Parent's Creek. Next, Pontiac divided his warriors into several bands and assigned them specific objectives.

One war party recrossed the river and passed around the fort to a farmhouse lying about a mile in the rear. It was owned by a Mrs. Turnbull, who lived there with her two sons. The Ottawas killed and scalped the three of them. Three death halloos were heard in the fort, and the officers understood what had happened. This was their first notification that the Indians had spilled blood. It was an oral declaration of war. The Ottawas then burned the Turnbull house and drove off the cattle.

Another war party took to their canoes and landed on Isle au Cochon (modern Belle Isle) to seize the king's cattle which grazed there. Two soldiers were on the island as herdsmen, and James Fisher, a retired sergeant of regulars, occupied a farm there with his wife, four children, and a maid. This day there was another soldier visiting on the island, and a French sawyer named François Goslin, who was squaring some building timbers. The Ottawas killed Fisher, his wife, one child, and two of the soldiers. The serving woman, the other soldier, and the three remaining Fisher children were taken prisoners.[4]

[4] One little Fisher girl was taken to Saginaw, according to St. Aubin. *Mich. P. & H. Coll.*, VIII, 352. Another, Marie, aged 15 months, died in October in the fort. Little Betty Fisher was brutally murdered in 1764 on the Maumee River, as will be related. Mons. Peltier recounted a local legend about the difficulty of burying James Fisher. *ibid.*, p. 360.

The frightened Frenchman, who did not believe his life was to be spared, attempted to escape and was killed by an Indian who mistook him for an Englishman.

By the time these two detachments returned and reported their nine murders to Pontiac, the rest of the Ottawas had established a camp on the north shore east of the fort. The braves now turned their attention to the fort. One group was able to get within one hundred feet of the stockade and take protection in a gardener's house belonging to La Butte, the interpreter. From this vantage point they fired on the fort and on the schooner *Huron*, which was anchored off the upper corner of the fort. No damage was done, and occasionally the *Huron's* guns blasted back at them. Pontiac sent out warnings to the French that if they took any provisions into the fort or helped the garrison in any way, they would be put to death.

Late in the afternoon further good news was brought to Pontiac by a band of Chippewas from Saginaw Valley. They told him of their successful attack, May 6, on the military party under Lieut. Charles Robertson. This group numbered twelve and included Sir Robert Davers, John Rutherford (nephew of James Sterling's partner), six soldiers, two sailors, and a Pawnee slave. On learning from Pontiac of their approach, the Chippewas had moved down the Ste. Claire River and had lain in wait for them at its mouth. Robertson and Sir Robert Davers were killed along with the two sailors; young Rutherford, the six soldiers, and the Pawnee were taken prisoners. Robertson's body was eaten, and the skin from one arm made into a tobacco pouch. Rutherford was claimed by Chief Perwash of the Chippewas as a household servant.

The Chippewa delegation had with them Peter Desnoyers, a carpenter who had been working for several days in the pine woods above Lake Ste. Claire. He was allowed to enter the fort, where he reported the attack to Major Gladwin. The commandant heard the news grimly. He asked La Butte to go out and talk with Pontiac and try to learn his immediate plans. The interpreter was respected as an emissary, but he could discover little. He went back and forth several times that evening, probably carrying threats and counter-threats, until Pontiac grew tired of this fruitless communication and warned him not to show his face again.

The night passed with only desultory firing aimed at the schooner. But about four o'clock in the morning the Indians turned on the fort, presenting a moving fire as they passed around three sides. Later they resumed shooting at the schooner and sloop. If they hoped to sink the vessels with muskets they were wasting ammunition. The replies from the garrison were no more effective than the Indian fire, for the savages found good cover behind the houses, outbuildings, and fences near the fort.

The impatient Pontiac called a council of French and Indian leaders at the house of Antoine Cuillerier, between the fort and the camp, in the forenoon of Tuesday, May 10. This *habitant* was an intimate of Pontiac and the person whom the chief planned to place in command of the fort after driving out the British. He was also the brother-in-law of Bellestre, the late French commandant. The purpose of the council was to discuss means for a speedy reduction of the fort. Several of the *habitants* were friendly to Pontiac's aim, if not his methods, and would have liked to see the British humiliated and forced to give up the fort, even though the surrender might be temporary. They hoped to hide their collaboration with the Indians so that if the British mustered enough strength to take revenge only the Indians would suffer.

The decision of the council was to propose to Major Gladwin an armistice, or cessation of hostilities, while terms of peace were discussed. Whether Pontiac was sincere in this proposal or only seeking a fresh opportunity for treachery is not known. Besides Cuillerier, the names of five other Frenchmen who participated in the subsequent negotiations are known: Dr. Jean Chapoton, Laurence Gamelin, Jacques Godfroy, Thomas Gouin, and Pierre La Butte, the interpreter. If Pontiac was actually intending a trap, the question still remains whether these *habitants* knew it when they assisted in the parley. Cuillerier and Godfroy did, however, shortly espouse the Indian cause openly.

Be that as it may, Chapoton, Gamelin, and Godfroy informed Gladwin of Pontiac's desire to talk peace, and the major signified his willingness. La Butte returned to Cuillerier's house with the three Frenchmen to initiate the discussion. Soon Pontiac sent them back to the fort with four chiefs to request that Captain Campbell be sent out to speak for the garrison. Apparently there was some discussion in the fort of retaining the four chiefs as hostages for the safe return of Campbell, but Gladwin allowed himself to be overruled on this precaution by the promises of the *habitants*. He gave his consent for Campbell to go out, but did not order him to go. Campbell was anxious to serve and believed that because of his long acquaintance with Pontiac he might bring him to reason. Lieut. George McDougall volunteered to accompany him. Thomas Gouin now appeared on the scene and was so suspicious of Pontiac's design that he warned Campbell not to go, but the doughty Scotsman set off with his party.

Campbell and McDougall found some French and Indians assembled in the largest room of Cuillerier's house. The owner was seated in the center wearing a laced hat and coat. The Indians were eating bread. Angélique and her mother probably were hiding. Pontiac greeted the two officers and then ignored them. After awhile he addressed himself to Cuillerier, saying that he looked upon him as his father and as the commandant of Detroit until the French returned. Then the chief turned to the surprised British officers and told them that if they wanted peace they could have it on the same terms by which the French gave up the fort—namely, by laying down their arms, giving up their baggage, and being escorted to the frontier settlements by the Indians.[5]

Campbell and McDougall, however, were not permitted to carry those terms back to the fort. The French emissaries took the ominous news to Gladwin with the additional stipulation that Campbell and McDougall would be taken to the frontier if the terms were accepted. Sensing treachery, Gladwin warned them and Pontiac that he would do nothing until his two officers were returned to him. Pontiac was violating even the Indian tradition of respecting ambassadors, although he said he would keep them only two days. The *habitants* realized at last, if they had not known it before, that they were parties to a broken faith.

Pontiac seemed to be proud of his deed and in the evening sent messengers to the Potawatomies and the Huron band that supported him with news of his prize catch. He had kept the Potawatomies disposed at a distance around the fort so as to intercept any Englishmen going toward the post. They had captured two men whom the commandant of Fort St. Joseph had sent with letters to Gladwin. The prisoners were brought to the camp of Pontiac, and he ordered them killed. He now asked Ninivois, the Potawatomi chief, to place about twenty of his braves in ambush near the fort to capture any Englishmen who might venture out. Gladwin utilized the time of the truce in buying and having moved into the fort

[5] "Gladwin Manuscripts" in *Mich. P. & H. Coll.*, xxvii, 641.

all the provisions which the friendly *habitants* would sell. The work went on all night and the next day. Jacques Duperon Baby was particularly helpful in supplying the garrison.

The next morning, Wednesday, May 11, the Indians and French conferred again about proper terms of capitulation and obliged Campbell to write them out for presentation to Gladwin. The only concessions were that the garrison would be allowed to embark in the two vessels with their arms, but all merchandise and ordnance must be left behind. Curiously enough, Pontiac specified that he must have the Negro boy belonging to merchant James Rankin for a valet! Some *habitants* delivered the new proposals, but Gladwin was adamant. He said he would treat with them only after his two officers had been restored; until then he would defend the fort to the last man.

There were no hostilities during the day. While the negotiations were pending, Pontiac took four chiefs—Macatepilesis, Breton, Chavinon, and his nephew—through the woods around the fort and visited the *habitants* living in the section southwest of the fort. He required them to furnish him with powder and shot on pain of being plundered if they resisted. These supplies were shared with the Potawatomies.

With the four chiefs Pontiac then recrossed the river for a council with the christianized band of Hurons to threaten them with disaster if they did not ally themselves with him. They had taken no part in the hostilities so far, and Pontiac warned them that if they didn't join him he would attack them. As these Hurons could muster only about sixty warriors, they had to acquiesce. Teata, their chief, won some delay by declaring that they would not go to war until after mass next day, which was the Feast of the Ascension, or Holy Thursday. Pontiac agreed not to resume his attack on the fort until the Hurons joined him.

Next morning after mass, the Christian Hurons took up their muskets and tomahawks, crossed the river, and joined the Potawatomies below the fort. Their combined war whoops signaled to Pontiac to begin firing on the fort from above. Acting together they kept up a heavy fire all day long. The shots of the reluctant Hurons proved more effective than those of any of the others. One party of Indians rushed out of the woods and took possession of some barns at the rear of the fort, about a hundred yards distant. Gladwin fired on the barns with hot shot from his three-pounder and set them on fire. The surprised and frightened Indians were forced to flee and suffered several casualties before they regained the woods. Altogether the British had three men slightly wounded, while the savages lost at least three or four men and had nine or ten wounded. In the evening Pontiac sent in by Mons. Gamelin a proposal for another truce so that the dead could be buried. It was granted. He still kept Campbell and Mc-Dougall prisoners at Baptiste Meloche's house.

Farther south the Indians achieved a minor victory. The pagan Hurons had been watching the lower Detroit River for any traders or soldiers bound for the fort. Late that day two unsuspecting traders moved into their ambush. They were Chapman Abraham, a Jew who had put ashore at Mons. St. Louis', and Rackman, a Dutchman with five boats of merchandise from Niagara. The capture was an important one, for besides rum and trade goods the Indians obtained seventeen barrels of gunpowder.

News of this event reached the fort early next morning, Friday, May 13, and the rascally Frenchmen who brought it said that the Hurons were all drunk from the rum. Their ruse was very nearly successful. Gladwin immediately ordered twenty-five volunteers under Captain Hopkins, now second in command, to board the sloop, go down and burn the Huron village, and rescue the powder. Before they got half way the wind shifted and blew against them. Gladwin signaled for their return. He learned later that more than 120 Hurons—very sober—were waiting in ambush to greet this sally.

Joseph Hopkins deserves almost as much credit as Major Gladwin for the valiant defense of Fort Detroit. He was foremost in leading sorties out of the fort against the savages. His ready daring seemed almost habitual. Hopkins came from Maryland and once belonged to the 18th Regiment. He was not a commissioned officer, but must have been a sergeant, for on the formation of the Queen's Independent Rangers during the late war, he obtained a captain's commission.[6]

As the Indians did not come close to the fort that day, Gladwin improved the afternoon by sending out two detachments to burn the nearby house and barns which the Indians used for cover in their attacks. The parties were unmolested. Pontiac was holding another council at his camp to which he had summoned the more substantial French residents. He urged them to become combatants against the English. In particular, he wanted them to show him how to dig entrenchments for siege operations.

[6] After his valiant service in Detroit, he went to England late in 1764 where he was granted a coat of arms, but otherwise seems to have been disappointed in his expectations. He joined the French service and by 1766 was a colonel stationed at Cape François, St. Domingo. While there he wrote to his friend, Major Rogers, and urged him to join the French. Hopkins was a brigadier general in 1770 and governor of Aux Cayes. When the American Revolution broke out he appealed to Silas Deane in Paris to aid him in enlisting in the American cause. Apparently he did not succeed. He was reported still living in France in 1795 and trying to obtain command of a French vessel. Information adapted from *Docs. Rel. Col. Hist. N.Y.*, VII, 934, and Burton's note in the Navarre *Journal*, p. 88.

Pontiac realized that his methods so far were not proving effective, and obviously he had learned somewhere about the digging of parallels and approaches toward besieged objects. Most of the Frenchmen were unacquainted with such military operations, and those who knew something of the proper procedure assured him that they also were ignorant.

Pontiac then tried to frighten the fort again. He called La Butte and Campbell and dictated a letter for the captain to write to Gladwin. Pontiac again offered to let the garrison retire in the vessels and leave the merchants' trade goods. If Gladwin refused these terms Pontiac threatened to carry the fort by assault and put the captives to torture. He demanded an immediate reply. The letter was dispatched by a Frenchman.

Pontiac was chagrined and enraged to receive a verbal reply from Gladwin. The commandant merely reminded him that he had not been sent to Detroit to give up the fort, and he advised Pontiac to save his ammunition for hunting. The Briton's cool indifference was not lost on Pontiac. He ordered his braves out to fire on the fort, but they found less cover than the day before and consequently were less effective from a greater distance.

Gladwin did fear an assault on the fort, but he was reassured by those who knew the Indian mind better that the savages would never attempt a storm, since it was certain to involve a loss of life which they would not willingly accept. Gladwin knew, however, that he was constantly in danger of fire from burning arrows. He had ordered all tubs and barrels in the fort set around the streets and filled with water from the well. The use of fire apparently did not occur to Pontiac for several days, or if it did he probably hesitated to burn the traders' stores, which contained goods he wanted to seize.

The next afternoon, Saturday, May 14, Pontiac was surprised to be visited by a delegation of twelve prominent *habitants*. They asked to hold a council with him, so he summoned some other chiefs and all proceeded to Baptiste Meloche's house. These Frenchmen had been solicited by Father Potier, Jesuit missionary to the Hurons, to talk with Pontiac in an effort to persuade him to abandon his war. Father Potier himself had immobilized the Christian Hurons, first by refusing to administer the sacraments unless they remained neutral and then by persuading them to move to another location until the war was over.

The eldest *habitant* opened the council by asking Pontiac plainly what his war aims were. The chief replied that he was trying to expel the British from the fort and the land in preparation for the arrival of a French commandant who was on his way. This was the old rumor so frequently circulated by the disaffected French. The spokesman then argued that if he expected a French officer so soon, he need only wait for his arrival and then drive out the English with his help. Pontiac demurred; he said he had promised to have the place ready for his "father" and he wished him to find it so.

The *habitants* protested that the war was ruining them by stopping all trade. Pontiac cleverly replied that if they wanted relief they had only to join forces with him and expel the British, then peace would be restored. The French said they could not take such a part because they had sworn to be loyal to the British in 1760. Unable to come to any agreement, they retired and reported their failure to Father Potier.

The war was a week old. Pontiac had inflicted far more casualties than he had suffered, having killed fifteen English men and women, wounded five, and captured fifteen.

10

The Problem of Supplies

SUNDAY, MAY 15, passed tranquilly. Pontiac had resolved to await the arrival in force of the Chippewas from Saginaw Bay and from the Thames River. He had already broadened the theater of war by dispatching two parties to promote other attacks at Sandusky and St. Joseph. They will be heard from later.

Gladwin made use of the lull to destroy the last house and fence which would afford protection to an assailant of the fort. Holes were cut in the stockade on either side of the western gate, and the six-pounder cannon rolled up to command the road.

A week of war had already raised for Pontiac the problem of supplying his warriors with food, since they had no stocks in reserve at this time of year and were not hunting. He took the four chiefs of his nation and on May 17 again visited the settlers along the shores to levy assessments of food on threat of butchering their livestock. There was, moreover, some system to this levying. The Ottawas were to be fed at the expense of the settlers living north and east of the fort; the Potawatomies by those living to the southwest; and the Hurons by those living across the river.

As soon as this business was settled, Pontiac called a council at his camp of the principal Huron and Potawatomi chiefs as well as the Ottawa. They realized that the *habitants* who still went to and came from the fort were carrying information about the Indians to the enemy, or words of good cheer to the settlers outside. It was decided to maintain a guard of twenty braves on the east and west sides of the fort to stop this traffic.

Another idea had occurred to Pontiac since his failure either to surprise the fort, attack it successfully, or frighten the commandant. He called into council all the chiefs and many of the *habitants* on May 18. Probably the meeting was held outdoors at the Ottawa camp, because of the large number attending. The prisoners, Campbell and McDougall, were also present. Taking up a war belt, Pontiac addressed the French as follows:

"My brothers, you are ignorant of the reasons which have induced me to act, although I have spared no pains to keep you informed of my sentiments. But as I fear that our father will not come and take possession of the fort soon enough after I have expelled or killed the English, and that the Indians may insult you if there is no commandant here to obviate this difficulty, I have resolved to send to the Illinois some of our French brothers with some Indians to carry our war belts and our words to our father, Mons. de Neyon, and ask him to send us a French officer for a commandant to guide us and replace the English. You, my brothers, will do me a pleasure to write to our father in this matter, joining your words to mine."[1]

This speech was an elaborate deception. Pontiac had already arranged to put the command of the fort in the hands of Antoine Cuillerier pending the arrival of a French commandant, and it is doubtful if he was concerned about French-Indians relations during that interval. He had quickly realized the strength of the fort in defensive action, and the only alternative tactic was a siege to starve out the garrison. Pontiac knew there was a particular way to conduct an effective siege and that he did not have this technical information. Neither did any of the *habitants*, he had learned. Consequently, what he

[1] Navarre, *Journal*, p. 110.

sought from Illinois was a French officer skilled in the white man's art of siege warfare. The arrival of such an officer would also hearten the *habitants* along the Detroit River and swing them to the Indian side.

Pontiac thereupon dictated the following message to one of the Frenchmen for the Illinois commandant:

"Listen, you French brethren, who are prisoners as well as we: It is vexing that the English, whom we are willing to adopt as brethren, should deceive so many nations. All that the Delawares and Shawnees told us is now come to pass. They warned us not to trust the English, as they seek only to deceive us, and so it happens. Without the help of the French merchants who gave us credit and without some small reserves which we had for buying our fall needs, we would have been lost.

"Since our father, Mons. Bellestre, went away, we have no news; none but the English receive letters. Is it possible that our father never writes? No Frenchman receives any letters. This is to let our father at the Illinois know our situation and to request him to inform us what is going on, that we may know if we are abandoned.

"The English tell us incessantly, 'What, you savages, dare you speak? See what we have done. We have overthrown your father and the Spaniards; we are masters of all these lands and of all that belonged to your father, for we have conquered him, and we possess all these countries even to the Illinois, except a small edge which is trifling.'

"The Delawares told us this spring that the English sought to become masters of all and would put us to death. They told us also, 'Our brethren, let us die together, since the design of the English is to destroy us. We are dead one way or another.' When we saw this, we decided to say to all the nations who are your children, to fall in here at Detroit, which they have done. We pray our father at the Illinois to hasten to come to our succour, that he may have pity on us, notwithstanding that the English tell us constantly, 'From whom will you get what you stand in need of?'

"When our father, Mons. Bellestre, left here, he told us, 'My children, the English today overthrow your father. As long as they have the upper hand you will not have what you stand in need of; but this will not last.' We pray our father at the Illinois to take pity on us and say, 'These poor children, who wish to restore me.' Why do we what we are doing today? It is because we do not want the English to hold these lands, this is what causes your children to rise and strike everywhere.

"We pray thee, my father, send us an answer speedily by these couriers. Tell us your thought and your wish. We will put in your hands the one who expelled you; no harm will come to him. We will say to you, 'Behold, here he is.' We beg of you also, my father, to treat kindly our couriers. We are the cause of the fatigue which they are going to suffer."[2]

To this speech the Chippewas present added a word of their own approving of Pontiac's message. The perturbed Frenchmen conferred among themselves and composed a brief note to explain their predicament:

"Gentlemen:

"We are obliged to submit to what the Indians exact from us. The English are blocked up, and all the passages are shut up. We cannot express to you our perplexity. It would be necessary in order to judge of the calamities which threaten us and which appear to us inevitable that you saw with your own eyes what is going on here. God alone can prevent our becoming the victims of the English and savages.

[2] Amherst Papers, vol. 2, Clements Library; a crude translation is found in the "Gladwin Manuscripts," *Mich. P. & H. Coll.*, xxvii, 644.

"These couriers bear to you the talks of the nations here. We look upon it as a happiness to have it in our power to acquaint you of our deplorable situation. We certainly have never contributed thereto by our conduct. The English on their part never gave us occasion. Instruct us what we can do. We look upon you as protectors and mediators who would be willing to employ themselves efficaciously to pacify two contending parties who threaten us with an unexampled desolation."[3]

The messages finished, Pontiac designated the Indians and Frenchmen who were to carry them to Illinois. The *habitants* appointed were Jacques Godfroy, Mini Chesne, a Cuillerier, a Chauvin, and one of the Labadies. All of them were sympathetic with Indian aims and ready to be of aid. The group departed the next morning after Pontiac had solicited provisions for their journey. He seems also to have given them secret instructions and a belt of war wampum to promote attacks on Fort Miamis and Ouiatenon along their way.

For the next two days things were quiet around the fort. The sloop *Michigan*, Captain Newman, was sent down the river on May 21 to wait at the mouth of the river to convoy an expected reinforcement. The same day Pontiac was joined by 120 Mississaugi-Chippewa braves under Chief Sekahos from the Thames River. This addition, however, was largely offset next day by the secret defection of the pagan Hurons under Také. They sent into the fort their interpreter, Jacques St. Martin, with a message to Gladwin. They complained that they had been forced into the war by Pontiac, but were willing to release the traders they had captured and pay them for their seized goods if the commandant would make peace with them. Gladwin replied that if they would carry out this offer, remain quiet, and try to separate Pontiac from his other

[3] "Gladwin Manuscripts," *ibid.*, p. 645.

⟨ 149 ⟩

followers, he would recommend them to the general. Pontiac appears to have remained unaware of this treason among the Hurons.

In the week following, Pontiac led two attempts against the sloop, which was hovering around the mouth of the river. He had about four hundred braves in thirty war canoes. They engaged the ship's crew and the soldier-guards on board, but were prevented from getting close. A fortunate breeze sprang up, and Captain Newman maneuvered away from his attackers. Pontiac had brought Captain Campbell with him to use as a shield and as an English interpreter. He now dispatched the canoe in which Campbell rode in pursuit of the slowly moving vessel. Campbell was made to hail the ship, and the captain allowed the canoe to come within speaking range. Campbell said he was obliged by the Indians to order the ship to halt and turn into shore, but added that the master knew his orders and should get on his way as soon as possible.[4] The ship proceeded, and the Indians gave up.

Likewise concerned about provisions, Gladwin appointed a committee of three to act against hoarders. They visited the house of each Frenchman in the fort and removed surplus food supplies into a communal storehouse. They collected wheat, peas, corn, flour, tallow, oil, etc., giving receipts and keeping accounts. The French now found themselves in the plight of all neutrals who cannot isolate themselves. They were plundered by the Indians and forced to contribute to the British. Those living outside the fort especially feared a long siege, during which time the savages would be living off them. Both those who favored the Indian cause and those who preferred peace with the British agreed on their own present discomfort.

Accordingly, on May 25 they sent fifteen of their num-

[4] Wilkins to Amherst, June 15, 1763, Amherst Papers, WO34, XXII.

ber who were known and esteemed by Pontiac to talk
with the chief. He was surprised by this unexpected visit,
but when they proposed a general council he willingly
sent for the Potawatomi and Huron chiefs. The Chippewas were on hand, encamped with the Ottawas. After
all were assembled, one of the elder *habitants* explained
their point of view. He complained of the loss of livestock
and flour to the Indians, who had promised that their
brothers would not be harmed by the war. He mentioned
the domineering attitude of the Indians toward the
French. He did not appeal for a cessation of hostilities
but for a stricter limitation of the war to Indians and
British.

"Avenge the insults which have been offered you—we
do not object, but remember that we are all brothers and
the children of your Great Father, the King of France.
You are expecting him back, you say. When he returns
to supply your needs, as he has already done, and sees
that you have killed us and taken all that we were preserving for him, what will he say to you? Do you think he will
give you presents to cover up the wrong you have done us?
On the contrary, he will regard you as rebellious children
and traitors, and instead of petting you he will make war
upon you, and then you will have two nations upon you,
the French and the English. Consider whether you want
to have two enemies, or whether you will live as brothers
among us."[5]

Pontiac had listened attentively and now he arose and
delivered his answer. He was a war chief, but he knew
something of diplomacy as he soon demonstrated in his
patient and brilliant reply.

"My brothers, we have never intended to do you any
injury or harm, neither have we pretended that any should
be done you; but among my young men there are some,

[5] Navarre, *Journal*, p. 122.

as among you, who are always doing harm in spite of all precautions that one can take. Moreover, it is not for personal vengeance merely that I am making war upon the English; it is for you, my brothers, as well as for us. When the English have insulted us in the councils which we have held with them, they have insulted you, too, without your knowing it. And since I and all my brothers, also, know that the English have taken away from you all means to avenge yourselves by disarming you and making you sign a paper which they have sent to their own country—a thing they could not do to us—for this reason we wish to avenge you equally with ourselves, and I swear the destruction of all that may be upon our lands.

"What is more, you do not know all the reasons which oblige me to act as I do. I have told you only what concerns you, but you will know the rest in time. I know very well that many of you, my brothers, consider me a fool, but you will see in the future if I am what people say I am, and if I am wrong. I know very well, also, that there are some among you, my brothers, who side with the English in making war upon us and that grieves me. As for them, I know them well and when our Great Father returns I shall name and point them out to him and they will see whether they or we will be most satisfied with the result in the end.

"I do not doubt, my brothers, that this war causes you annoyance because of the movements of our brothers who are coming and going in your homes constantly; I am chagrined at it, but do not think, my brothers, that I inspire the harm which is being done you. As a proof that I do not desire it just call to mind the war with the Foxes, and the way I behaved as regards you seventeen years ago. Now when the Chippewas and Ottawas of Michilimackinac, and all the northern nations, came with the Sauks and Foxes to destroy you, who was it that defended you? Was it not I and my men?

"When Mackinac, the great chief of all these nations, said in his council that he would carry the head of your commander to his village and devour his heart and drink his blood, did I not take up your cause and go to his village and tell him that if he wanted to kill the French he would have to begin first with me and my men? Did I not help you rid yourselves of them and drive them away? How does it come then, my brothers, that you would think me today ready to turn my weapons against you? No, my brothers, I am the same French Pontiac who helped you seventeen years ago; I am French, and I want to die French, and I repeat that it is altogether your interests and mine that I avenge. Let me carry out my plan. I do not demand your assistance, because I know you could not give it; I only ask you for provisions for myself and all my followers. If, however, you should like to help me I would not refuse; you would please me and get out of trouble the quicker, for I promise when the English shall be driven away from here, or killed, we shall all withdraw into our villages, following our custom, to await the coming of our French Father.

"Thus you see, my brothers, what my sentiments are. Do not worry. I shall see to it that neither my followers nor any other Indians harm you any further, but I ask that our women may have permission to raise our corn upon your fields and fallow lands. By allowing this you will oblige us greatly."[6]

This masterly clarification of Pontiac's attitude toward the French made the complainants appear like naïve school boys rather than the secretive collaborationists they pictured themselves to be. He let them know that he was fighting for them as much as for himself and that he was

[6] ibid., pp. 122-126.

aware of the men—quislings we would call them today—
who played up to the British. Victory would take care of
them. Meanwhile, he admitted his discipline was not perfect, yet he did not think that the inconvenience suffered
by the *habitants* was an unjust contribution on their part
to the war effort. He overlooked their unwillingness to
fight because they had no arms and were bound by the
surrender of Canada, but there was something positive
they could do.

The Frenchmen who had come to complain of trespassing and petty thievery found themselves without satisfactory arguments to escape the turn which Pontiac had
given the conference. They agreed to his proposal, and
that very afternoon a number of squaws began work in
the corn fields. Some of the French even ploughed fields
for their planting. As good as his word, Pontiac went
along both shores giving orders regarding future rations
and warning the warriors that nothing more was to be
taken from the French by force.

This success on the diplomatic front was followed by
news that evening of his first military victory. Fort Sandusky had fallen on May 16 before a surprise attack carried out by a few Ottawas and Hurons from Detroit supported by the Hurons living around Sandusky. They had
approached the gate of the blockhouse and told the sentry
that they wished to speak to the commandant. Ensign
Christopher Pauli came out and, recognizing his neighbors, admitted seven of them to council. They entered a
cabin, smoked for a short time in silence, then one of
them raised his head. At this signal the Indians on either
side of Pauli seized him and tied him. As he was carried
from the room, he saw his sentry dead and other soldiers
of the fifteen-man garrison lying around slain. Pauli was
the only survivor. Even the merchants who maintained a
storehouse at the fort were dead, and the Indians were

carrying off their goods. The attack had been as complete as it had been noiseless.[7]

The victorious party was coming up the river now in their canoes, one of them flying the red British flag and bearing their only prisoner, Ensign Pauli. They were wildly received at the Ottawa camp. The warriors lined up in a double row and made Pauli run the gantlet, striking him as he fled between the lines. Bruised and beaten he reached the end of the gantlet and figuratively fell into the arms of a widowed squaw, who at once adopted him as her second husband. In this way he was saved from further torture and even exempted from hard work. He escaped into Fort Detroit on July 3.

The victory at Sandusky was much to Pontiac's liking. It was complete and yet the Indians suffered no casualties. It strengthened his confidence, heightened his prestige, and underscored his remarks to the French. It also gave him expansive ideas.

[7] "Gladwin Manuscripts," op. cit., p. 636; Gladwin to Amherst, July 8, 1763, Parkman Papers, 22, p. 293.

11

Victories Beyond Detroit

THE PRESENCE OF THE SLOOP at the mouth of the Detroit River day after day had given unmistakable intelligence to Pontiac that she was expecting something, provisions or reinforcements or both. Consequently a band of Indians moved eastward along the north shore of Lake Erie to intercept whatever might be coming from Niagara. The savages were also in control at Sandusky in case approaching boats should hug the south shore, or in case pack horses should come up the Great Trail from Fort Pitt.

Lieut. Abraham Cuyler of the Queen's Rangers had in fact left Niagara on May 13 with 96 men and 139 barrels of provisions in ten bateaux. A bateau was a sturdy French boat usually with flat bottom, pointed ends, and high sides, propelled by oars or a sail, and used chiefly to transport goods. Cuyler was ignorant of any Indian trouble at Detroit, of course. His party landed on May 28 about ten o'clock at night at Point Pelee, about twenty-five miles from the Detroit River. The beach was about forty yards wide before the woods began. The soldiers started to prepare camp, unaware that they were being watched by Indians among the trees.

A man and a boy wandered along the beach looking for firewood. Suddenly the boy was seized by dark-skinned figures, but the man ran terrified back to the camp. Lieutenant Cuyler had just time to post his men in a semicircle before the Indians rushed them. Crashing into the center of the line, they threw the soldiers into fatal confusion. The Rangers broke for the boats, and in close fighting were killed or stunned. Five boats were pushed off, but the savages seized two other boats and rounded up the five. Lieutenant Cuyler found himself with only six men left on the beach trying to push off one of the heavy bateaux. They succeeded and headed out into the lake. Their boat was pursued for a mile before the Indians gave up. The officer could find but one other escaped boat, and the two hoisted sails and crossed the lake. Next day the party approached Fort Sandusky and found it burned. Cuyler had only forty men left, five of them wounded, including himself. Nine barrels of provisions and a little ammunition remained. As it was useless to proceed to Detroit, the survivors turned back to Presqu'Isle and Niagara.[1]

The victorious Indians gathered their prisoners and booty into the eight bateaux and rowed to the mouth of the Detroit River. Here they should have encountered the sloop *Michigan*, but Captain Newman, fearing a third attack and having given up hope of meeting any reinforcements, had sailed away to Niagara. The Indians proceeded up the river and early on the morning of May 30 passed the fort with much hallooing. The garrison thought at first that these bateaux were their reinforcements. The soldiers lined the stockade to hail their approach. Their joy was shortlived, however, for they soon discerned Indians in each boat with the soldiers.

As the insulting parade was passing the fort, the four soldiers in the first boat suddenly threw overboard their two Indian captors and made a break for the anchored schooner. One of the soldiers was pulled under water and drowned by the Indians, but the other three made good their escape and brought in seven barrels of provisions besides.

[1] Cuyler's report, transcript in the Parkman Papers, 22, 109-110.

On the Ste. Claire River the day before, another party of Indians had captured two bateaux containing a woman and eighteen soldiers and boatmen under Sergeant Shaw, who had been sent up to Fort Michilimackinac with provisions in April.

Three victories in quick succession—against Fort Sandusky, Cuyler's detachment, and the escort returning from the north—put the Indians in high spirits. Moreover, as the loot included much rum the Indians celebrated in their accustomed manner. They drank, danced, boasted, quarreled, and fought, while the squaws and children kept out of the way. The drunken spree lasted three days, during which time hardly a shot was fired at the fort. Blood ran freely, however, from the prisoners of Cuyler's detachment. All of them reportedly were killed in running the gantlet or during the orgy that followed.[2]

Recovering from the celebration, Pontiac was quick to believe that although Detroit was holding out against him, the smaller forts would be easy prey. On June 2 he sent a fleet of canoes down the river carrying two hundred warriors on a secret mission. Under this new strategy which Pontiac developed the theater of war was broadened, and the destruction of Fort Detroit was no longer a first requisite.

Within the fort that day, Major Gladwin received news that must have brought him a wry smile. A Frenchman brought in a letter by which he learned, while sitting in

[2] Accounts of Gouin, Parent, and St. Aubin in *Mich. P. and H. Coll.*, VIII, 347, 353, 358. Mme. Meloche, *ibid.*, p. 344, relates the story of a trunk found among the loot of Cuyler's defeat. It was being sent to a Mlle. Deriviere in Detroit, and she learned that it was with the goods seized by the Indians. Taking La Butte with her to Pontiac's camp, she told the chief she was expecting the trunk and believed it had been captured by his warriors. Pontiac ordered a search to be made, the trunk was found, and he gave it to her with no objection.

the hottest spot in North America, that the definitive treaty of peace between France and Great Britain had been signed in London on February 20. The great Seven Years' War was officially ended, and France's first empire was lost. There would be no reconquest of Canada by the French, and no help for the Indians from Illinois or anywhere else. Pontiac stood alone—but he did not know it and he was far from discouraged. The war he had started was still gaining momentum, attracting new Indian allies. Those allies were achieving victories for him elsewhere among the Great Lakes.

The first British fort to fall was Sandusky, as we have noted. Next was Fort St. Joseph (Niles, Michigan), commanded by Ensign Francis Schlosser and garrisoned by fifteen men. On the morning of May 25 he was informed that a party of Potawatomies had arrived from Detroit to visit their relatives in that neighborhood and wished to greet him. As he prepared to leave his quarters, a local Frenchman entered with the news that the visiting Potawatomies had come to make trouble. Alarmed now, Schlosser ran to the barracks to get his men under arms. He found the building already full of Indians mingling with the soldiers, so he spoke his orders to a sergeant and left, returning to his quarters to talk with the chiefs, under Chief Washee, who had assembled there. Hardly had they made their greetings before he heard a cry from the barracks. Immediately the Indians seized him. All but six of the soldiers were killed in about two minutes, and then the fort was plundered. Schlosser was taken to Detroit and on June 14 delivered over to Gladwin.[3] The pattern of attack followed closely the treachery at Sandusky and the scheme planned for the capture of Detroit. There could be no doubt as to the ultimate author.

[3] "Gladwin Manuscripts" in *Mich. P. & H. Coll.*, xxvii, 636.

Miamis (Fort Wayne, Indiana) was the third fort to fall to the Indians. Pontiac's couriers to Illinois showed a directing hand in the attack. The tactic used at the other two forts could not be repeated here, because Ensign Robert Holmes knew that some sort of Indian trouble was astir in the region. He did not know that Sandusky was taken, but on May 23 a passing Frenchman mentioned hearing cannon fire from near Detroit. Holmes gauged the temper of the Indians and set his men to making cartridges.

On their way up the Maumee River, Godfroy, Chesne, and the rest of Pontiac's embassy seized one Welch, an English trader, and took him with them to the vicinity of the fort. They spoke to the Miamies and doubtless realized that Holmes would never allow a party of Indians inside the fort. If the Miamies did not know of Pontiac's war before this, they at least were willing to take the word of the couriers and to cast their lot with the other tribes against the English. They took three soldiers from the fort prisoners on May 25.

Then the conspirators learned that Holmes kept as his mistress a Miami girl who apparently bore him no love. She consented to decoy him to his death. This tactic was an improvement on anything Pontiac might have suggested. On May 27, before Holmes knew the fate of his three soldiers or learned of the visitors from Detroit, his nameless mistress entered the fort and told the young officer that another squaw was lying ill in a cabin nearby. Would he not come and bleed her, as white people were treated? Holmes consented and followed the girl to a cabin about three hundred yards from the fort. As he approached it, two shots rang out and Holmes dropped. The sergeant heard them and ran out of the fort to investigate. He was immediately seized by the Indians. The eleven remaining soldiers quickly shut the gates and climbed up on the stockade to look over.

Welch was now brought up by Godfroy and Chesne and called out in English their order to surrender and be saved, or face death if they resisted. The men consulted among themselves and decided to surrender. Four of them were carried to Detroit to be exhibited before Pontiac, but whether the others were kept prisoner by the Miamies or massacred is not known.[4]

Pontiac's embassy, which had become a military force en route, jubilantly continued on its journey down the Wabash River. Reaching Fort Ouiatenon (Lafayette, Indiana) about May 31, they told the local Indians—Weas, Kickapoos, and Mascoutens—of Pontiac's war and its successes to date. The couriers seem to have carried along a war belt from Detroit and with this wampum they persuaded the tribes of Ouiatenon to seize the fort.

On the morning of June 1 they sent in a request to Lieut. Edward Jenkins to meet several chiefs in council at a cabin outside the fort. As soon as he entered he was seized and bound. He saw that a few of his soldiers had already been taken. The Indians demanded that he order those remaining to surrender, or all would be killed. Jenkins did so, and the whole garrison of twenty was taken without bloodshed. They were held captive for more than a month, until taken down to Fort de Chartres early in August.[5] Eventually Jenkins went down the Mississippi and reached New York by ship.

Beyond Ouiatenon British authority did not yet extend. The high land below it (Terre Haute) marked the boundary between Canada and Louisiana. Vincennes, like Fort de Chartres, lay in Louisiana and was free of a British garrison, although formally surrendered to England in the

[4] *ibid.*, pp. 637 and 660.
[5] *ibid.*, p. 635; *Ill. Hist. Coll.*, x, 11-19.

⟨ 161 ⟩

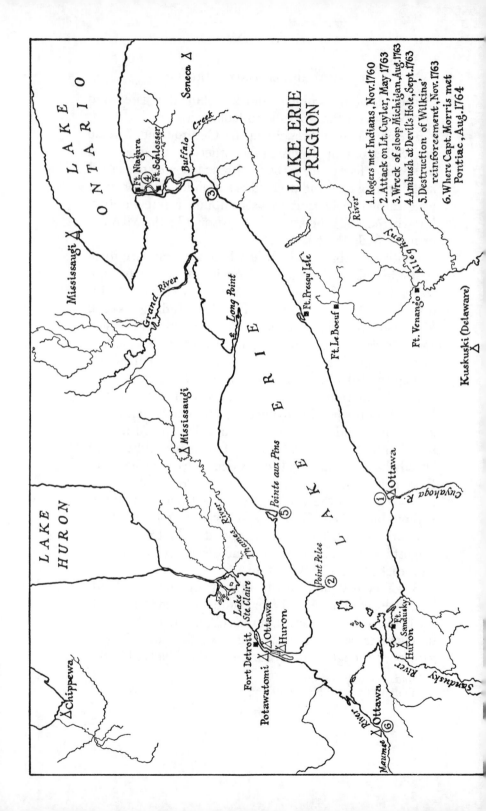

LAKE ERIE
REGION

1. Rogers met Indians, Nov.1760
2. Attack on Lt. Cuyler, May 1763
3. Wreck of sloop Michigan, Aug.1763
4. Ambush at Devil's Hole, Sept.1763
5. Destruction of Wilkins' reinforcement, Nov.1763
6. Where Capt. Morris met Pontiac, Aug.1764

final treaty. Pontiac's embassy passed into friendly territory.

These four forts had fallen easily. The next one to go was the largest of them all and its capture the bloodiest. Fort Michilimackinac had a garrison of 35 men commanded by Capt. George Etherington, including the handful under Lieutenant Jamet from the burned Sault fort. They were all ignorant of the Indian war when on June 2 the neighboring Chippewas began a game of *baggataway* (lacrosse) against some visiting Sauks on the sand just outside the fort. Soldiers and officers alike strolled out to watch the game. The day was pleasant, the contest between the teams entertaining. Some of the squaws wandered into the fort.

In the seeming excitement of the game one of the players hooked the ball high over the stockade. Shouting, the Indians ran pell-mell past the sentries into the fort after it. Once inside, however, they dropped their sticks, grabbed weapons concealed on their squaws and began massacring the soldiers and the English traders. Captain Etherington and Lieutenant Leslye were seized at the outset, but Lieutenant Jamet fought bravely with his sword until overcome by numbers. When he fell wounded, the savages cut off his head. Twenty soldiers were killed on the spot. The French retired indoors and were not disturbed. One trader was killed and the others plundered of their goods, which included fifty barrels of powder and lead in proportion.

Forty-six years later, Alexander Henry, a young English trader at Michilimackinac, could recall the day with horrible vividness. "Through an aperture which afforded me a view of the area of the fort, I beheld, in shapes the foulest and most horrible, the ferocious triumphs of barbarian conquerors. The dead were scalped and mangled; the dying were writhing and shrieking under the unsatiated knife and tomahawk; and from the bodies of some, ripped open, their butchers were drinking the blood, scooped up in the hollow of joined hands and quaffed amid shouts of rage and victory."[6]

The Chippewas had planned this surprise by themselves, after learning that Pontiac had begun a war to drive the British out of the country. They said they did not even tell the local French of their intention. Although the great chief of the Chippewas was Minavavana, called *Le Grand Saulteur* by the French, the war chief who led the assault was Matchekewis.[7] Successful as he was, he had neglected one diplomatic detail: he had not informed the neighboring Ottawas of the plot or invited them to join.

As soon as the northern Ottawas, living around L'Arbre Croche (Cross Village, Michigan), heard of the attack, they promptly betook themselves to the fort, twenty miles north. They had already received a war belt from Pontiac urging them to join him, but apparently they had come to no decision. What they resented now was the fore-handedness of the Chippewas in beating them to the local objective and thereby obtaining all the loot. Under Chief Okinochumake, they reached Fort Michilimackinac in the evening of June 4 and seized all the British prisoners.

The astonished Chippewas protested, and a two-day conference was held. The upshot of it was that the Otta-was were given a portion of the plunder and returned to the Chippewas a trader and four soldiers while taking two traders, eleven soldiers, Captain Etherington, and Lieu-tenant Leslye back to L'Arbre Croche. A Chippewa chief who arrived on June 8 killed the four soldiers held by his

[6] Henry, *Travels and Adventures*, chapters 9 and 10; Raymond McCoy offers an excellent summary of the fort's fate in his *Massacre of Old Fort Mackinac*.

[7] *Wis. Hist. Coll.*, VII, 188-194.

nation to make up for his having missed the surprise attack. One body was promptly cut up and boiled for eating.

As a repercussion of the fall of Michilimackinac, Fort Edward Augustus (Green Bay, Wisconsin) was abandoned. After notifying Major Gladwin of his plight, Captain Etherington sent a letter by a party of Ottawas to Lieut. James Gorrell at the bay ordering him to bring off his garrison to L'Arbre Croche.[8] Gorrell summoned the neighboring Sauks, Foxes, Menominees, and Winnebagoes to council and told them he must leave the fort in their hands. They were not interested in Pontiac's uprising, having long disliked the French, and they offered a delegation to accompany Gorrell and speak to the Ottawas and Chippewas. The commandant, his garrison, and allies set out on June 21 and crossed Lake Michigan to L'Arbre Croche. There he was received by the Ottawas and persuaded them to take their prisoners to Montreal and receive a large reward for them.

When the Chippewas learned of the proposed trip they threatened not to let the British troops pass. It was a last show of bravado. Reaction to their recent success had set in; their earlier self-confidence gave way to doubt and fear of revenge. They moved their village over to Mackinac Island as being a place easier to defend. Not much arguing was required to placate them, and the Ottawa band with its British charges started for Montreal on July 18, via the Ottawa River. They reached the city safely less than four weeks later and turned in their semi-captives.

With the passage of the garrison from Fort Edward Augustus and the survivors from Michilimackinac, not a

[8] Copied into James Gorrell's journal, which is printed in *Wis. Hist. Coll.*, I, 39. The original is in the Maryland Historical Society Library; a shorter journal covering the same events is in the Clements Library.

single British post remained in the western Great Lakes region except besieged Detroit.

Meanwhile, the news of Pontiac's war and the destruction of the forts was being carried south and east by hot young braves anxious to enlist the help of other tribes. The Delawares received a war belt from the Hurons at Sandusky informing them that the fort was taken and Detroit was under attack. This news was all that was needed to set them off, since they had long been vacillating between the exhortations of their own Prophet, supported by the machinations of the French, and the promises of George Croghan for the English. The Delawares were readily joined by the Mingoes, but for a time the Shawnees held off.

Led by Chief Wolfe, the Delawares and Mingoes, after selling a quantity of pelts for powder and lead, swept southward up the Monongahela River on May 27. Next day they fell on Col. William Clapham's little settlement (West Newton, Pennsylvania), about twenty-five miles below Fort Pitt, and brutally massacred Clapham, one of his men, two women, and a child. Returning to Fort Pitt the Indians found two soldiers outside at the saw mill on May 29 and killed them.

Capt. Simeon Ecuyer, commanding in Colonel Bouquet's absence, ordered all the settlers to move into the fort for protection and formed the men into two companies of militia. Houses outside the fort which might give protection to the Indians were burned, and the savages themselves burned other houses, including George Croghan's new residence up the river. Fort Pitt was besieged, but Captain Ecuyer was not alarmed. He had a better fort than the one at Detroit; there was a good ditch around it and sixteen pieces of cannon mounted on the stockade. His garrison consisted of 250 men, regulars and militia.

Meanwhile, at the Delaware town of Tuscarawas about May 21, a party of fourteen English traders was warned by King Beaver to depart because an Indian war had been started "against you" by the "Ottawas and Chippewas." The traders heeded the warning and set off for Pittsburgh. On reaching Beaver Creek next day, however, they were fired on by Indians—Delawares, no doubt. Several traders were killed on the spot and only four reached Fort Pitt.[9]

A party of savages ventured as far east as Fort Ligonier (Ligonier, Pennsylvania, 45 miles southeast of Pittsburgh) and fired on the post from a harmless distance on June 2. Lieut. Archibald Blane disdained to reply until towards evening, when he sent out a detachment which scared them off. But they moved forty miles east and molested Fort Bedford (Bedford, Pennsylvania).

The Shawnees joined the Delawares against the English early in June. The Senecas entered the war about the same time, possibly on invitation from Pontiac, more likely by their own volition as soon as they heard that the western nations had attacked Lieutenant Cuyler. While a siege was maintained at Fort Pitt, the main Indian effort was directed at the forts to the north of it. The Senecas of Geneseo took the initiative and struck first at Fort Venango (Franklin, Pennsylvania), eighty miles north of Pittsburgh.

Lieut. Francis Gordon commanded a garrison of perhaps fifteen or sixteen men at this post. Apparently the only respectable construction at the place was the blockhouse, and when the Senecas struck, the soldiers took refuge there. As there were no survivors, the date cannot be set exactly, although the attack probably occurred about June 16. The only account of it available is what a Mohawk chief told Sir William Johnson. According to this report the Senecas butchered the whole garrison without mercy and then forced Lieutenant Gordon to write down on paper the reasons why they had risen against the

[9] *Bouquet Papers*, Series 21649, pp. I, 121-122.

English. They dictated two complaints: the scarcity and dearness of powder for the past two years, and the fact that the English kept possession of so many forts that the Indians believed they intended to possess all their country. After Gordon had finished writing this peculiar form of declaration of war, the Senecas burned the blockhouse and slowly roasted the lieutenant to death.

Undoubtedly it was these same Senecas who moved on northward to Fort Le Boeuf (Waterford, Pennsylvania), commanded by Ensign George Price and garrisoned by thirteen men. Price knew of the Indian attack on Detroit, but apparently was not expecting an echo in his own vicinity. He was attacked suddenly on June 18. The Indians gained the cover of one building and fired burning arrows at the blockhouse in which the soldiers were gathered. This blockhouse was a rectangular stronghold, 24 by 32 feet. The garrison held off the savages until night and then escaped into the woods. Price and seven men made their way to Fort Venango and found it destroyed. They continued southward and reached Fort Pitt on June 26. Four more soldiers came in next day.

The victorious Senecas moved up to Fort Presqu'Isle (Erie, Pennsylvania), a stronger post containing 29 men under Ensign John Christie. Here the Senecas joined forces with about 200 Ottawas, Hurons, and Chippewas from Detroit, the detachment which Pontiac had sent off by canoe on June 2. Two hills very near the fort gave attackers an advantage, and on the night of June 19 the savages took possession of them, throwing up breastworks to protect themselves. This was scientific siege operation suggesting the presence of a white man, a suspicion later confirmed.

At daybreak the Indians opened fire on the post. The garrison retired into the blockhouse, but the attackers shot burning arrows into the roof and set fire to it several times. The soldiers were able to extinguish the fires with water from reserve barrels, but with those emptied they dared not expose themselves on the parade to reach the well. Some of the savages got into the ditch that ran around the stockade, but were routed from there. They then began digging a trench, or tunnel, from one of the hills to the fort. As the soldiers could not stop this approach, they occupied themselves in sinking a new well within the blockhouse itself.

Firing was resumed next day, and that night from their trench the Indians set fire to the commandant's house and the stockade. Despite fatigue the besieged soldiers kept on firing at close range until midnight. Finally Ensign Christie called out to ask if there was anyone among the savages who spoke English. An Englishman, formerly a captive but now a tribal member, was fighting with them. He answered Christie that the Indians wanted only the fort, and the garrison could go where it pleased.

Christie apparently believed him and gained an armistice till morning. He then sent out two soldiers to treat with the chiefs and observe their entrenchments. When these two signaled to Christie that the approaches were effective, he went out to talk terms. It was agreed to permit the garrison to retire to Fort Pitt, but as soon as the surrender was completed the soldiers were divided among the four tribes and taken away.[10]

Four soldiers, a woman, and Christie were taken by the Hurons to Detroit. There at the Huron village two of the soldiers were killed. Christie, the woman, and another soldier were delivered over to Major Gladwin on July 9. One soldier of the garrison escaped and made his way to Fort Pitt, believing himself to be the only survivor. No doubt many of the soldiers were killed in victory celebra-

[10] Gladwin's report in his letter to Amherst, July 8, 1763, Parkman Papers, 22, pp. 293-300.

tions after the capitulation. Colonel Bouquet hoped that Christie had not survived his disgraceful surrender of the fort. Bouquet may not have realized the effectiveness of the Indian attack, but he did know the strength of the blockhouse for he had superintended the construction of both Presqu'Isle and Le Boeuf in the summer of 1760.

Thus it was that in less than a week the Senecas and Pontiac's detachment from Detroit had wiped out the three forts on the communication between Pittsburgh and Niagara. After the Detroit Indians retired from this theater, the Delawares, Mingoes, and Shawnees renewed their attack on Fort Pitt with more confidence and struck at Fort Ligonier a second time.

Hailing Fort Pitt on June 24, a chief and a principal warrior of the Delawares spoke to the Indian commissary. They informed him of the loss of the upper posts and advised the English to give up the fort before a great army of Indians reached there. Captain Ecuyer thanked them, but insisted that he was strong enough to defend his post. His garrison had increased to 338 men, although smallpox had broken out among them. He told the chiefs to urge the other Delawares to make their peace. He then gave them a present of two blankets and a handkerchief from the smallpox hospital![11]

A Swiss soldier of fortune, Ecuyer regarded the Indians as savage enemies to be eliminated by any means available. A fatal epidemic was as lawful a method as shooting. A white captive among the Delawares later testified that smallpox raged among them, the Shawnees, and the Mingoes all summer and was still prevalent the next spring.[12] It certainly affected their vigorous prosecution of the war.

[11] William Trent's journal, as edited by A. T. Volwiler, *Miss. Val. Hist. Rev.*, XI (1924), 400.

[12] Examinations of Gersholm Hicks in Grant's letters to Gage, Apr. 15 and 26, 1764, Gage Papers.

12

The News Travels East

Sir Jeffery Amherst, His Majesty's commander-in-chief of the armed forces in North America, fumed impatiently in his headquarters in New York. He hoped every day to receive permission from London to go home. After all, he had conducted no military campaign in almost two years. The war was won, peace was signed, and he had been in the field more than five years. He disliked America and particularly New York in the summertime. He wanted to go home now!

It was about three o'clock in the afternoon of June 6, a warm, lazy day, when his aide brought in two letters which had just arrived by express from Colonel Bouquet in Philadelphia. Bouquet was a man after his heart—dependable, careful, serious, a thorough professional. Too bad there weren't more officers like him among the British. Amherst broke the seals and found four letters: two short notes from Bouquet enclosing Captain Ecuyer's letters of May 29 and 30 from Fort Pitt. Amherst read the latter with irritated interest.

In his first letter Captain Ecuyer reported that some Delawares and Mingoes had gone down the river to Clapham's and killed four persons. His second letter announced that two more men had been killed outside Fort Pitt, while a party of traders at Beaver Creek had suffered a similar fate. News had also been brought in that Fort Sandusky had been captured and Detroit was being attacked. The captain believed the uprising was general and feared for all the western posts.

Amherst was annoyed by this fresh disturbance thrust across his desk. Captain Ecuyer was frightened and even gullible. Those rumors about Sandusky and Detroit were rubbish, of course. The savages weren't daring enough— or fools enough—to start anything like that. Something had upset the Indians around Fort Pitt and they had murdered some settlers and traders, as they always did. Probably by this time they had come to their senses and were regretting their behavior. Nevertheless, certain precautions must be taken, meaning a good deal of tedious detail on a hot afternoon.

This was primarily a job for the Indian agents, but Johnson was on the Connecticut shore for his health. Where was George Croghan anyway? Still in Philadelphia? He ought to be in Fort Pitt, his headquarters, right now if he was going to be of any use. The general called his aide and made inquiry for Croghan's whereabouts. He then dictated orders to Major Campbell of the 42nd Regiment to gather the light companies of his regiment, the 17th, and the 77th and take them over to Staten Island and encamp. They should be ready to march to Philadelphia at a moment's notice, should Bouquet indicate a wish for reinforcements to take west with him. Information was produced that Croghan had already set out from Philadelphia for Fort Pitt. Amherst then replied to Bouquet's express. After acknowledging receipt of the letters and indicating the steps he had taken, he gave his opinion of Ecuyer's news:

"Altho' I have thought proper to assemble this force, which I judge more than sufficient to quell any disturbances the whole Indian strength could raise, yet I am persuaded this alarm will end in nothing more than a rash attempt at what the Senecas have been threatening and which we have heard of for some time past. As to their cutting off defenceless families, or even some of the small posts, it is certainly at all times in their power to effect such enterprises; particularly while we ourselves supply them with powder and lead, as appears from Captain Ecuyer's letter of the 29th May to have been the case with those villains, who are suspected to have committed the mischief. The post of Fort Pitt, or any of the others commanded by officers, can certainly never be in danger from such a wretched enemy as the Indians are, at this time, if the garrisons do their duty. I am only sorry that when such outrages are committed, the guilty should escape; for I am fully convinced the only true method of treating those savages is to keep them in proper subjection and punish, without exception, the transgressors."[1]

Amherst was no friend of the Indians like Johnson and Stuart and Croghan, but he thought he knew better how to deal with them. He wouldn't bother the superintendents with this affair at Fort Pitt, lest they interfere with all their interminable rigmarole of councils, presents, medals, recommendations, etc., etc. He and Bouquet would handle this as insubordination should be handled. Meanwhile he would say nothing publicly about it.

For almost a week nothing happened. No news doubtless was good news. Then on the night of June 11 came another express from Bouquet with tidings that Fort Pitt was surrounded and unable to make contact with Venango to the north; moreover, Fort Ligonier had been attacked, and settlers were pouring into Fort Bedford for protection. Grudgingly Amherst supposed he had better order those reinforcements on to Philadelphia for Bouquet to use. The affair appeared to be somewhat more serious than he had thought. Nevertheless, he slept on it and issued his orders next day. At that time he wrote to Johnson to inform him of what was going on.

"You will no doubt have heard," he began, "that the

[1] *Bouquet Papers*, Series 21634, p. 182.

Indians near Fort Pitt have been doing mischief; and it would seem that the affair is more general than I had once apprehended. I herewith inclose you copies of what I have received from Colonel Bouquet. The last part of the intelligence seems to be greatly exaggerated, as I cannot entertain a thought that they have been able to cut off the garrison of the Detroit, or any of the posts where officers are stationed."[2]

Three days later, June 15, Amherst decided he ought to tell John Stuart, the superintendent of Indian affairs in the South, what was going on in case the business should spread into Virginia. "It is not as yet known who are the principal promoters of this mischief," he wrote, "tho' in general it would seem as if the Senecas and Shawanese have been at the bottom of it; and in a message sent to Fort Pitt by some of the chiefs of the Delawares they accuse the Ottawas and Chepawas as the nations that have now, according to their languages, taken up the hatchet against the English. I imagine the affair will drop after some outrages which they may commit against the defenceless inhabitants before assistance can be sent to them."[3]

Next day, however, Amherst's dream that the Indian uprising was a minor incident in western Pennsylvania was rudely broken. Expresses from Maj. John Wilkins at Niagara reached him on June 16 with the shocking news of Lieutenant Cuyler's rout on Lake Erie. Fifty-six soldiers massacred! One hundred and thirty barrels of provisions taken! Those mad savages! Was he going to have an Indian war on his hands?

"Various are the opinions at this place," Wilkins had written on June 6, "concerning the cause of what has happened. Some say the want of ye rum trade, others that

[2] *Johnson Papers*, IV, 138-139.
[3] Amherst Papers, vol. 3, Clements Library.

⟨ 174 ⟩

a squaw was put to death at Detroit; others will have it that the French are concerned." In a postscript he added that some Iroquois just leaving Fort Niagara had begged a squaw living with Decouagne, the interpreter, to go back to her people because "they, and all the Indians in America, was just going to war with all the English."[4]

Amherst could hardly believe they would persevere in their hostility. Nevertheless, strong measures were demanded. Detroit might yet be subjected to attack.

Amherst dispatched his own aide, Capt. James Dalyell, to Albany to collect reinforcements there and along the route west. At Niagara he was to leave only as many men as were necessary to safeguard that fort and proceed to Detroit with the others, should such a move be judged necessary. Amherst also wrote a letter to Major Gladwin describing this movement and adding, "but I flatter myself, notwithstanding the reports we have heard, that I shall have the pleasure to find you and your garrison are all well, and that you have been able to defeat the weak attempts of the Indians, if they have been so rash as to make any."[5]

But even this hope was denied the general five days later, for on June 21 arrived Gladwin's alarming letter of May 14 from Detroit. At last Amherst was getting a true view of the insurrection. The main attack was on Detroit, and the affair in western Pennsylvania was only an echo by allies of this fellow Pontiac. Doubtless the general congratulated himself on having already sent off Captain Dalyell with reinforcements. He would certainly move on to Detroit now, and with added strength Gladwin could quell this uprising. Wilkins, who had forwarded Gladwin's letter, said he was sending 54 men again under Lieutenant Cuyler to Detroit at once on the sloop. Gladwin could take care of himself, Amherst felt sure, al-

[4] Amherst Papers, WO34, 22, 187. [5] ibid., 49, 73.

though he did wish the major had seized Pontiac on his second visit to the fort and nipped the revolt in the bud.

Meanwhile, the news of the massacre on the frontier was circulating rapidly through the seaboard colonies. Philadelphia naturally received word first, and the *Pennsylvania Gazette* published on June 9 an extract of a letter from Fort Pitt dated May 31. This same extract was picked up by the *New-York Mercury* and published there June 13. The *Boston News-Letter* put the item in its issue for June 16. The *Newport Mercury* reprinted the same extract on June 20. The *South Carolina Gazette* issued an extra supplement, July 4, with the news. Each week thereafter news from the frontier increased in quantity and importance. In general the New England papers obtained their news overland from Albany and Niagara, while New York and Philadelphia got it from Fort Pitt mainly and copied from each other and from other papers. Officers' letters were quoted, and plundered traders were interviewed.

At Amherst's suggestion Governor James Hamilton called a special session of the Pennsylvania Assembly in order to provide assistance to His Majesty's forces in safeguarding the province's western frontier and stopping the flight of the panicked settlers. The assembly convened on July 4 and displayed a Quaker-like reluctance to take any military action needed, but finally called for wagons and voted to raise 700 men.

Amherst realized it would not be long before the news reached London; therefore he ought to make a formal report to the secretary of state, the Earl of Egremont. He wrote the painful letter on June 27, hoping it would not delay his leave to return to England. Still confident that his policy in applying the ministry's order for economy was wise, he could not see any pretext for what had happened.

"It is difficult, my lord, to account any causes that can have induced these barbarians to this perfidious attempt. They have pretended to be very dissatisfied at not getting rum, when in every formal meeting that has been held it has generally been a request of their chiefs not to permit any. From a declaration of one of their prisoners it appears they strike the blow to revenge the death of two of their chiefs that were killed in the action at Niagara [1759]. I think it is most likely to have derived from the belt that was sent to the Miamies, which Sir William Johnson supposes to have come from the French some time ago and has lain by, and I believe the savages have really long meditated this mischief and have been waiting an opportunity."[6]

Being but slightly acquainted with the western tribes, Amherst could not believe that the fire was blowing from west to east, not from east to west. He had never tried to understand Indians, and he was ignorant that they felt themselves mistreated and reacted to it in their own fashion. They were peculiar, unpredictable savages to Amherst, and he let it go at that. His reaction to their mode of warfare was never that of a generous opponent, and his contempt increased to wanton cruelty as news of each fresh disaster reached him during the summer.

Sir William Johnson, who thought he knew everything that happened among the Indians, even before it happened, was taken by surprise at this outbreak. The nation which gave him the most trouble was the Senecas. He did not think the Delawares and Shawnees would ever start anything without first consulting his Iroquois, and he believed he had pacified the distant Lakes tribes. Of the nations in the Illinois country he knew almost nothing. News of the uprising reached him first from Niagara and then from Fort Pitt via Bouquet and Am-

[6] Transcript in Parkman Papers, vol. 22.

herst. He realized the generality of the outbreak at once and was apprehensive as to the fidelity of the Iroquois. He sent messages to them calling a council at the German Flats (across the Mohawk River from Herkimer, New York) for the middle of July.

Before the conference took place, he learned of the active part taken by the Senecas. He had never been able to impress them with the generosity and justice of the British, the sacredness of their promises, or the terror of their arms. Consequently, only five nations were represented at the council. They renewed their loyalty to the English, blamed the western nations and the French for this foolish warfare, and promised to talk with the Senecas and bring them to their senses.

London had news of the Indian war ahead of Amherst's official communication. The *London Chronicle* evidently received an American newspaper and on July 16 published the news of "an Indian insurrection at Fort Pitt, Sandusky, and Detroit." The *Gentleman's Magazine*, a monthly literary periodical that also reviewed the happenings of the month, referred to it in the August issue. Neither Detroit nor Pontiac was mentioned then. The editor must have been a thorough provincial, for even in his September issue, although he offered an "Account of the Disturbances in North America" and talked about Detroit, he identified it as "the French fort on the Illinois." Pontiac did not achieve personal mention until October 18 in the *London Chronicle*.

His Majesty's ministers knew where Detroit was, however, and recognized a full blown Indian revolt when they saw it. They had been discussing the desirability of a boundary between red and white settlements in America, both as a gratification to the Indians and as a curb to English migration for fear that interior towns might set up manufacturing in competition with the mother country.

News of Pontiac's war caused the ministry to hasten its deliberations. The crest of the Appalachians was set as the western limit of white settlement, and the line was announced on October 7 by royal proclamation. Whatever satisfaction the Proclamation of 1763 might have given the Indians, it came too late to prevent a war and its effectiveness was promptly offset by the refusal of westward-pushing frontiersmen to observe it.

13

Progress of the Siege

BACK IN DETROIT Pontiac continued his siege of the fort during the month of June without the slightest visible progress. For an Indian his perseverance was remarkable. No doubt he was heartened by the success of his allies, news of which he received as fast as each fort was captured. The growing number of nations uniting with him in this war likewise increased his prestige along the Detroit River. Although unified command was lacking except on this river, Pontiac was looked to by the more distant tribes as the nominal leader because he had dared begin the war and because he had sent them war belts.

Confident as these victories made Pontiac, they apparently did not stir in his mind a picture of the inevitable reaction among the English. He did not seem to realize that once the news was carried east, the reinforcements sent to Detroit and the avenging attitude of the enemy would be in direct proportion to the Indians' degree of success. Had he perceived this development, he must have sensed the necessity for speeding up his operations for destroying Fort Detroit. Every day that this island of resistance continued to stand brought nearer the day when it would be reinforced and prepared for the offensive; whereas if it were destroyed the British could not strike within Indian territory, but must fight their way westward from the Niagara-Pittsburgh line.

To be taken, Fort Detroit must be stormed. To be stormed, the lives of many Indians must be sacrificed, yet once they broke through the stockade victory was virtually certain because of their overpowering numbers. Pontiac was allowing himself to be defeated because he would not or could not alter the traditions of his race in war. The Indians would fight hard in a surprise attack and endure much privation for the sake of revenge, yet they would not undertake a tactic which they knew in advance would certainly require the death of some of their warriors. They believed too thoroughly in individualism to accept the sacrifice of a few for the sake of the many. Pontiac had no expendables. Even if he was able to perceive this hampering weakness of his people, he could not enforce the discipline necessary to change it.

Unwilling or unable to marshal his forces for a direct assault on Detroit, Pontiac relied on the weaker tactic of preventing reinforcements from reaching the fort. For this task, however, he lacked proper equipment, having no cannon and possessing only canoes and a few bateaux with which to oppose armed ships.

On June 4 Pontiac was tremendously cheered by hearing that Fort Miamis was taken and Fort Pitt attacked. The latter news meant, of course, that the Delawares had heeded their own Prophet and Pontiac's example and had declared war. Next day several traders and two barges of merchandise, captured on Lake Erie, were brought up the river to Pontiac's camp. Two days later some Potawatomies returned from Fort St. Joseph with the news that it had fallen and that prisoners would arrive soon.

Inspired to a new offensive, Pontiac called a council at the Potawatomi village for June 7. There methods of attacking the schooner *Huron*, still anchored near the fort, were discussed. A night assault was the only feasible venture, and the barges recently captured would carry a sufficient number of warriors to constitute an effective boarding party. To divert the attention of the garrison and the crew, a hot fire was to be kept up against the fort.

Sound as the plan was fundamentally, it was never tried, possibly because of ensuing diversions.

Perhaps the first interruption was the arrival from the Thames River the next evening of forty-five Chippewas belonging to Sekahos' tribe. With this addition, we now have the first detailed census of Pontiac's strength before Detroit. The figures are supplied by an intelligent French diarist of the war who lived outside the fort. He listed the enemy warriors as:

150 Potawatomies under Ninivois
50 Hurons under Také; the Hurons under Teata who had given up the war are not counted
250 Ottawas under Pontiac
250 Chippewas from Saginaw Bay under Wasson; whose arrival is not chronicled
170 Mississaugi-Chippewas from the Thames River under Sekahos

———

870 Warriors[1]

About 200 fighting men were off on the expedition against Fort Presqu'Isle, which our French reporter may not have included in the above figures as of this date. Similarly, of the Potawatomies who had gone to attack Fort St. Joseph, not all had as yet returned.

A second delay in the projected attack on the vessel may have been caused by the arrival on June 9 of a war party with three barges of goods and eleven traders captured by the Mississaugi-Chippewas at the mouth of the Grand River on the 2nd. That night some Potawatomies from St. Joseph brought in their prisoners, the commandant and six soldiers. Doubtless there was feasting and drinking from the traders' supplies, and celebration in the form of making the prisoners run the gantlet

[1] Navarre, *Journal*, p. 160.

and probably of killing one or two to be boiled and eaten. This was not cannibalism in the sense that human flesh comprised part of their diet, but a wartime ritual by which the Indians supposedly endowed themselves with the strength of their enemies.

The Potawatomi newcomers were disappointed to learn that two of their St. Joseph band were prisoners in the fort, one of them a chief. The newcomers sent four of their chiefs with Mons. Gamelin as interpreter to arrange for an exchange of prisoners. Major Gladwin did not admit them, but spoke to them over the stockade. In Indian fashion they said they had been led into the war by Pontiac. Gladwin advised them to desist and go about their hunting and planting before the war ruined them. They wanted to know how many Englishmen he would ask for their two tribesmen. Gladwin demanded all of their prisoners, but they came away without giving an answer.

There was no firing on the fort next day, yet an incident occurred which opened the first rupture in Pontiac's ranks. A French trader by the name of Jacques Lacelle, Jr., arrived from Montreal with two canoe-loads of merchandise and liquor which he unloaded at the house of the Widow Gervais on the south side of the river. The Potawatomies, learning of his arrival, went over and demanded the liquor. To get rid of them, Lacelle gave them two barrels of wine.

Hearing of this transaction, Pontiac went to the widow's and ordered Lacelle to move his liquor and goods up to Mons. Labadie's house near Pontiac's camp, where it could be better protected. However, in payment for this "protection" Lacelle had to give five barrels of liquor to the Ottawas. The drunken brawl that followed resulted in the butchering of several prisoners, whose bodies were thrown into the river. The Potawatomies liked neither this highhandedness in regard to the liquor nor the massacre which followed. When a reinforcement of 30 Chippewas from Saginaw came in next day, the Potawatomies apparently complained to them.

Three of the Potawatomies went back to the fort on June 13, spoke to their two prisoners there and then to Gladwin. They said they disliked the war and repeated that Pontiac had dragged them into it. Gladwin asked if they were slaves of Pontiac and warned them that the Ottawas yet would kill Pontiac for having started this war, which in the end was bound to ruin them. The Potawatomies came away impressed.

Rain that day kept warriors away from the fort. The gloom was relieved in the Ottawa camp, however, by the arrival of messengers with news that Fort Ouiatenon on the Wabash had been taken by local Indians.

Two days later Chief Washee and several of the St. Joseph Potawatomies went to the fort for the third time and took Ensign Schlosser and two soldiers to exchange for one of their prisoners. They expected to receive the chief, but Gladwin cleverly released the less important savage. Dissatisfied with their bargain, the Potawatomies departed, obliged to give up more prisoners if they were to obtain the release of the chief.

Next day at noon Chief Washee and two others returned and brought with them two Saginaw Chippewas from the newly arrived band. One of them was named Mindoghquay. They spoke to the commandant with wampum. The Potawatomies asserted that they spoke for their whole nation and wished to bury the hatchet. They would turn in all their prisoners and go to their homes. One of the Chippewas said that they had not yet taken part in the war, and since their hearts were inclined the same way as the Potawatomies they did not intend to.

They promised further not to let Pontiac pass if he should try to go to Michilimackinac.

Gladwin commended them for their wisdom and urged them to go about their hunting.

That same afternoon Teata and the chiefs of the Huron band which had taken no part in the war since Father Potier had threatened them went into the fort and discussed terms of peace. Gladwin could not make peace independent of General Amherst, but he listened and gave them a flag.

Whatever progress the British may have thought they were making against Pontiac's encirclement was offset on June 18 by the arrival of Father Du Jaunay, the priest at L'Arbre Croche, with the news of the massacre at Fort Michilimackinac and the abandonment of Fort Edward Augustus on Green Bay.

Accompanying Father Du Jaunay were seven Ottawas from L'Arbre Croche and eight Chippewas from Michilimackinac under Kinonchamek, son of Minavavana, the great chief of the Chippewas. His arrival caused a suspension of hostilities. Kinonchamek and his party encamped about a mile above Pontiac's village and was soon waited on by a delegation of lesser chiefs. He told them to inform Pontiac that he wanted a council with him the next afternoon and he was rather brusque about it.

Two canoes of Delawares and Shawnees arrived at the Huron village down the river next morning. When they learned that the son of the great Chippewa was in the vicinity, they went on up to his camp, significantly passing Pontiac's settlement without paying their respects. The Delawares and Shawnees conferred secretly with Kinonchamek. Two or three Frenchmen were called in to answer questions about local conditions and apparently they complained of their situation. It was evident that the visitors were gathering information independent of

Pontiac and before their scheduled council with him. Early in the afternoon the northern Chippewas and Ottawas, with the Delawares and Shawnees, proceeded in a body to Pontiac's village and took their places in a circle for the council. Pontiac and his allied chiefs joined them.

Kinonchamek spoke first, in the name of his father:

"We have learned at home, my brothers, that you are waging war very differently from us. Like you, we have undertaken to chase the English out of our territory and we have succeeded. And we did it without glutting ourselves with their blood after we had taken them,[2] as you have done; we surprised them while playing a game of lacrosse at a time when they were unsuspecting. Our brothers, the French, knew nothing of our plan. The English found out that they were the ones we had a grudge against; they surrendered. We made prisoners of them and sent them unharmed to their father in Montreal. The soldiers tried to defend their leaders; we killed them, but it was done in battle. We did not do any harm to the French, as you are doing; on the contrary, we made them guardians and custodians of our captives."

Ominously, Kinonchamek faced Pontiac directly. "But as for you, you have taken prisoners upon the lake and the river, and after having brought them to your camp you have killed them and drunk their blood and eaten their flesh. Is the flesh of men good for food? One eats only the flesh of deer and other animals which the Master of Life has placed on the earth. Moreover, in making war upon the English you have made war upon the French by

[2] This statement is not true, of course, in view of Alexander Henry's account of the Chippewa chief's slaying of the four English prisoners, one of whose bodies was then cut up into five chunks and boiled for eating. Kinonchamek must have been aware of this butchery, yet he and his father may well have disapproved of it, and the murderer may have suffered the disapproval of most of his tribe.

⟨ 186 ⟩

killing their stock and devouring their provisions, and if they refuse you anything you have had your followers pillage them. We have not done so; we did not rely upon provisions from the French to make war; we took care when planning to attack the English to lay in provisions for ourselves, our wives, and our children. If you had done likewise, you would not be in danger of incurring the reproaches of our Great Father when he shall come. You await him, and we too, but he will be satisfied with us and not with you."[3]

It is plain that the Indians had a code of rules governing their warfare. Even though a Chippewa chief had wantonly killed four prisoners, and one of the victims had been cut up and cooked for eating, apparently Minavavana and his royal family did not approve of such conduct. Pontiac had violated that code in the same manner and also by pillaging his allies, and Kinonchamek felt honor bound to reprove him, even as the Chippewa may have been reproved. It is an interesting commentary on Pontiac's relative status as a war chief, that the son of the great Chippewa chief should not hesitate to take him to task. Pontiac was visibly surprised and chagrined.

A Shawnee chief continued the castigation, offering a new version of the Delaware Prophet's message.

"My brothers, we have also fallen upon the English because the Master of Life by one of our brother Delawares told us to do so, but he forbade us to attack our brothers, the French, and you have done so. Is this what we had told you by means of the wampum belts which we have sent you? Ask our brothers, the Delawares, what the Master of Life had told them: it is all right to kill during battle, but afterwards, and when one has taken prisoners, it is no longer of any value; nor is it to drink the blood or eat the flesh of men. Since you are French as well as we,

[3] Navarre, *Journal*, pp. 172-174.

ask our brothers, the French, if, when they make war and have taken prisoners, they kill those whom they have brought home with them. No, they do not, but they keep them to exchange for their own men who are prisoners among the enemy.

"We see well what has obliged you to do what you have done to our brothers, the French: it is because you have begun the war ill-advisedly and are now in a rage at not having been able to take the English in the fort; you are bound to have our brothers, the French, feel your bad humor. We desired to come to your assistance but shall not do so, because you would say that all the harm which you and your followers have caused our brothers, the French, was caused by us. For this reason we do not desire to put ourselves in a bad light with our Great Father."[4]

These were stinging words, and having no excuses Pontiac accepted them in silence. He saw himself looked upon as a weak and lustful leader by three of his principal allies, who in consequence would give him no help at Detroit. He might have reminded them that since they had all struck the English they had better hang together in common defense, since the English would not differentiate among them. But, individualists to the last, they would not have believed such a thing even if Pontiac had thought to argue it. Moreover, they were all expecting a French army to arrive, now that they were opening a way, and protect them from English counterattack. So Pontiac made no reply and the visiting delegation withdrew.

Two days later, June 21, news reached Pontiac's camp that the sloop *Michigan* was returning from Niagara and had reached the mouth of the river. Pontiac put his warriors in motion southward to intercept the vessel. They were given further excitement next day by the return of

4 *ibid.*, pp. 174-176.

the war party which had gone eastward and now was bringing back prisoners from Presqu'Isle, and news that Le Boeuf and Venango were also taken. Doubtless these developments raised the spirits of Pontiac once more and made him indifferent to the departure of Kinonchamek homeward.

He concentrated his men on Turkey Island (Fighting Island today) and directed them to build breastworks of tree trunks and earth on the shore facing the channel where the sloop must pass. Captain Newman started his ship up the river on the evening of the 21st, but as the wind died out when he was opposite Turkey Island he anchored. The Indians were overjoyed by this favorable turn of events. Captain Newman, however, expected to be attacked and in coming up the river kept the reinforcement of 55 soldiers he was bringing from Niagara below decks. Only the crew members were visible, and the Indians believed they could take the ship easily from them.

As soon as it was dark the Indians pushed off from Turkey Island in their canoes and paddled noiselessly toward the dark and silent vessel. A lookout saw them coming, but did not shout. Captain Newman let the soldiers crawl up on deck to take their places along the gunwales. The Indians slipped in closer. Suddenly they heard a hammer blow on the deck. The next instant the whole ship lighted up with gunfire as the cannon boomed and muskets barked. Fourteen savages were killed and as many more wounded. The others turned their canoes around hurriedly and dashed back to their entrenchments. They did not make a second attempt. Next morning the sloop dropped back down to Lake Erie to await another favorable wind.

The rest of the week passed quietly, with only desultory firing at the fort. On Sunday, June 26, Pontiac attended mass at the Huron mission across the river. No doubt he did this to influence the French favorably. After mass he impressed three gigs from the *habitants* and had himself and two attendants driven along the shore in search of provisions. Whenever he took any cattle or grain he gave the owners a receipt or bill of credit signed with his mark, said to be a picture of a raccoon. All the goods were collected at Meloche's house, and old Cuillerier acted as commissary. Kinonchamek's tongue lashing over Pontiac's treatment of the French was having some effect.

Next day Pontiac dictated another letter to Captain Campbell and had Mons. Gamelin carry it to the fort. It was another summons to Major Gladwin to surrender, this time because Kinonchamek would return within ten days with eight hundred warriors whom he (Pontiac) would not be able to control. This was pure bluff, as Gladwin may have known, in view of Kinonchamek's attitude toward Pontiac. Gladwin replied that he would give no answer until Campbell and McDougall were restored to him. Pontiac answered this rebuff by saying that he had too much regard for the two officers to send them into the fort, because "as the kettle was on the fire he would be obliged to boil them with the rest."

Next day the sloop found a favorable wind which carried her up to the mouth of River Rouge before dying out. The ship lay at anchor all next day unmolested. On June 30 another wind lifted her upstream. As she passed the Huron village, Captain Newman directed a broadside of grapeshot into the cluster of cabins, wounding some savages and scattering the rest. The *Michigan* came safely to anchor before the fort, and the garrison welcomed not only the reinforcement under Lieutenant Cuyler, but the 150 barrels of provisions and the ammunition he also brought along.

Detroit had now demonstrated that not only could it maintain itself, but it could obtain reinforcements and supplies. A better military mind than Pontiac's would have realized that a fort in such circumstances will not fall by siege. The chief was sufficiently disturbed that he called a meeting of the heads of the French families for July 1. They assembled uneasily, suspecting some kind of threat. At the council Pontiac arose with a war belt in hand and addressed them:

"My brothers, I am beginning to grow tired of seeing our lands encumbered by this carrion flesh [the English], and I hope you feel the same. I believe you are about ready to conspire with us to destroy them; still, it has seemed to me that you have been abetting them to our hurt. I have already told you, and I say it again, that when I began this war it was for your interest as well as ours. I knew what I was about.

"I know Fort Presqu'Isle has fallen. I say I know it, and this year all the English in Canada, no matter how large their force, must perish. It is the Master of Life who commands it; He has made known His will unto us, we have responded, and must carry out what He has said, and you French, you who know Him better than we, will you all go against His will? I have not wished to speak, hoping that you would let us take our course; I have not wished to urge you to take up arms against them, for I did not think you would side against us. I know very well you are going to say that you do not side with them, but you are siding with them when you report to them all that we do and say. For this reason there is only one way open today: either remain French as we are, or altogether English as they are.

"If you are French, accept this war belt for yourselves, or your young men, and join us; if you are English we declare war upon you, which will show our valor all the more because we know you to be children of our Great Father as well as we; to make war upon our brothers for the sake of such dogs pains us, and it will cost us an effort to attack you inasmuch as we are all French together; and if we should attack we should no longer be French. But since we are French it is wholly the interests of our Father, yours and ours, that we defend. Therefore answer, my brothers, that we may come to an understanding; and behold this belt which makes its appeal to you and your young men."[5]

It was a tidy ultimatum. Much as the French would like to see the British disgraced by defeat, they were too hard-headed to put their heads in a noose by openly taking part in this rebellion. If Pontiac persisted in forcing them from their affected neutrality, he was more likely to push them over to the British side than to draw them over to his. One of the *habitants* had brought with him a copy of the Capitulation of Canada of 1760. He held it up now and reminded Pontiac of its meaning.

"We do not hesitate an instant to follow you and with you defend the interests of our Father, but first you must remove, if you can, the bonds which tie our hands and which the Father of the French and the Father of the English have knotted about us as the only hindrance to our accepting this war belt."

Pontiac, of course, did not understand the niceties of European diplomacy and could not realize that France was, moreover, too exhausted to shoulder a war begun for them by the Indians. Nevertheless, he recognized that the *habitants* were trying to put off the day of decision by hiding behind a legalistic barrier. Pontiac announced that if the older men, the family heads, would not join him, he would appeal directly to the young men and the bachelors.

[5] *ibid.*, pp. 194-196.

Fearing he might be successful, the French asked for a day's delay before replying. However, one of the *habitants*, named Zacharias Cicotte, rose and picked up the war belt offered by Pontiac.

"I and my young men," he said, "break away from our bonds; all accept the war belt which you offer us and are ready to follow you! We shall go and find other young men to join us—there are enough of them—that you may see how soon we shall capture the fort and all that is in it."[6]

The more prudent Frenchmen immediately withdrew from council, but Cicotte and some others stayed. They began counting up the number of young men available as allies to the Indians. Young Alexis Cuillerier was ready. Labadie had two sons and a son-in-law who wanted to fight. Charles Dusette, who had Sir Robert Daver's rifle and Lieut. Charles Robertson's powder horn, and Pierre Barthe were commissioned to raise the young men of the vicinity. Mayerin assured Pontiac that they would take up arms. One report states that about three hundred Frenchmen, both without and within the fort, would be willing to fight with the Indians.

At this council, or at a later one, a plot was hatched to secure entrance to the fort and massacre the garrison. Through some traitorous Frenchmen living inside the stockade, keys to one of the gates were to be made and used to open the gate on the night of the attack. For some reason the plan was never executed, but the traitors within the fort did their part, for three keys were afterward dug

[6] *ibid.*, p. 198. The diarist also relates the story of one father who returned to Pontiac the war belt which his son had accepted. He berated the chief for involving the young men of the river and warned him that his French father would credit the *habitants* with driving out the English, rather than the Indians, as a consequence. Pontiac replied: "Thou art right, my brother, and I thank thee for the warning thou hast given me." (p. 202.)

⟨ 193 ⟩

up from their hiding place.[7] Observing how the wind was now blowing, several French families moved into the protection of the fort, lest they be compelled to take up arms.

Before dawn of July 2, Lieutenant McDougall, a Dutch trader from Schenectady named Abraham Van Eps, and an English trader somehow made their escape from the Indians and reached the fort. McDougall reported that he had tried to bring Captain Campbell with him, but that officer being both fat and near-sighted, feared to make the attempt. Pontiac made no retaliatory move beyond requiring Robert Navarre to write Gladwin a last demand for surrender of the fort.

Growing bolder, Gladwin posted parties in two small, detached blockhouses that stood on higher ground just north of the fort. On July 4 he sent out a detachment under Lieutenant Hay to destroy an entrenchment northeast of the fort which had been thrown up by the Indians and their new French allies. The savages and French held their ground, and Gladwin ordered Captain Hopkins out with reinforcements. He came up on the Indians' flank, and shortly routed them from their cover. The encounter was not particularly important, except that in the pursuit two Indians were killed, and a soldier who had once been prisoner among them stopped and scalped his victim. Some of the fleeing Indians saw this act. Unfortunately for the British, the warrior who was killed and scalped happened to be the nephew of Wasson, chief of the Saginaw Chippewas.

When Wasson heard of the fate of his nephew, he went at once to Pontiac's camp and spoke to the great chief. He was angered by this death in his family and he abused Pontiac for his inactivity. Finally he demanded custody

[7] "Gladwin Manuscripts," *Mich. P. & H. Coll.*, xxvii, 656, 659, 660.

of Captain Campbell for purposes of revenge. "My brother, I am fond of this carrion flesh which you guard. I wish some in my turn. Give it to me."[8]

Pontiac meekly ordered Captain Campbell delivered up to Wasson. The Chippewa chief marched the prisoner to his camp, stripped him of his clothes, and promptly killed him with his tomahawk. Then he scalped him and otherwise mangled the body, tearing out the officer's heart and eating it then and there. Finally the body was thrown into the river. It floated down toward the fort, was recovered, and given burial.[9]

Hearing of this affair, the Ottawas were insulted, not so much by the loss of Captain Campbell as by the contempt shown their prisoner by a neighboring tribe. In a curious sort of revenge they set out to demand a prisoner from one of their allies to butcher. They determined to take Ensign Pauli, late commandant of Fort Sandusky, from the Hurons. Pauli, however, having heard of Campbell's murder, looked to his own safety and that very afternoon luckily made his way across the river. He burst into the fort at supper time, dressed and painted and clipped like a savage since his adoption. He informed Gladwin of Campbell's grisly fate.

The French were now beginning to show their colors, as their neutrality grew daily more untenable. Those within the fort were mustered into a militia company by Gladwin and elected the Irish trader, James Sterling, as their leader. Some of those outside the fort gathered at the Huron mission and declared themselves opposed to giving any aid to the Indians. Navarre read to them a copy of the

[8] Navarre, *Journal*, p. 208.

[9] A later commandant of Fort Detroit, Captain George Turnbull, placed a railing around Campbell's grave and a stone on it in November 1767. Turnbull to Gage, Nov. 11, 1767, Gage Papers.

final treaty of peace between France and Britain which Gladwin had sent out to him. The text had been delivered by Lieutenant Cuyler.

Gladwin now ventured an offensive move. He sent the sloop *Michigan* upstream on July 6 to shell Pontiac's camp. Captain Hopkins and Ensign Pauli were put aboard to direct the fire. The wind, however, was so weak that the vessel moved slowly, and Pontiac, guessing the enemy's intention, removed the women and children out of the village. Nevertheless, the 'ship's cannon did considerable damage to the flimsy tepees and their contents. Pontiac saw the possibilities in a repetition of this kind of attack, so he ordered his Ottawas to move the encampment northeastward to the other side of the swamp or *Grand Marais*. The new site was three miles above the old, or five miles from the fort.

While the cannonading was taking place, a delegation of Potawatomies was admitted to the fort and held a council with Gladwin. They said they had heard of the peace treaty between the French and the English and believed it. Therefore, they were going to leave Pontiac and they wished to exchange two English prisoners for the Potawatomi chief whom Gladwin still held. The major reminded them that they had fired on the sloop a few days ago when it came up the river. Notwithstanding this, he said he would release their chief and recommend them to General Amherst as soon as they brought in all their prisoners. He also offered them a belt of wampum to carry to the rest of their nation around Fort St. Joseph, emphasizing the generous treatment they could expect if they kept the peace.

Next day the Potawatomies returned to get the wampum before setting off to round up all the prisoners held by their nation. Some Hurons entered the fort with them as a result of the sloop's attack on Pontiac's camp, perceiving that their village was likewise vulnerable to shelling from the vessel. They related the old story about being forced into the war by Pontiac. Gladwin had nothing to lose by answering that he believed them and he said he would recommend them to the general if they would bring in all their prisoners and remain at peace.

The Hurons returned promptly on July 9 and delivered up Ensign Christie, the former commandant of Fort Presqu'Isle, and eight other prisoners. They spoke of retiring from the vicinity and of fortifying themselves against Pontiac in case he should attack them.

Pontiac had not yet learned of this double defection by the Potawatomies and Hurons. He was busy with a new scheme which may have emanated from his own brain, but more likely was suggested by one of the Frenchmen. It was a plan to burn the schooner and sloop by launching fire rafts which would float downstream and collide against the vessels. Four captured bateaux were lashed together and filled with faggots, birchbark, and tar. On the night of July 9 this huge raft was pulled out into the river by the Indians, set on fire, and dispatched with the current. The crews guarding the two ships saw the inferno coming and slipped one cable of their anchors. The vessels swung around with the current, and the blazing raft passed harmlessly down the river.

This failure was rendered more irritating to Pontiac by his discovery next morning of the intentions of the Hurons. Taking fifteen of his best warriors he crossed to the Huron village and threatened his erstwhile allies for making peace with the enemy. He dissuaded some of the Hurons from giving up, but Teata remained firm in his decision. Pontiac was in no position to attack the Hurons while engaged in another war; a victory would do more to win the Hurons back to his allegiance. Accordingly he set about trying the fire raft scheme again.

This time two rafts were constructed. The second was to be set on a new course after the first had forced the vessels to veer away. They were launched about midnight of July 11. Captain Hopkins, who lay aboard the *Michigan* that night, fired a cannon at the first raft as soon as he saw the blaze. This shell so frightened the Indians who stood in the river holding the second raft that they let loose of it before it was lighted. It floated harmlessly away, and the British snared it as it passed and pulled it ashore.

It was growing time to send one of the ships to Niagara again for provisions. Gladwin dispatched the *Huron*, asking Major Wilkins also for another reinforcement of fifty men. It departed late the next afternoon in ballast, thus foiling Pontiac's attempt to destroy both vessels at once.

The Potawatomies entered the fort that day with their prisoners: the trader Chapman Abraham, the trader Hugh Crawford and one of his employees, and seven soldiers. Gladwin was about to give them their chief in exchange when Abraham spoke up and told him there remained other prisoners among this nation. Thereupon Gladwin changed his mind and accused them of not having brought in all their captives. The Potawatomies turned sullen. Then Lieutenant McDougall, who was present, recognized an Ottawa in their midst. He informed Gladwin, who pointed out the spy and said he must remain as a prisoner. Frightened and thwarted, the Potawatomies took their leave.

Pontiac was still obsessed with the idea of fire rafts. He ordered two barns pulled down to obtain timbers. It was reported at the fort that he was making six rafts, then that he was constructing a float three hundred feet long, and later that he was building twenty-four rafts. A token siege was maintained by occasional firing on the fort.

Meanwhile Gladwin had two bateaux fitted out with thick, oak planking above the gunwales to protect the rowers, and installed a swivel gun in each. On July 24 he sent them up the river to investigate the construction of the fire rafts. They found nothing, but by cruising up and down in midstream they drew the precious ammunition of the Indians who lined either shore to fire at them. The prowling of these two bateaux caused the Indians to abandon their rafts, as they saw they would be intercepted before they could reach the sloop.

The same day a band of 70 Chippewas from Michilimackinac, accompanied by five Menominees from Wisconsin, arrived at Pontiac's headquarters. The nature of their council with Pontiac is not known. However, some Delawares and Shawnees had arrived down at the Huron village and sent up a request for a joint council next day at the Huron town. This council lasted for two days, July 25 and 26, yet its deliberations are but vaguely reported. Apparently the whole strategy of the war was canvassed. If there were disagreements Pontiac triumphed finally. He insisted that the Master of Life had ordered him to make war upon the English and that he would not give up. He instilled fresh enthusiasm in his allies, and when in conclusion he caught up his tomahawk and began to chant a war song against the English, the assembled chiefs joined in with him, even the Potawatomies and most of the Hurons. His oratory must have been superbly convincing.

While the council was convening, Jacques Godfroy and Mini Chesne and their party returned from the Illinois country, bearing replies both to the Indians and to the *habitants*. The letters were not encouraging to the Indians. Maj. Neyon de Villiers, the commandant at Fort de Chartres, advised the French to take no part in the hostilities. He told Pontiac he could not send him any aid just at that time, because he had heard rumors that peace between France and Great Britain was signed.

However, he had dispatched couriers to New Orleans to learn the truth, and should the report not be true he would do what he could.

Thus matters stood on the 28th of July. The day passed uneventfully and the night ushered in a heavy fog that hung low over the river. About 4:30 in the morning was heard the muffled sound of muskets cracking and of what seemed to be small cannon firing from the direction of the Huron village. Immediately the fort was put on the alert, and the stockade manned. Could the schooner be returning already? The mist held its secret.

Captain Hopkins took a dozen volunteers out the water gate and quietly pushed off in a bateau to investigate. Silence fell again, but gray dawn was lightening the sky. Suddenly out of the fog a bateau materialized, then another, and another, each filled with red-coated British soldiers. The garrison of Detroit, standing on the firing platform to overlook the stockade, burst into cheers. The procession of boats lengthened incredibly as the fog released one after another. There were twenty-two of them altogether, holding a reinforcement of 260 men commanded by Capt. James Dalyell—more men than Gladwin commanded within the beleaguered fort.

14

From Bloody Bridge
to Bushy Run

CAPTAIN JAMES DALYELL was an ambitious young officer with the right connections. A younger son of a baronet, he obtained a lieutenancy, January 1756, in the Royal Americans, a regiment newly raised for the war. After service in this country he went with Colonel Thomas Gage as a captain into the new 80th Regiment Gage was raising in December 1757. With the help of patrons or relatives back home, Dalyell was transferred in September 1760 to the 1st Regiment, an old unit with much military and social prestige. He also was taken into General Amherst's official family as an aide-de-camp. The chance to relieve Fort Detroit and to subdue the Indian revolt doubtless appealed to him as an exploit which must result in his promotion to major.

On his march westward Captain Dalyell had picked up at Albany Maj. Robert Rogers, the Ranger who had received the surrender of Detroit in 1760, and 21 New York Provincials. He collected also several companies of the 55th and 60th Regiments and reached Fort Niagara on July 6 with 220 men. He demanded of Major Wilkins all the remaining men of the 80th Regiment at Niagara, but finally settled for forty of them. So eager was he to be off that he would not wait for the schooner to escort his boats.

Putting his men into bateaux on Lake Erie, he proceeded along the south shore to Presqu'Isle, where he stopped to inspect the ruins of that fort. He continued his dangerous voyage, hugging the shore, to Sandusky Bay. Again he ventured inland beyond the ruined fort and destroyed the Huron town of Junundat, about three miles farther, the inhabitants having fled on sight of the troops.

Dalyell's danger from attack increased hourly as he swung around the western end of the lake to the mouth of the Detroit River. But luck sailed with him. All that saved the detachment from running a gantlet of fire and possibly being routed was the providential fog that hung over the river during his night ascent. Even so, he was discovered in passing the Huron village and suffered fourteen men wounded before he reached the water gate of the fort.

His successful voyage and the rousing welcome he received did nothing to chill his desire to strike a spectacular blow against the Indians. He allowed his men to rest on July 29 and 30 and then felt himself ready for action. Although he was supposed to place himself under the command of Major Gladwin, Dalyell did not hesitate to argue with his superior over tactics. Besides being ambitious and self-confident, the captain had absorbed Amherst's contempt for Indians as intelligent fighters. All he feared now was that Pontiac, hearing of the reinforcement to the garrison, would abandon the siege and slink away into the forest before Dalyell had a chance to win glory by drubbing him in battle.

On the evening of July 30 Dalyell went to Gladwin's quarters and urged a surprise attack immediately on Pontiac's encampment. Gladwin, who once might have argued that way himself, had learned a good deal about Indian warfare in the last three months. He pointed out to Dalyell that the Indians were not fools and a surprise would be impossible. The road from the fort to Pontiac's camp was lined with spies, who were Frenchmen when not Indians. Dalyell persisted in believing that now was the time to seize the offensive. Gladwin reminded him that he was still far inferior to the Indian force, and the only thing that made him superior was the protection afforded by the fort. Doubtless Dalyell mentioned Amherst's name, as he had to Wilkins at Niagara. He could imply that he knew the general's mind and his expectations. The general wanted the Indians broken up and wiped out. He, Dalyell, had been sent out for that purpose and he was not afraid to make the attempt.

Gladwin deliberated. After all, the young man was pretty close to the general and it would not be prudent to anger him or convey the impression of respecting the enemy too highly. The fact that Dalyell wanted to lead the attack did not escape his calculations. Admittedly, there was a slim chance of success. Against his better judgment, Gladwin gave his consent for a sortie in force before dawn.

Fearing an attack on their village, the Hurons, with a great show of burning articles no longer wanted, had embarked in their canoes with baggage and dogs, on July 30 and paddled down the river out of sight. They wished to give the impression that they were leaving their town for their winter's hunting. However, they soon landed and hid their women, children, and goods in the woods, while the braves circled back to the edge of their village. There they waited two fruitless days in ambush for the British to come and destroy the town. Then chagrined, they all moved back into their cabins again.

Pontiac, of course, had been informed of Dalyell's arrival and knew enough to be on his guard for some offensive operation out of the fort. The French allied with him evidently feared he might be intimidated by this strengthening of the fort and told him it was no reinforcement at all, but a ruse by Gladwin, who had sent out a number of men in the night fog to return at daylight and deceive the Indians. But Pontiac could count, and he realized that more men and more boats had arrived than Gladwin had on hand. He maintained his alert.

A geographical factor also endangered the success of a surprise movement out of the fort. The fort was built on a slope running up from the river, as has been noted; consequently a person standing across the water could look over the near side of the stockade and see into the upper part of the fort. Unless Dalyell could assemble his men quietly and without lights, the French or Indians across the river would spot some movement.

Captain Dalyell was allowed 247 officers and men for his detachment, over half from the 55th Regiment. He took mainly the troops he had brought with him, with the addition of a company of Queen's Rangers. For officers he had Capt. Robert Gray of the 55th, second in command, Capt. James Grant of the 80th, third in command, and Maj. Robert Rogers, who should have led the whole force. The subalterns mentioned included Lieuts. George McDougall, acting as adjutant, Dietrich Brehm, acting as gunner, and James MacDonald, all of the 60th; Lieuts. John Luke, Archibald Brown, and Francis Nartloo of the 55th; Lieuts. James Blain and Abraham Cuyler of the Queen's Rangers; Lieut. Edward Abbott of the Royal Artillery; Ensign Christopher Pauli of the 60th; Ensigns Robert Anderson and Garrett Fisher of the 55th. Messrs. Baby and St. Martin were to act as guides.

The men were roused in the middle of the warm night and quietly assembled. At 2:30 they began moving out of the fort through the east gate. They were stripped to their jackets and wore sabers in addition to carrying muskets. The expedition marched two abreast up the river road. Lieutenants Brehm and Abbott followed alongside

⟨ 204 ⟩

in the two gunboats, each mounting a swivel gun. They were to convey dead and wounded back to the fort and cover the retreat. The men were grimly silent, but the tramping feet and inevitable rattle of arms broke the stillness. About a mile and a half from the fort, the detachment was formed into platoons, with Lieutenant Brown commanding the advance guard of 25 men. Then followed Captains Dalyell and Gray with the main body. The rear was commanded by Captain Grant. In this order the force approached the narrow timber bridge that crossed Parent's Creek in front of Baptiste Meloche's house. The creek was two miles from the fort.

There Pontiac was waiting for them.

He had been informed by his French allies, who had learned it from their brethren inside the fort, of the coming attack before the troops even marched out. He sent the Indian women and children into the woods away from his encampment behind the swamp. Only the old men were left in occupation. Pontiac mustered more than four hundred warriors, probably all Ottawas and Chippewas, although a few Hurons crossed the river and joined him later. He divided his force into two parties and deployed them carefully. The larger band of 250 braves he sent around through the woods to the Chauvin farm, only about two-thirds of a mile from the fort, where they had already watched the British pass. Thus his main strength was directed at cutting off the retreat of the British. Pontiac was planning on annihilation, not mere repulse, of the attackers.

The other band of warriors, about 160 in number, was sent down to Parent's Creek. They spread themselves around Meloche's house and garden fence, and a number took cover behind a ridge just beyond the bridge and facing the advancing British. The moon was bright enough to light the road clearly. Pontiac's order to fire evidently was explicit: when the soldiers reach the middle of the bridge. . . .

Lieutenant Brown's platoon set foot on the bridge and tramped noisily over the planks. A few yards in front of them dark heads sighted down musket barrels. Suddenly a wall of fire blazed up before them. Shouts, screams, curses, savage war whoops rose with the crescendo of musket reports which reverberated around toward the house. Lieutenant Brown dropped, wounded in the thigh, and several of his men lay heaped on the bridge they would never cross.

Troops from the main body ran up and forced their way over the creek and dislodged the Indians behind the ridge. The widespread arc of Indian fire swept the side of the main column, too, and Captain Dalyell was hit in the thigh, though not seriously. The soldiers discharged their muskets wildly, being confused in the darkness. Far to the rear Captain Grant heard the sudden heavy firing ahead and knew the enemy had been met. Then abruptly he was fired on from his left. Recognizing the makings of a bloody trap, he faced his men around quickly and gave the invisible enemy a full volley. The Indians drew back, and Grant's men advanced after them. Dalyell had heard the firing in the rear and also realized his dangerous encirclement. He sent orders to Grant to take possession of the houses and fences on his flank so as to keep the road back to the fort open.

Meanwhile, the main body of troops farther up the road was desperately engaged. At the sound of the first burst Major Rogers had looked for cover. Throwing a party of Rangers into the first house he saw, Jacques Campau's, he used it as a blockhouse. By this prudent measure he was able to prevent the Indians from closing in on that part of the detachment's extended flank.

After sending back one of the armed boats filled with

wounded, Dalyell limped to the rear and spoke to Grant. He seemed to be undecided what to do, and Grant urged him either to press on or retreat before they were surrounded. It was growing light when Dalyell returned to the head of his column and gave instructions for the retreat. The main body began withdrawing in good order, protected by Rogers' defense post. Dalyell sent word to Grant to fall back to an orchard and a house which Mons. Baby would show him.

The Indians still occupied one strong position commanding the road. They were entrenched behind a pile of cord wood and in the basement excavation for a new dwelling. Here they held up the retreat for an hour. Only a charge would force them out, and Dalyell led it. Ambushed as he had been by his own imprudence, he fought bravely in battle. But in the charge he was shot dead, reputedly by an Indian named Geyette who was called Pontiac's brother-in-law. Captain Gray led the storming party on and fell seriously wounded in the shoulder and belly, but the savages scrambled off before the onslaught. Lieutenant Luke was also wounded. The retreat was resumed. Gray, Brown, and Luke and several of the wounded men were carried to the water's edge and placed in Lieutenant Abbott's boat. Having run out of ammunition, he was going back to the fort for more. For some reason, Dalyell's body was not recovered.

The troops passed on, leaving Rogers at last exposed on all sides in his house. Lieutenant McDougall informed Grant that he was now in command of the expedition, and Lieutenant Blain brought news of Rogers' precarious position. Grant acted swiftly and intelligently. He ordered the armed boat of Lieutenant Brehm to move up and try to rout the savages sufficiently to allow Rogers to withdraw. At the same time he sent Ensign Pauli and twenty men back to the excavation to hold the road open for

Rogers' men. Both maneuvers were successful, and Rogers brought off his troops. The several protecting parties which Grant had posted along the way withdrew in succession, one covering the other as they flowed into the main column.

By eight o'clock the unlucky expedition was safely back in the fort. Casualties were numerous. Captain Dalyell, one sergeant, and eighteen men had been killed. Three officers and 34 men were wounded, three of whom soon died of their injuries. Others were taken prisoner. As James Sterling admitted, the savages had given the troops a "damn'd drubbing." "The enemy's loss cannot be ascertained," Lieutenant MacDonald wrote, "as they always conceal that from everybody. It's believed to be seven killed and a dozen wounded. . . ."[1]

The Indians found the body of Captain Dalyell and took it back to camp with their own dead. They exulted in having killed the commander of the troops sent against them. In a barbaric orgy of celebration they cut out his heart and wiped it on the faces of their prisoners. They also cut off his head and mounted it on a pole. Jacques Campau recovered the remains of the body next day and took them into the fort for burial.

Several of the soldiers killed at Parent's Creek had fallen into the stream and the water ran red with their blood. Ever afterward the innocent brook was known as Bloody Run.

Relating a story told him long afterward by his grandfather, Col. James Knaggs said: "After his triumph Pontiac invited the leading French residents, including Peter

[1] Letter to Horatio Gates, Aug. 8, 1763, Clements Library. Besides this letter, accounts of the battle are found in Hay's diary, Gladwin's letter of Aug. 8, Rogers' letter printed in the *Pennsylvania Gazette* Sept. 11, 1763, and elsewhere, and John Duncan's letter in *Can. Hist. Rev.*, XII (1932), 184-188.

Descompts Labadie, who afterward became the father of my mother, to a grand feast in honor of the victory. There was plenty of fish and fowl but no liquors. After the feast was over Pontiac said to Labadie, 'How did you like the meat? It was very good young beef, was it not? Come here, I will show you what you have eaten,' and Pontiac then opened a sack that was lying on the ground behind him and took out the bloody head of an English soldier. Holding it up by the hair, he said with a grin, 'There's the young beef.' "[2]

Signal as was the victory for Pontiac, it was a success of only immediate importance. He had foiled a surprise and saved his encampment; he had routed the enemy and inflicted many more casualties than he had suffered; he had enormously increased his prestige among his allies and thereby attracted some reinforcements. Creditable as these accomplishments were, they did not improve Pontiac's long-term military position. He had failed to annihilate Dalyell's force, as he had hoped to do. Consequently, Fort Detroit stood greatly reinforced and was further from surrender than ever.

Following their victory the Indians to the number of 250 hovered around the fort each night, watching for another sortie and hoping to catch small parties outside. Far from avoiding conflict, Gladwin felt himself in a position to assume the offensive from time to time. One night he sent out a detachment of sixty under Captain Grant to post itself in houses which the Indians approached during the day, but the savages did not come near them next morning.

The schooner *Huron* appeared in sight of the fort late in the afternoon of August 5 and dropped anchor for the night. The Indians did not attempt an attack, and next morning the vessel moved up to the fort's water gate. She

[2] Palmer, *Early Days in Detroit*, pp. 370-371.

carried a further reinforcement of sixty men of the 17th Regiment, eighty barrels of provisions, some naval stores, and merchandise. She was unloaded and made ready with the sloop to return to Niagara.

The indefatigable Captain Hopkins tried a surprise attack by water on one of the cabins in the Potawatomi village in the early foggy morning of August 8, but his boats became separated in the mist, daylight revealed them to the savages, and they returned empty handed.

The *Huron* and *Michigan* sailed on August 13 without molestation from the Indians. Perhaps they were in council, since Pontiac had received reinforcements of 200 warriors, whose tribal identity is not mentioned. Gladwin put on board the ships fifteen of the most seriously wounded soldiers and about the same number of traders who had been captured and plundered by the savages, then turned in at the fort.

Pontiac moved a great part of his encampment on the night of August 17 down to the River Rouge, on the southwest side of the fort, to keep track of the incoming vessels and to be in a better position to intercept them in the narrowest channels. The move was all the more necessary since the withdrawal of the Potawatomies from active warfare. Next day Wasson, the Chippewa chief, took it upon himself to dictate a letter to Gladwin and advise surrender of the fort. Possibly the letter was intended only as a feint to allay suspicion while a fresh blow was plotted at the other end of Lake Erie. If Pontiac could not stop the supply ships from reaching Detroit, perhaps he could prevent them from starting at Niagara River.

Although the war in the West had just passed a new climax of victory for the Indians, farther east it had taken a turn for the worse for the Delawares, Shawnees, and Mingoes. The military force being assembled under Colonel Bouquet made rendezvous at Carlisle, whence a company was hurried along to reinforce Fort Ligonier. He had two Scottish regiments, the 42nd (already famous as the Black Watch) and the 77th, reduced to 214 and 133 men respectively, fit for duty; a battalion of Royal Americans (60th), and a party of Rangers—460 in all. While he was held up waiting for horses and wagons, he received word on July 3 of the loss of Forts Presqu'Isle, Le Boeuf, and Venango. The reluctance of the settlers, fleeing from and fearful of the Indians, to act as wagoners kept Bouquet at Carlisle until July 18.

When he reached Fort Bedford on July 25, he was obliged to leave another company. As Pennsylvania had done nothing about garrisoning Fort Lyttleton, a provincial fort at modern Fort Littleton, Bouquet stationed some farmers there and furnished them with provisions and ammunition. The encumbered brigade reached Fort Ligonier on August 2. Fearing for the safety of Fort Pitt, from which he had not heard for more than a month, Bouquet left the wagons and hurried on with the troops and 340 horses loaded with flour.

Pittsburgh was in little danger, however. The siege had been carried on half-heartedly for a month. On July 26 the chiefs of the Delawares and Shawnees asked to speak to the commandant. Captain Ecuyer admitted them and listened to their accusation that the English had provoked the war by taking possession of this country and to their demand that he leave the fort. The captain replied next day with the familiar argument that the English had taken the forts from the French, not the Indians, and that he would defend his post against all the Indians in the woods. Angered, the chiefs departed without the customary farewell handshake.

Next afternoon the savages opened fire on the fort in earnest. Captain Ecuyer was wounded in the leg by an arrow. The fort answered with muskets and cannon. With great audacity the Indians crept into the ditch below the stockade and fired at close range, protected by the bank. But the soldiers changed weapons and lobbed hand grenades just over the stockade into the ditch. Abruptly on August 1, the Indians withdrew and the firing ceased. They were seen moving off with horses and luggage. Captain Ecuyer felt little relieved, however, for he knew they were marching eastward to attack the relief column coming up under Bouquet.

At Edge Hill, twenty-six miles east of Pittsburgh, on August 5 Bouquet's advance guard was suddenly attacked by Delawares, Shawnees, Mingoes, and Hurons from Sandusky. The assault broadened until the troops were surrounded, but they fought back stubbornly. The firing ceased only with darkness. The soldiers camped on the hilltop in a circle, their wounded and the pack horses in the center. Early next morning the Indians resumed the battle. The long march of the previous day, the fighting and standing guard, and especially the want of water distressed the troops. They could hold off the enemy but not disperse them.

Anticipating that victory must ultimately be theirs, the Indians fought cautiously, rarely exposing themselves and making their shots tell. At length they thought they saw the effect of their sustained attack. Two companies of soldiers retired within the circle, and others filled the gap thinly, flattening the circle on one side. Sensing a weakening, the Indians gathered themselves for a charge. They rushed headlong into the thinning ranks for the final massacre.

But they reckoned not with Colonel Bouquet, who knew a thing or two about deception. At the height of the furious clash, the two companies which had disappeared into the circle reappeared on its periphery and tore into the flank of the savages. Surprised and dismayed, the Indians now turned to fight their way back to the woods. Just before they reached the trees they were struck again by the full fire of two more companies which had followed upon their rear. In wild flight the Indians dispersed into the forest.

Bouquet moved his brigade on a mile to Bushy Run, where water was available for the thirsty and wounded. The skirmish took its name from this locality rather than from Edge Hill where it was fought. The victory had not been easy for Bouquet, despite his stratagem. He lost fifty killed, including three officers, sixty wounded, and five missing. The Indians fired on the encampment at Bushy Run once and then withdrew for good. Their losses are only guessed at; they were believed to be as heavy as those suffered by the troops. Of greater importance was the fact that two Delaware chiefs, Kittiuskung and his son, Wolfe, were among those slain.

Bouquet destroyed all the flour, as the remaining horses were needed to convey the wounded. The column proceeded to Fort Pitt without further incident, arriving on August 10. A detachment returned to Ligonier and brought up all the wagons of provisions, then went back again with the women and children from Pittsburgh. The crisis in western Pennsylvania was past; only a few Indians showed themselves around Fort Pitt again. They were reported collecting their braves at the head of the Scioto River. Bouquet, however, was in no position to move offensively against them.

15

The War on the Settlements

BESIDES ATTACKING FORTS, the Indians raided the lonely cabins of settlers exposed on the western edge of Pennsylvania, Maryland, and Virginia. This war along the frontier was the inevitable accompaniment of conflict between soldiers and savages. Houses and barns were burned, horses and cattle run off or butchered, and pioneers killed or carried into captivity. Tales of individual heroism, suffering, and escape abound. What Pontiac had unleashed did not make a pretty war. It aroused the implacable hatred of westward-looking frontiersmen and popularized the notion that "the only good Injun is a dead Injun." George Croghan estimated that the Indians "killed or captivated not less than two thousand of His Majesty's subjects and drove some thousands to beggary and the greatest distress."[1]

At the first alarm of Indians being on the warpath in Pennsylvania, settlers in the vicinity of Bedford flocked into the protection of the fort early in June. As days passed without sign of an Indian, the farmers grew chagrined at their flight and anxious over the cultivation of their crops. Families left the fort and made their way home again about the middle of the month. Waiting for some such exodus, the savages now showed themselves and fell on a number of families along Dunning's Creek, murdering, scalping, and burning. Needless to say, the

[1] Croghan to the Lords of Trade, PRO Plantations General Papers, R 19, 54, as quoted in the Parkman Papers, 27, p. 441.

other farmers who had ventured homeward hastened back to Fort Bedford.

Farther east, thousands of frightened settlers poured into the little town of Carlisle, which could neither shelter nor feed them. Luckily the evacuees could camp out, it being summer. Yet the scene was indeed pitiful, as one resident observer related: "Every day almost affording some fresh object to awaken the compassion, alarm the fears, or kindle into resentment and vengeance every sensible breast, while flying families obliged to abandon house and possession to save their lives by an hasty escape; mourning widows bewailing their husbands, surprised and massacred by savage rage; tender parents lamenting the fruits of their own bodies cropt in the very bloom of life by a barbarous hand; with relations and acquaintances pouring out sorrow for murdered neighbors and friends present a varied scene of mingled distress."[2]

War parties numbering from a dozen to fifty warriors ravaged independently up and down the frontier, usually following the river valleys. Their tribal affiliations seldom were known by their victims, if there were any survivors. A war party moved up the Juniata River, north of Carlisle, early in July. On the morning of the 10th they struck first at the house of William White, who had three men and a boy with him to harvest. Hearing a noise outside, White opened his door and was shot dead. Then the savages set fire to the house. When the four occupants tried to get out, another was shot. The boy and one of the remaining men tried to make their escape through a window in the loft, and both were mortally wounded. The last man managed to break a hole through the roof and escape before the fire consumed the house and the four bodies within it.

[2] *Pennsylvania Gazette*, July 21, 1763.

⟨ 215 ⟩

By noon the same Indians had moved along a mile and a half to Robert Campbell's house on Tuscarora Creek, a tributary of the Juniata. Six men were gathered there to help harvest. In a sudden assault the war party broke into the house, killed two men, wounded most of the others, but withdrew quickly when one Indian was killed. The savages swept up Tuscarora Valley, ransacking two more farm houses and burning a third. By now a party of twelve Pennsylvanians was in pursuit. They ran into an ambush, however, and lost five men killed and one wounded. The Indians crossed into Shearman's Valley, between the Juniata and Carlisle, and next day killed Alexander Logan, his son, and two men. By July 13 Carlisle had heard of twenty-five deaths and four or five wounded in the past four days.

From Cumberland, Maryland, came the report that a party of Indians had fired on six men shocking wheat in Thomas Cresap's field, east of that settlement, on July 13. One worker was killed. Next day another man was wounded in Cresap's lane. The marauders moved on and the following day attacked Cresap's neighbor, Wilder, and killed him.

Down in Virginia (modern West Virginia) another war party of sixty to eighty Shawnees under Chief Cornstalk passed up the Kanawha River ostensibly bound for war against the Cherokees. They were fed by two families on Muddy Creek, Frederick Lea and Filty Yolkum. In payment for this hospitality the men were killed and their families made prisoners. The Shawnees then crossed into the adjoining valley and approached the settlement of Greenbrier, where half a hundred folk were gathered at Archibald Glendenin's house. Acting the part of friends, the Indians were invited to take part in a feast on three fat elk just killed.

One old woman showed a Shawnee her sore leg and

asked whether he could relieve it with his knowledge of healing herbs. He said he thought he could, and drawing his tomahawk instantly killed her. This was the signal for a general massacre of the startled settlers. All the men in the house were murdered. Glendenin was shot and scalped as he attempted to escape over a fence with one of his children in his arms. The women were spared, and dauntless Mrs. Glendenin, holding her baby, hysterically cursed the murderers, despite their threats to kill her. Finally to quiet her they lashed her face with the scalp of her husband.

One of Glendenin's guests had taken his horse out to hobble him just before the massacre started, and hearing the cries and shots, he mounted and rode to Jackson's River giving the alarm. Few settlers would believe him. Many of the Shawnees at Greenbrier followed his trail and fell on those unbelievers who had not fled. The rest of the Indians took their prisoners over to Muddy Creek and waited for the others to join them with additional captives.

On the day the whole party started into the wilderness, Mrs. Glendenin handed her baby to a neighbor, slipped into a thicket, and escaped. As soon as she was missed, one of the Indians remarked that he would "bring the cow to her calf." Seizing the baby he made it cry loudly. If the mother heard, she did not turn back. Disgusted, the Indian beat out the infant's brains against a tree and threw it on the trail. Mrs. Glendenin returned to her house and covered her husband's body with some rails.

In general the frontier of Virginia was ravaged less than that of Pennsylvania, because the government of the former acted with resolution and dispatch in raising 1,000 militia for defense. In companies of about thirty men each, the militia pursued the war parties and often recovered prisoners and loot as well as killing some of the

Indians. Once in the fall, however, a detachment of sixty militia under Captains Moffat and Phillips was ambushed on Jackson River in Augusta County and suffered heavy casualties. One report had thirteen killed, another half of the detachment. This attack was promptly revenged by a pursuing party.

In Pennsylvania the General Assembly, dominated by Quakers living safely around Philadelphia and opposing war on religious grounds, voted to raise a militia of only 700 and then forbade them to engage in offensive operations or to move beyond the settled parts. They were only to protect the farmers while they gathered in their crops. This pious nonsense angered not only General Amherst and Colonel Bouquet, but the frontiersmen as well, who regarded themselves as abandoned by their own province.

Bouquet's successful relief of Fort Pitt in August put a stop to most of the war parties from the West. A motley band of Delawares living high on the Susquehanna River, however, was not intimidated. They made occasional bloody forays late in the summer, and volunteer groups of Pennsylvanians, ignoring the objections of the Assembly, moved against them twice, once routing a party of fifty warriors and later destroying their towns and fields. One group of these Delawares swept down into Northampton County early in October and plundered four houses in one neighborhood, killing seven persons at one place and four at another. Retreating northward the party fell upon the settlement of Wyoming, near modern Wilkes-Barre, peopled by emigrants from Connecticut. Hearing the news, some Pennsylvanians set out after the Indians. Arriving too late at Wyoming on October 17, "they buried the dead, nine men and a woman, who had been most cruelly butchered; the woman was roasted and had two hinges in her hands, supposed to be put in red hot; and several of the men had awls thrust into their eyes, and spears, arrows, pitchforks, &c. sticking in their bodies."[3]

Such massacres provoked retaliation that was often disgraceful to civilized Englishmen and sometimes criminal. Seeking revenge for sufferings on the frontier, a party of 57 Pennsylvanians under Lazarus Stewart attacked a band of twenty peaceful Indians—seven men, five women, and eight children—who had long been settled at Conestoga in Lancaster County. On December 14, 1763, these so-called "Paxton Boys" killed and scalped eight of the innocent and defenseless Indians in their cabins. Philadelphia was horrified, and Governor Penn promptly issued a proclamation for arrest of the offenders. In reply the outlaws returned to Conestoga and murdered the remaining fourteen Indians on December 27. They then marched on Philadelphia after some Indians who had taken refuge there. They got as far as Germantown and found the city in arms against them. After threats against the Quaker-dominated government, the mob was persuaded to go home unpunished. It is some satisfaction to know that Stewart at least was killed by Indians in 1778.

It is unfortunate that the frontier has always attracted some of the worst examples of white mankind. The congenitally dissatisfied, the fugitives from justice, the army deserters, the debtors, the swindlers, all were churned out of seaboard society and thrown to the frontier. Some of them were squatters who had seated themselves without title on lands acknowledged as Indian property. Others traded with the savages and cheated them at every turn. Not all the frontier settlers can be regarded as innocent victims of unprovoked cruelties. A hatred of Englishmen individually had been built up in the Indian mind at the same time that British policy was proving so exasperating.

[3] *New York Gazette*, Oct. 31, 1763.

This war on civilians with its attendant barbarities had the result usual in Indian wars. The savages, by giving full vent to their feelings, were in turn made the victims of them. That is, their outrages committed on the settlers aroused such a disproportionate amount of fury that simple defeat of the Indians did not satisfy the English. The red man was tracked down, overwhelmed, fought when already beaten, his villages and fields levelled, until the tribe was annihilated, dispersed into neighboring tribes, or reduced to servility. This pattern was repeated for the next century as the frontier was pushed steadily westward.

There are fashions in war just as there are fashions in apparel, and some of the older customs seem as ridiculous today as do older styles of dress. In the eighteenth century war was definitely a professional business, with its rules of correct behavior. Soldiers engaged in it; civilians did not. Deceit was a prime element in tactics, yet both spying and attack by ambuscade were regarded with contempt. Firing was done by platoons drawn up together in the open, not by individuals hiding behind trees and rocks. Prisoners of war were humanely, not to say gallantly, treated, and usually were exchanged at intervals by the opposing sides. In the successive Indian wars the savages violated parts of this military code. They attacked civilian settlers, they laid traps for unwary British soldiers and fired from cover, and they tortured and sometimes ate their prisoners. They paved the way for the eventual abandonment of some of these European rules, but even in 1763 their violation was viewed with horrified resentment—as Pontiac learned to his dismay. This conflict of basic concepts of war explains the extreme measures of revenge which General Amherst came to advocate.

16

The East End of Lake Erie

THE RELATIVE CALM around Detroit after Dalyell's defeat and around Fort Pitt after Bouquet's victory was simply an ominous lull in the Indian war. The savages never pursued a defensive policy; either they attacked, or planned fresh assaults, or retired and gave up fighting. They were now in process of changing fronts in order to break up the source of supplies bound for Detroit. The most vulnerable spot on the "communication" was the portage, or "carrying place," around Niagara Falls.

Fort Niagara stood at the mouth of Niagara River, where it flows into Lake Ontario. Supplies from Montreal and from New York and Albany destined for the western posts passed by this fort. The loaded vessels pushed up the river a short distance to the landing place (Lewiston, New York), were unloaded, and the supplies carried by wagons up a tortuous, winding road of nine miles to the top of the falls. A small fort standing there was called Little Niagara or Fort Schlosser, after the officer who built it (the father of Ensign Schlosser of Fort St. Joseph). Above the falls the wagons were unloaded into boats which proceeded around Grand Island and up through the rapids to Lake Erie. The vessels from Detroit anchored at the mouth of Buffalo Creek (Buffalo, New York), close to the source of Niagara River, where they were loaded and unloaded.

Several times in the latter part of August, Indians were seen along the portage, but though they acted hostilely they offered no resistance to the armed escort of the supply wagons. They were probably Senecas, who had taken little part in the war since their bloody victories in north-western Pennsylvania in June. But there were 150 Ottawas and Chippewas who had been reported hiding around Presqu'Isle since August 17,[1] waiting for any party of soldiers that might return to the post which connected Fort Pitt with Niagara and Detroit. Their prescience, if it were no more than that, was marvelous, for Amherst had in fact ordered both Bouquet at Pittsburgh and Wilkins at Niagara to reestablish the fort at Presqu'Isle as soon as possible. Only local conditions prevented execution of the command. The Ottawas and Chippewas did not wait in vain, however.

The *Huron*, which had sailed with the *Michigan* from Detroit, arrived at Buffalo Creek on August 16; the *Michigan* came in later with its cargo of wounded men. Wilkins hurried the reloading of both vessels. In this work he was assisted by Lieut. John Montresor, an engineer officer whom Amherst had dispatched from New York with letters to Gladwin. Montresor had been waiting impatiently at Niagara for passage since July 31. The *Michigan* was finally made ready to sail on August 26, with provisions and a detachment of seventeen men of the 17th Regiment under Capt. Edward Hope.

The wind failed the first day, and then blew up a hard storm the next. The sloop got into the middle of the lake when she sprang a leak. While the pumps were manned, the soldiers began throwing provisions and artillery over-board. The gale carried the ship back to the southeast shore and drove it on the bank in battered wreck near Catfish Creek (Eighteenmile Creek, New York). All hands were saved.[2]

[1] *Bouquet Papers*, Series 21634, p. 257.
[2] The account of the shipwreck and the events following are taken from Montresor's journal as published in J. C. Webster,

As engineer, Lieutenant Montresor took charge of preparing a defensible camp. He laid out a post on a bluff seventy feet up from the water and put the men to work leveling brush, cutting timber, digging, and setting up barrels of provision as breastworks on the land side. An express was sent off to Wilkins asking for reinforcements until the sloop could be repaired. The reinforcement of one hundred men arrived on September 2 at Montresor's already respectable fortification.

Before daylight next morning the camp was attacked, presumably by the band of Ottawas and Chippewas from Presqu'Isle, although Montresor thought they were Hurons. They crept within fifty yards of the post from two sides and opened fire. The troops rallied and turned a swivel gun on them. The attack lasted until ten o'clock, when the Indians withdrew. Three soldiers were killed. The savages hovered around, but did not attack again.

The sloop was found to be irrecoverable on September 6, and another express was sent off to Niagara with this news. Meanwhile Montresor strengthened his post as if he were constructing a permanent stronghold. It was a remarkable performance. He completed a secure fort by September 16.

Witless Major Wilkins sent another detachment of 240 men in 23 boats to take the sloop apart and raft it down to Fort Schlosser, but he sent them off without a single tool! The embarrassing situation was relieved by the return of the schooner *Huron* from Detroit. The sloop was taken apart, the schooner loaded with the remaining provisions, the reinforcements returned to Niagara, and Montresor's camp was evacuated on September 18. Cap-

"Life of John Montresor," in *Transactions of the Royal Society of Canada*, Section II, Series III, Vol. XXII (May, 1928), 1-31.

tain Hope's detachment and Montresor continued their interrupted voyage to Detroit via the *Huron*.

While this action was taking place on Catfish Creek, the Senecas plotted an assault on the portage. Whether any of the Ottawas and Chippewas who had attacked Montresor's camp cooperated with them cannot be ascertained.[3] Between 300 and 500 Indians took part. On September 14 they lay in ambush along the trail near the whirlpool, at a place called Devil's Hole today.

A convoy of twenty-five horses and ox-drawn wagons wound down the trail from Fort Schlosser toward Fort Niagara, escorted by an officer and thirty men. Where the chasm yawned on their left and the woods pushed close on their right, they were struck by a heavy volley of musket fire. Then the Indians burst out of the trees in a furious rush. Teams broke away in stampede and plunged over the abyss onto the rocks below. Drivers leaped from the wagons, but some became entangled in the harness and were dragged to their death. Amid the frightened, kicking animals, the soldiers tried to rally, but the savages were upon them with tomahawks before they could form or reload. With the chasm behind them there was no retreat. Overwhelmed, the soldiers fought hand-to-hand with the yelling Indians or in panic fled backward too far. Only two men managed to evade death and escape through the underbrush.

The firing was heard by two companies of the 80th Regiment that were encamped on the landing place. Totaling about eighty men, they advanced on the run. But the Indians awaited them in a new ambush about a mile below Devil's Hole. Hurrying along in close forma-

[3] Bouquet thought so. He had heard that 800 Indians from Detroit had gone to Niagara in August to take post on the carrying place. Although the number of savages obviously was exaggerated, because no such exodus was noticed at Detroit, some Detroit Indians may very well have assisted the Senecas. *Bouquet Papers*, Series 21653, p. 219.

tion the troops were caught in a withering blast of fire that dropped half of them. The savages closed in on the others. Again the soldiers engaged in individual combat, with little chance to use their muskets. One after another was cut down. Only a few escaped and fled back to Fort Niagara.

Wilkins summoned almost the entire garrison and marched out to the scene. Not an Indian was in sight. The dead soldiers and sutlers lay scattered along the road, stripped of their clothes and their scalps. Five officers and 67 men were slain, and eight of the survivors were wounded, in the two ambuscades. The British loss was greater than at Bushy Run or Bloody Bridge or any of the forts.[4]

Farther east, meanwhile, Sir William Johnson had opened a second conference with the Iroquois at his Mohawk Valley home on September 7. Six Senecas from two villages which had hesitated to follow the bloody trail of their brethren attended. In addition, a delegation from eight nations in Canada had been sent down by Johnson's deputy with a wampum belt they wished to carry to the western tribes demanding an end to this war. The atmosphere was cordial and Anglophilic. The Iroquois messengers who had gone to argue with the belligerent Senecas at Geneseo had not been heard from, so Johnson's hope that he might be able to neutralize this tribe was again postponed. All the superintendent could accomplish, after thanking the nations for their steadfastness, was to urge them to strike the western tribes themselves. Even this oratorical accomplishment, however, was nullified by Amherst, who replied to Johnson that he would not employ Indians.

It is remarkable how ineffective His Majesty's Indian agents proved to be once the war got started. Although they understood the cause of it, as Amherst did not, they

---

[4] The account of this ambuscade is based on letters to be found in the Bouquet, Amherst, and Gage papers.

were financially and militarily prevented from stopping it or localizing it. They could only stand by and hope to patch up a peace after the Indians had sued for one. Even as Johnson concluded his conference, the Senecas, over whom he had direct jurisdiction, were administering the worst drubbing of the war to British arms.

In New York City, General Amherst, whom we left in a frenzy at the end of June, continued to receive a stream of bad news from the West. His rage and inhumanity increased as each Indian victory or depredation emphasized his seeming helplessness. He wrote sharp, impatient letters to the governors of New York, Pennsylvania, and Virginia, urging them to permit their militia to augment the regular army in its pursuit and chastisement of the enemy. He wrote to Gladwin that if any of the enemy Indians fell into his hands they should "immediately be put to death, their extirpation being the only security for our future safety, and their late treacherous proceedings deserving no better treatment from our hands."[5]

He wrote to Bouquet that he wanted to hear of no prisoners being taken on his march westward to relieve Fort Pitt. As if in reply he heard from Bouquet on July 7 of the bloody loss of Venango, Le Boeuf, and Presqu'Isle. Detroit was now an isolated outpost in the savage wilderness beyond Niagara and Fort Pitt. In a postscript to his reply to Bouquet, Amherst made a startling proposal: "Could it not be contrived to send the small pox among the disaffected tribes of Indians? We must on this occasion use every stratagem in our power to reduce them."[6] Bouquet answered that he would try to spread an epidemic with

[5] Amherst Papers, PRO, WO34, LIV, 171.

[6] Transcripts of the Bouquet papers in the Canadian Archives, Series A, IV, 232; original in the Bouquet papers in the British Museum, Series 21634, f. 243. Although this postscript bears no date, Bouquet's letter of July 13 is clearly in reply to it. The next postscript by Amherst is attached to his letter of July 16 in the

infected blankets and mentioned a wish to hunt "the vermin" with dogs. Amherst replied on July 16: "You will do well to try to inoculate the Indians by means of blankets, as well as to try every other method that can serve to extirpate this execrable race. I should be very glad your scheme for hunting them down by dogs could take effect, but England is at too great a distance to think of that at present."

Regiments returning from the victorious, though harrowing, siege of Havana, provided Amherst with needed strength, and he dispatched them to the northern and western posts so as to relieve other regiments for Niagara and Detroit. At the end of July he received word of the murder of Captain Campbell at Detroit. He formed a corps of one hundred discharged men, reenlisted for a short term, and dispatched them westward under Capt. Lieut. Valentine Gardiner with instructions that the Senecas and the Indians of the Lakes were to be treated "not as a generous enemy, but as the vilest race of beings that ever infested the earth, and whose riddance from it must be esteemed a meritorious act, for the good of mankind. You will therefore take no prisoners, but put to death all that fall into your hands of the nations who have so unjustly and cruelly committed depradations."[7] He also promised a reward of one hundred pounds to the man who should kill Pontiac, and another hundred pounds to

Canadian Archives transcripts of the Amherst papers, WO34, XLI, 227; it is unattached in the transcripts of the Bouquet papers, Series A, IV, 231. Oddly enough, neither postscript is mentioned in the calendar of the Bouquet transcripts in the *Report* of the Canadian Archives for 1889; nor is either one printed in the *Bouquet Papers* just published by the Pennsylvania Historical Commission from photostats in the Library of Congress. Francis Parkman's London agent, Henry Stevens, had no difficulty finding them among the Bouquet papers in the British Museum, and Parkman quotes them in his *Conspiracy of Pontiac* (6th ed.), II, 39-40.

[7] Parkman Papers, 22, pp. 413-414.

the person who should kill the chief that butchered Captain Campbell.

Settling back then, Amherst awaited news from Bouquet and Dalyell. Word of the former's success at Bushy Run and of his safe arrival at Fort Pitt reached him on August 26. But in less than a week it was offset by the black tidings of Dalyell's defeat and death. In a new fit of impotent rage Amherst doubled the reward for Pontiac's head. He ordered the post of Presqu'Isle to be reestablished from Niagara, and he still had hopes that Bouquet could send part of his troops on to Detroit. Bouquet informed him, however, that he could not forward any men or move against the Delawares and Shawnees for want of supplies and guides. Then came news that the *Michigan* was lost on Lake Erie, and two companies and a platoon wiped out on the Niagara portage. Erecting another fort at Presqu'Isle was now out of the question. The main problem was to get a really large reinforcement to Detroit so Gladwin could take the offensive. Such a corps was being formed under Wilkins to leave Niagara in October.

If Amherst had been dogged by failure in getting adequate relief to Gladwin, he was more successful in obtaining a mark of his esteem for the major personally. He sent a note to Gladwin on September 19: "It is always a great satisfaction to me when I can promote an officer of real merit, and should the enclosed succeed to my wishes, it will give me much pleasure, as it will be of service to you, as well as proof of the sense I have of your distinguished conduct. Success attend you."[8]

The "enclosed" did succeed. It was a request to the secretary at war to approve Amherst's appointment of Major Gladwin as deputy adjutant general in America and promotion to the rank of lieutenant-colonel. The secretary heartily approved.

[8] Amherst Papers, PRO, WO34, XLIX, 695.

17

The Siege is Raised

BACK AT DETROIT, Major Gladwin was still trading blows
with the Indians, sending out detachments which shot
one or two savages and usually suffered one or two wounded soldiers. He was impatiently waiting for a reinforcement of six or seven hundred men which would enable
him to meet the Indians on an equal footing and drive
them, he assured Amherst, out of the region. It was a
heartbreaking kind of war for a British officer to fight.
The enemy was all around, but melted away from every
party sent out, then flowed back to fire on the fort as soon
as the returning detachment shut the gate behind itself.

Pontiac seems undoubtedly to have been marking time,
hoping for good news from Fort Pitt and Niagara, perhaps
undecided himself what to do until circumstances provided an opportunity. He suffered the loss of a Mississaugi-Chippewa chief on August 31, and next day the
nephew of an Ottawa chief was killed. On September 2,
however, he was cheered by two arrivals. Two Frenchmen
from Illinois reached Detroit, having left Fort de Chartres
about August 6. They said that as yet there was no official
news of peace having been signed, and that Maj. Neyon
de Villiers had furnished the Weas with powder and lead.
Wanting desperately to be reassured that France had not
given up the war, Pontiac must have grasped at this news
as evidence of French support to come.

The other arrival was the schooner *Huron* at the mouth
of the river. It had dropped anchor there and let off six
Mohawks, who had come from Sir William Johnson to

speak to the Huron band under Teata. Two Frenchmen went aboard next morning to sell greens to the crew. They were surprised to find the ship under the command of a Captain Horsey, with only eleven men, part of whom were soldiers, constituting the crew and protective guard.

The two hucksters lost no time in reporting the ship's inviting condition to Pontiac, and he immediately called for an attack that night. The Hurons cooperated to the extent of holding the Mohawks in their village. Some 340 savages, probably almost all of the Ottawas and Chippewas, pushed their canoes silently into the river as soon as darkness fell and paddled down to the schooner, which had moved up into the channel between Turkey Island and the west shore. Screened by rushes, they approached within a hundred yards of her before they were seen. With a cry the boatswain rallied the crew into instant action. The Indians answered the cry with their own shouts and yells as they propelled their canoes forward.

The crew got one shot at the onrushing mob from the bow gun before the savages darted in under the bow and stern and swarmed all around the vessel. The Englishmen took to their swivel guns and small arms and managed a few shots. The momentum of the attackers had not reached its height yet, and it carried some of the bravest up the sides of the ship in boarding efforts. Captain Horsey and a soldier fell dead, but the others repelled the boarders with spears. Four of the crew were wounded in this close fighting.

One party of Indians had been hacking at the heavy anchor cable and finally severed it. To their surprise the vessel swung around in the current, brushing their canoes out of the way like so many waterbugs and spreading momentary confusion. This fortunate repulse enabled the six remaining crewmen to use their muskets and swivels again. They rallied themselves with the cry to fight to the last man, and Jacobs, the mate, sang out for the last man to blow up the ship. It was said that Adam Brown, a white captive among the Indians, heard this last command and communicated to them the danger of explosion.[1] Whether it was this fear or the determined effort of the crew, the attack was beaten off. The canoes turned back to the shore. The Indians had suffered eight killed and twenty wounded, of whom seven later died of their wounds. Although the casualties were small relative to the size of the attacking force, they were large for Indians to bear.

As soon as Gladwin heard the attack he sent down four armed boats which arrived after the battle was over. Captain Hopkins and twenty men stayed on board and brought the vessel up to the fort next day. She carried 47 barrels of flour and 160 of salt pork. Gladwin distributed one hundred dollars among the ten survivors of the gallant crew, and General Amherst ordered medals for them, at the same time berating Major Wilkins for sending off the *Huron* with so few persons on board. The French whispered that the Mohawks had betrayed the weakness of the ship to Pontiac, and it was almost four weeks before Gladwin learned of the true instigators. He sent the *Huron* away again on September 8, when it picked up the shipwrecked passengers of the sloop, as we have seen.

There was no victory celebration in the Indian villages. They had failed to capture the ship or any prisoners, and they had suffered what were to them heavy casualties. Pontiac's stroke did not enhance his prestige as a war leader. As a measure of petty revenge, his warriors set fire to Pierre Reaume's barn, which contained a thousand

[1] Peltier's account in *Mich. P. & H. Coll.*, viii, 361; *Burton Hist. Leaflet*, iv, 66.

bushels of wheat that they feared might reach the garrison.

Seventy Potawatomies from Fort St. Joseph arrived on September 9, but they came to make peace. Whether they counselled with Pontiac and notified him of their separate truce is not known, but certainly he learned of their intentions. Forty of the Potawatomies left in a few days, and by the 19th the others had departed. Their decision provoked murmuring among the Chippewas and Ottawas. Faith in the cause and in Pontiac's generalship gave way to scepticism. For the first time a faction among the Ottawas asserted itself and disowned Pontiac as chief. The dissenters banded together under one Manitou, who seemed to favor making peace. Pontiac's grip was slipping.

About this time Pontiac must have enlisted the aid of a Shawnee war chief named Charlot Kaské to send another appeal to the French commandant of Fort de Chartres. He gave Kaské a letter and a belt to carry to Major de Villiers again asking for French aid and ignoring the business of a peace treaty between France and England.

The siege was not relaxed, however, as one luckless victim discovered. A sergeant was killed outside the fort on September 24. A boat that Gladwin sent out on patrol was attacked, and one man was killed. A week later Lieutenants Brehm, Hay, and Abbott were sent up the river with four armed bateaux to Isle au Pêche, at the mouth of Lake Ste. Claire, to examine the possibility of getting wood from it for the fort. The Ottawas began firing on the boats from foxholes they had dug in the shore to conceal themselves. As the boats did not stop, the Indians pushed off twenty-five canoes and bateaux to pursue them. Up above Isle au Cochon (Belle Isle) the savages began to close around the British boats. Lieutenant Brehm loaded a four-pounder with grapeshot and at a distance of only forty or fifty yards fired it into the side of an Indian war canoe. Of the fifteen or sixteen occupants only two were able to paddle it ashore. This loss frightened the others, and they all pulled away to the shores.

Next day, October 3, the *Huron* returned to Detroit, bringing the salvaged cargo and shipwrecked reinforcements from the lost *Michigan*. Only 185 barrels of provisions had been saved, and Captain Hope's detachment was too small for offensive use. Gladwin was as alarmed by the former circumstance as he was discouraged by the latter. The punitive force which was to take the field against the Indians had better come soon if it was going to act this year. Meanwhile, his large garrison was insufficiently provided for. He had flour for only three weeks. With but one small ship now shuttling across Lake Erie, he hurried her back to Niagara for more supplies. Captain Gray and Lieutenant Brown, both of whom had been wounded at Bloody Run, sailed with her, as well as Lieut. James MacDonald of the original garrison, who went down to settle the long overdue accounts with the paymaster. Captain Gray, incidentally, was appointed aide-de-camp by General Amherst in the room of the late Captain Dalyell.

Undoubtedly Major Gladwin wished that he were going along, too, in the schooner. The fatigue and disappointments he had suffered since spring provoked him to blurt out to Sir William Johnson: "I am brought into a scrape, and left in it; things are expected of me that cant be performed; I could wish I had quitted the service seven years ago, and that somebody else commanded here."[2]

Pontiac was in no happier situation than his opponent. Wabbicomigot, a principal Mississaugi chief from Toronto, had arrived on the Detroit River with twenty-four men on October 1, possibly as a result of the death of another

[2] Oct. 7, 1763; original in the Burton Historical Collection.

Mississaugi chief weeks before. Apparently he canvassed the sentiment of his own tribe's warriors and that of his relatives, the Chippewas, and he may have spoken to Pontiac. Wabbicomigot had lost his taste for the war. On October 7 he sent in word to Gladwin that he would like to enter the fort and talk terms of peace. Next day one hundred Miamies from the headwaters of the Maumee arrived to learn how the war was progressing. They found divided councils. Half of the Miamies started home at once; the other half stayed and agreed to do whatever the Hurons decided to do.

Wabbicomigot held three conferences with Gladwin inside the fort on October 11, 12, and 13. In usual fashion the chief said he had had nothing to do with the war and wished only to secure forgiveness for his warriors who had mistakenly taken part. But the powerful old chief had also laid the groundwork for a general peace. He said he was interceding in behalf of the Chippewas and Ottawas, who could also be brought into a truce. Then he talked privately with Gladwin about the origin of the war as he understood it, telling of the war belt he had received from the French.

Such was Wabbicomigot's influence with the nations that the Chippewas next went into the fort on October 14 to turn in six prisoners as evidence of their desire for peace. Some local Potawatomies followed them in an effort to get their last prisoner from Gladwin. Further councils were held with the Chippewa chiefs in the fort. As a portent of what suffering was in store for them if they should procrastinate, the first snow of the season fell that day, a four-hour squall of giant flakes. The Chippewas apparently were urging the Ottawas to follow their lead, and on October 17 Wasson with three Chippewas and Manitou with three Ottawas entered the fort together for a peace council. The sands of revolt were fast running out.

The momentum of this general movement to end the warfare might have carried the obdurate Pontiac along with it. But aside from his stubborn perseverance, a Frenchman from the Illinois country arrived and brought him news that he could expect a detachment of French troops under Captain de Beaujeu and forty packhorses loaded with ammunition and goods. This lie appeared to be the last subterfuge of the renegade French to keep the war going awhile longer. Though Pontiac could not stem the tide of peace, he would not bow his head. In sadness and bitterness he saw the last of the Potawatomies depart and ten canoes of Chippewas and Ottawas go off together to hunt. He was now up against not so much weak hearts, which could be strengthened by his oratory and his threats, but hearts torn between a desire to oust the British and an urgent, visible need to provide food for their wives and children. The immediate and elemental need was winning them away from his vision of a sovereign race allied with the French.

The French inhabitants could see how the wind was blowing. They realized now that the fort would stand, that the Indians could not succeed. They began sending in a little wheat, which the garrison needed so desperately. The renegades among them, who had assisted the Indians or had bought at bargains the goods which the savages had plundered from English traders, foresaw the day of reckoning and began sneaking off to the Wabash and Illinois country with their loot.

Pontiac made a final appeal for war in a last grand council. Lieutenant Montresor counted sixty canoes loaded with Indians passing down the river on October 20 to the mouth of the Rouge. What speeches passed there, no one tells us. The net result is fairly clear: Pontiac was

⟨ 235 ⟩

only partially successful. A delegation of Chippewas went back to the fort on October 23 to continue their peace negotiations. Pontiac and his faction skulked around the fort looking for scalps. It was a last gesture of defiance. How long it would have lasted before Pontiac would have found himself finally alone cannot be known. On the 29th a hard frost made the ground solid and was followed by four inches of snow. Pontiac's dwindling siege grew more impossible to maintain.

The last blow fell on him that night. Cadet Dequindre of Illinois came up the river with letters from Major de Villiers to Pontiac, to the French, and to Gladwin. He had left Fort de Chartres on September 27, and the letters bore that date. Dequindre had delivered similar messages to the tribes on the Wabash en route. Pontiac listened while the message addressed to the "French children," the nations of the Great Lakes, was read in translation. The Master of Life, De Villiers wrote, had inspired the great king of the French and the great king of the English to make peace. All their chiefs and warriors were asked to bury the hatchet. "What joy you will have in seeing the French and English smoke with the same pipe, and eating out of the same spoon and finally living like brethren." Forget the evil talks which the wind carries. The French king has not given away your land; he has ceded only that which was his. Leave off spilling the blood of your brethren, the English; our hearts are now as one. You cannot strike the one nation without having the other for an enemy also. The French will never abandon their children and will always supply them from the far side of the Mississippi. I bid you all farewell. Live in peace.

Pontiac's dream was broken off. There would be no help from the French, no army coming up the St. Lawrence or up the Mississippi. The French were through fighting the English, and the English were masters of the

Pontiac's note of capitulation, October 31, 1763

Pontiac's "signature"

Sir William Johnson

French forts and dominions. He, Pontiac, was fighting a hopeless war. There could be no victory if the French opposed him too.

The letter to the French residents was more mature and business-like. De Villiers said that proof of the signing of the treaty had been received. Fort de Chartres was to be delivered up to British troops on their arrival. If any Frenchmen wished not to remain under English rule, they might retire to the lands ceded to Spain west of the Mississippi. The *habitants* were expected to maintain the peace which he had demanded of the Indians. As to their folly in supporting the savages in the first place, De Villiers said nothing. One result of the message was that in the next four days the *habitants* sold 8,000 pounds of their hoarded wheat to the needy garrison, enough to relieve Gladwin of anxiety over his communications.

Dequindre entered the fort next day, October 30, and delivered his letter to Gladwin. De Villiers had written that as soon as he was officially notified of the treaty of peace and its provisions, he had sent out messages to quiet the Indians and now stood ready to deliver up his fort to the proper British authorities.

Pontiac hesitated, but only one course lay open to him. He must assume a mask of humility and then depart. He dictated a note to Gladwin that was translated into French and carried into the fort, presumably by Dequindre. In English what Pontiac said was:

"My Brother

"The word which my father has sent me to make peace I have accepted; all my young men have buried their hatchets. I think you will forget the bad things which have taken place for some time past. Likewise I shall forget what you may have done to me, in order to think of nothing but good. I, the Chippewas, the Hurons, we are ready to go speak with you when you ask us. Give us an answer. I am sending this resolution to you in order that you may see it. If you are as kind as I, you will make me a reply. I wish you a good day.

"Pontiac"[3]

Gladwin replied at once, pointing out that if he had started the war he would be able to grant peace; but as Pontiac had begun it he must await the pleasure of the general. Meanwhile, Gladwin would communicate Pontiac's peaceful inclination to Amherst and would notify him of the general's decision as soon as he received a reply.

Of course, Gladwin was relieved at this sudden dissolution of the long tension of the siege, but he regretted that the opportunity to attack and chastise the Indians passed with it. Now the Indians were preparing to scatter to their hunting grounds, and the punitive force Gladwin had been expecting for so long had not yet arrived. The situation was complicated by the invitation of that sly Frenchman, De Villiers, for the Indians to retire to the other side of the Mississippi. They would accept, too, if the British tried to punish them, thereby ruining the fur trade for the English. Gladwin summarized the situation to Amherst on November 1 with statesman-like vision:

"They have lost between 80 and 90 of their best warriors; but if your Excellency still intends to punish them further for their barbarities, it may be easily done without any expense to the Crown by permitting a free sale of rum, which will destroy them more effectually than fire and sword. But on the contrary, if you intend to accommodate matters in the spring, which I hope you will for the above reasons, it may be necessary to send up Sir William Johnson.

"I believe as things are circumstanced it would be for the good of His Majesty's service to accommodate matters

[3] Amherst Papers, vol. 7, Clements Library.

in the spring; by that time the savages will be sufficiently reduced for want of powder, and I don't imagine there will be any danger of their breaking out again, provided some examples are made of our good subjects, the French, who set them on. No advantages can be gained by prosecuting the war, owing to the difficulty of catching them; add to this the expense of such a war which, if continued, the entire ruin of our peltry trade must follow, and the loss of a prodigious consumption of our merchandises. It will be the means of their retiring, which will reinforce other nations on the Mississippi, whom they will prejudice against us and make them our enemy forever. Consequently, they will render it extremely difficult (if not impossible) for us to possess that country, as the French have promised to supply them with every thing they want."[4]

Gladwin's estimate of the number of Indian braves killed must be accepted for want of information from any other source, although the figures apply only to the locality of Detroit. Additional warriors lost their lives in the attacks on the other western posts, of course. Even so, Pontiac's war ended with much greater losses on the English side. The reader who wishes can go carefully through this book and count more than 400 British regulars and provincials who lost their lives in the war.[5] That figure does not include all of those taken prisoner and later sacrificed to savage fury or drunkenness; those deaths would swell the total. But 450 soldiers, say, equalled a full British regiment plus almost half of another. And these calculations omit the hundreds of civilians slaughtered on the frontiers of which no accurate count is possible. We

[4] *ibid.*

[5] According to a letter from Amherst to Wilkins, Oct. 29, 1763, Bouquet had recently reported that 137 men of the 60th Regiment, First Battalion, were "killed or prisoners with the Indians at the Detroit." Amherst Papers, vol. 2, Clements Library.

can only fall back on George Croghan's guess of "not less than two thousand" killed or captured altogether.

Pontiac asked to enter the fort and talk with Gladwin, but the major refused for the chief's own safety. If Pontiac had gone into the fort he might have been put to death by the soldiers, despite anything Gladwin could do. As for the rascally French, Gladwin had already taken down sworn testimony from prisoners about their guilt. He submitted those affidavits to Amherst and took no action himself beyond arresting Jacques Godfroy and Mini Chesne on November 2 for their treasonable part in the capture of Fort Miamis.

Although Pontiac did not see Gladwin again, the major learned on November 10 that the chief intended to set out in the next day or two with nine of his men to accompany Dequindre to Illinois. With all his mystical faith in the Delaware Prophet at stake, Pontiac had to go to Illinois to learn for himself why the English dogs must be admitted as brothers, why the French would no longer make war on them, why the Indians were left alone in a conflict for control of their ancient home lands. He could not believe that the French, who had been their friends and allies for generations, had suddenly ranged themselves on the side of their old enemy, the English. Here was a chasm in civilizations his mind could not bridge.

Pontiac may have had a more compelling reason for leaving, too. A large part of his village had turned against him because he had failed to win a victory and because he had held off suing for peace when all hope of victory was gone. Actually he had brought only death, sorrow, privation, and an uneasy future to his people. Some inveterate warriors and Anglophobes would follow him to a new location, but he had lost his leadership at Detroit. Under these circumstances he quietly took his leave of the locality.

⟨ 240 ⟩

The *Huron* returned on November 11 and brought the news of the Senecas' victory at Devil's Hole in September and of a later attack on Major Wilkins' expeditionary force of 600. This second attack, October 20, also took place on the Niagara portage as the troops were preparing to embark for Detroit. Two officers and six men were killed, and two officers and nine men, including Captain-Lieutenant Gardiner, were wounded. However, Captain Newman of the *Huron* and Lieut. Samuel Williams of the 17th Regiment, who commanded the guard of forty men aboard, assured Gladwin that Wilkins was continuing on his way and could be looked for very soon. Gladwin must have mused on the footlessness of such a reinforcement now. The prey had flown.

On November 18, the day after a heavy blizzard, two Mohawks entered the fort bearing from Maj. Thomas Moncrieffe to Gladwin a letter dated the 12th. Moncrieffe was accompanying Wilkins by Amherst's order to help Gladwin reduce and rearrange the regiments affected by the new military establishment. Moncrieffe's letter related a fresh tragedy. Wilkins' expedition, which had left Niagara in boats, encountered a violent storm on the night of November 7 off Pointe aux Pins. Three officers and 67 men were drowned, two boats and their occupants were missing, and 18 boats, 52 barrels of provisions, and all the ammunition were lost. The rest of the battered force had landed on the Point to collect itself and make repairs. The officers finally had decided to turn back to Niagara.

To Gladwin the bitterest aspect of the news was the fact that he himself could not be relieved, but must spend another winter in a place he had grown to detest. However, there was immediate work to do. As he lacked provisions and adequate barracks for the large garrison now on hand, and since any offensive action must be postponed until spring, he retained a garrison of 250 men and ordered Major Rogers, Captain Hopkins, Lieutenant Montresor, and 240 men to leave at once for Niagara and the East. They embarked on the 20th in nineteen bateaux and made a quick and uneventful passage to Niagara. There they learned that the Indians, probably Senecas again, had struck another blow on November 5 at the lower landing, falling on a party of ten men, killing seven and carrying off two. It was a last convulsion of Pontiac's war.

What no one knew, either at Detroit or Niagara, was that Pontiac's submission would not be known to General Amherst for weeks yet and would no longer particularly concern him. For early in October, Sir Jeffery had received His Majesty's gracious permission to return to England. He held a hurried conference with Sir William Johnson at Albany on Indian affairs, confident that Wilkins' expedition would enable Gladwin to punish the western savages as they deserved. Maj. Gen. Thomas Gage was summoned down to New York from Montreal to take over the command of the British forces in North America. Amherst left all the cares and problems of his office on his desk for Gage and joyfully embarked for home on November 17, never to return to this continent. But the ghost of Pontiac still followed him. A new king was on the throne, a new ministry in power, and Amherst's brilliant victories of 1759 and 1760 belonged to a war now ended. Instead, the Indian revolt in the West was in the news, and Amherst was pointed out as the general who had failed to subdue it.

18

Pontiac Escapes Punishment

PONTIAC did not go directly to Illinois after all. Probably he stopped off first around Sandusky to visit the Hurons, who had not yet asked for peace or given up hope of continuing the war. Then he found it necessary to hunt and provide for his family. He was accompanied from Detroit in the end by a great many Ottawa families, and along the Maumee River they fell in with several renegade Frenchmen who had found Detroit no longer safe for them: Baptiste Campau, Alexis Cuillerier, St. Vincent, and others. The Ottawas established an encampment, which grew into two villages, on the north bank of the river above the rapids of Roche de Bout. There Pontiac spent the winter.

During the cold season he took stock of his situation and found new fervor. His own position he could rationalize easily enough. He had not been defeated, he had not made peace. He had only asked for a truce because of cold weather and the necessity for hunting. There was indecision among the French over supporting the Indians, but as soon as he straightened that out, the war would be resumed. If the Detroit River Indians had lost their taste for war, there were other nations still hostile to the British. The loyal Hurons of Sandusky, the Delawares and Shawnees of Ohio, the Miamies and the Wabash tribes, the Senecas in the East had not submitted, and the Illinois Confederation could be stirred up to take the warpath. The prospect was stimulating.

In March 1764 Pontiac set out again for Illinois. He

went by canoe up the Maumee to the village of the Miamies on the portage between that river and the headwaters of the Little Wabash. The Miamies had a few English prisoners—traders probably and possibly soldiers from Fort Miamis. A dozen French and half-breed families lived in and around the powerless fort. The story drifted back to Detroit that when Pontiac learned one of the prisoners had beaten a Miami chief, he ordered the tribe to burn the unruly captive. The Miamies demurred, whereupon Pontiac threatened with his old belligerency to destroy the nation unless they complied. To satisfy him they burned the prisoner and shot another.

Pontiac continued on his way down the Wabash and passed the captured Fort Ouiatenon. He spoke to various tribes along the way—the Weas, Mascoutens, Piankashaws, Kickapoos—and probably paid his respects to the venerable Capt. Louis St. Ange de Bellerive, since 1736 the commandant of Fort Vincennes, where about a hundred French families were settled. He was now in the Province of Louisiana, which had not been ceded to the British until the treaty of peace and which was not yet occupied by them. Pontiac may have abandoned his canoes at the mouth of the Wabash and marched overland to avoid the long voyage down the Ohio and then up the Mississippi.

On April 12 Pontiac reached Fort de Chartres on the east bank of the Mississippi. Situated halfway between the mouths of the Missouri and of the Kaskaskia, this post was considered by some British officers as the finest fort in western America. Competently laid out by the French and rebuilt in 1753, it had heavy walls of stone and a stone barracks. The fort dominated the small settlement around its walls and comprised the main defense of the several villages stretching along the river bank above and below it. The commandant, Maj. Pierre Joseph Neyon de Villiers, was trying to do his duty so that he could get out of the wilderness and return to France. He didn't care for the British, but he would obey his orders to welcome them. He may have felt sorry for the Indians, but there was nothing he could do, and this war of Pontiac's was the maddest of all measures. De Villiers had asked for his own recall in the hope that when the Indians saw him leave they would finally believe the French were giving up the region to the British. He thought he had reconciled the Illinois Confederation to the coming of the British, who were to ascend the Mississippi from New Orleans. The last previous word from Pontiac had been on October 27, when the Shawnee war chief, Charlot Kaské, came into Fort de Chartres bearing a letter and a belt from Pontiac.[1] De Villiers had answered him unfavorably and in the presence of Lieutenant Jenkins, who had been carried off from Fort Ouiatenon.

Among the Illinois nations, however, Pontiac's name was known and respected. As soon as he arrived, Pontiac spoke to their chiefs and in two days proceeded to undo all of De Villiers' diplomatic spade work. He stirred up the Illinois to resist the English when they should approach.

A British force had already been stopped on the river, March 20, at Roche à Davion, 240 miles north of New Orleans, by a party of Tunicas, Ofogoulas, Choctaws, and Avoyelles inhabiting that vicinity. Long attached to the French, these tribes knew of the Indian war in the North and they may have acted as they did because of an appeal by messenger from Pontiac. At least he knew already that the British were on their way, and he gave De Villiers the first news of the expedition. Neither man yet knew that it had been turned back.

[1] *Ill. Hist. Coll.*, x, 52.

Pontiac called on De Villiers, April 15, and after the usual formalities of being seated and lighting a pipe presented a request for a general council.

"My father," he greeted him. "The Master of Life who deliberates every thing has had regard to the prayers which I have made to Him. It is a long time I have desired to see thee, my father; I do see you and am satisfied. Through one half of the road I have passed I was up to my neck in water; it is twenty-one nights since I left my home. I reckon all my trouble as nothing since I do see thee.

"I come to discover to thee my heart and to know of thee thyself what thou thinkest. I have left my army at Detroit, who continue there the war against the English and who will not end it until there are no more red men. They would rather die with their tomahawks in their hands than live in slavery with which the English menace them. Assemble all the French chiefs and the inhabitants; I shall be happy that they understand what I have to say to thee."[2]

Pontiac was not telling the truth about the status of his "army at Detroit," and De Villiers may have known it; but he was only too glad to acquiesce in calling a general conference so as to disillusion the chief and straighten out his thinking. The council was held at De Villiers' quarters two days later. Pontiac opened the meeting with a lengthy address:

"My father, Mons. de Neyon:

"I am not come here to tire thee with a useless dis-

[2] The minutes of this council were taken down by French interpreters and forwarded by De Villiers to Governor d'Abbadie at New Orleans. There the copy was shown to Lieut. Philip Pittman, who made an English translation and sent it to Maj. Robert Farmar at Mobile on July 10, 1764. Farmar transmitted it to General Gage on Dec. 21 (Gage Papers). Although Pittman's translation is literal and at times awkward, I have not felt at liberty to modernize it.

course. I am come here purposely to communicate to thee all which I have heard from the English. After the country was taken, the English called for me once, twice, and three times. I suffered myself to go at their demands. I was with them, and they said to me, 'My brother, we are charmed to see thee. We have trod down thy father. We would not thou shouldst be here without telling thee of it; perhaps if we had not done this thou might have beaten us.'

"My father, when they talked to me it was to re-engage me to bury my tomahawk, and that all the men [would] do the same, saying to me, 'We have always told thee that sooner or later thou must be abandoned and that we should become thy father. Notwithstanding, thou wilt always be fighting, and for what is it? For a few drams of brandy which he gives unto thee. We regard brandy as the water of the lakes. Thou canst tell this to all the nations; carry to them our word.'

"My father, when the English spoke to me, I did not make them the least answer and I have not told any thing with which they charged me for the nations. When Johnson came, he promised us that all the nations should be happy. There is the chain of our brothers which united us during some time, but we have broke it and trod it under foot; we are free. They said to us that we are hogs, notwithstanding we have not hair so long and so rude. The Master of Life that made us red, loves us as much as them, and we are as dear to Him as they are. It is Him that has inspired us to do what we do. Therefore, my father, meddle not in our affairs; it is the favor the red men ask of thee. What wouldst thou I should say to thee? They [the English] are liars and rascals. They speak not but with contempt of thy king and thee. They say they keep the French in their pocket, and that they knock them in the head as little flies that sting them, that for us they take us for a lump of earth which they break in their hands and give us to the winds to blow away like dust. Them who know not how to pray to the Master of Life cannot speak the truth, and thy children make war on them and will always carry it on.

"I have received the words, the belts, and the calumets of peace which thou hast sent to me and also to the other nations. Do not be angry, my father, if we have not obeyed in what thou mark't for us; things were too animated and the English have done too much. By the same words thou hast addressed to us thou hast informed us of thy departure to pass the great lake [Atlantic Ocean] according to the orders the king has given thee. I should have regarded it as a misfortune for us, if thou hadst gone before I could have had the pleasure to have seen thee. What made me come here was that I might charge thee to carry to the king the words of all the red men. It is I , my father, that loved thee without seeing thee. I see thee and I still love thee more. I know that thou knowest the red men. It is me, my father, that ought to speak to thee for them; therefore I pray thee harken to me. If I would, my father, thou shouldst not go from hence; I would stop thee. Think that I am able to do it, but no, I know how necessary it is that thou shouldst go and explain to the king the way of thinking of the red men. Let him know our attachment and for what I let thee go away. I am flattered it is to be thee that does it, because thou knowest and lovest the red men. It is me that am their interpreter and that speaks for all.

"My father, we pray the king to take pity on us. We hope the Master of Life will inspire him with something favorable for us. If our prayers are fulfilled, we hope to see again Mons. de Bellestre. You are the two chiefs we ask of the king. I pray thee not to abandon us, but to make the English liars who say he is pulled down and that we shall die slaves or at the foot of the trees for want of succour.

"My father, I pray thee to tell the governor of the Warm Town [New Orleans] to have pity on us or at least on our wives and children that they may have where-withall to live whilst we attend the answer of the king. I pray thee, my father, once more to have regard to our wives and children that they may have their supplies in powder to subsist them; we will not make the least use of it; it is for them only that we ask it.

"My father, the last summer we cleared the road that leads to thee. The English would have embarrassed it, but they have not succeeded, and we will always keep them as they are. Tell the king that all his children give him their hands and that they will never quit him. Thou canst assure him this by remitting to him the word I have given to thee in behalf of all the nations of the continent. [As for] the nonsense the English told us of the king and thee, we put ourselves in a condition to say we will give our bodies to revenge it, and it may be when the king knows this he will take pity on us.

"My father, if thou hadst come at my first demand, the red men would have made thee the greatest man in the world. Thou art a great chief, thou art our father, thou knowest the Master of Life; it is He who had put arms in our hands and it is He who has ordered us to fight against this bad meat that would come to infect our lands. If I was the first red man that held this opinion, thou might say, 'Pontiac is a liar'; but the Abenakies, the Iroquois, the Shawnees, the Chippewas, in short all the nations of the continent hold this discourse [doctrine?] and they are correct. All the answers to the demands I have made thee are to bury my tomahawk. Think then, my father, that thou goest against the orders of the Master of Life, and that all the red men conform to His will. Thus I pray thee to talk to me no more of a peace with the English, because I hate them.

"All thy children, my father, even when beat and conquered by the English love better to die than to fail the French in any thing. Be persuaded that we will not finish the war with the English whilst there remains one of us red men. That nation that had a desire to kill the French [the Hurons of Detroit], I took them myself to Quebec to have them punished by the Grand Chief; however, I asked pardon for them and obtained it. The last summer I obliged them to fight against the English, and they have done it.

"There, my father, is what I have had to say. Pardon me if I have spoke ill."

Pontiac sat down. De Villiers rose and answered him somewhat impatiently, endeavoring to explain that the king, their father, had ordered both the French and the Indians to maintain peace with the English.

"We, my father, make a peace with the English?" Pontiac interrupted. "No, I hate them. What thou tellest me is not the first, or second time. It is a long time thou hast told me the same thing. If this peace is made it will not hold forty moons, since it is true these are the sentiments of all thy red children. My father, thou art charged with my talk; recollect it is in behalf of thy children, the savages. The war will continue just to that moment."

De Villiers grew more emphatic, repeating his arguments and accusing Pontiac of continuing a war that was neither to his benefit nor to that of the French. He confessed his fear that the chief might provoke bloodshed in Illinois. At the end, he dismissed him with the advice to return to his village and be quiet.

Pontiac stood up again. "I accept, my father, the word thou bearest to me only for the French, and to prove to thee that I will live and remain in union with them and preserve that attachment I always had for them; that for the English is like a stone one throws over a precipice and never sees again. Be easy, my father, I will not spill blood upon thy lands. What I will spill shall be upon the water of thy river, which the current will carry away."

Sensing the threat, De Villiers asked him to reflect on their conversation and come back tomorrow to talk again. But Pontiac had no desire to hear more and he went away next day, incognito, it was said. Where he kept himself for the next two months has not been determined. As he did not return to his village on the Maumee River, he probably visited among the Illinois tribes exhorting them to war. Possibly he went back toward Fort Vincennes and appealed again to the tribes there.

When news of Pontiac's continued hostility eventually reached General Gage at headquarters in New York, the commander-in-chief was sufficiently alarmed to write at once to the Secretary of State, Lord Halifax. Having fought through the French and Indian War, Gage had far more respect for the Indians as warriors than Amherst ever had and he did not waste time despising Pontiac as an opponent. "There is reason to judge of Pontiac," he wrote, "not only as a savage possessed of the most refined cunning and treachery natural to the Indians; but as a person of extraordinary abilities. He [Governor d'Abbadie] says that Pontiac keeps two secretarys, one to write for him, and the other to read the letters he receives; and he manages them so as to keep each of them ignorant of what is transacted by the other."[3]

De Villiers left the Illinois in the middle of June, and Captain St. Ange was called down from Vincennes to command at Fort de Chartres. The garrison was reduced to forty soldiers. Pontiac promptly reappeared at the fort. Although St. Ange seems to have been less scrupulous

[3] Gage Papers, Apr. 14, 1764.

about dabbling in Indian affairs, nonetheless he dared not furnish Pontiac with more than a little ammunition for hunting. This lack of ammunition is probably all that prevented Pontiac from actively resuming the war in 1764. It affected not only himself and his own tribe, but also the Illinois nations and those on the Wabash who were disposed to join him. Unsuccessful in his principal mission, therefore, he left Fort de Chartres July 1 and returned to his village on the Maumee.

Affairs had not gone well in his absence. The war spirit had burned very low. He learned first that the Huron chiefs of Sandusky, those inveterate enemies of the English, had recently gone to Detroit to ask forgiveness and to sue for peace. Though he did not know it, the Senecas also had given up and made peace with Sir William Johnson. Moreover, Manitou, the collaborationist, was in Pontiac's village urging the Ottawas to return to their old settlement at Detroit, which they could do if they showed a properly contrite spirit to the British commandant.

Despite anything Pontiac could threaten or do, four influential Ottawas accompanied Manitou back to Detroit to throw themselves on the mercy of Lieutenant Colonel Gladwin. They told him that Pontiac was no longer listened to by his people, which may have been partly true, as the Ottawas had made two villages on the Maumee. The one on the north bank, opposite Roche de Bout Island (near modern Waterville, Ohio), was under a pro-English chief called Atawang. Pontiac had a settlement farther up the river on an island, now divided in two: Indianola Island and Vollmar's Island.[4]

---

[4] Captain Morris mentions the two Ottawa villages in his ms. diary (see note 6, below). He identified one as "Roche de Bout village of the Ottawas," and a French trader added that it was on the north side of the river. A railroad bridge now crosses the river at this place and is supported in the center by the rocky

Captain Thomas Morris

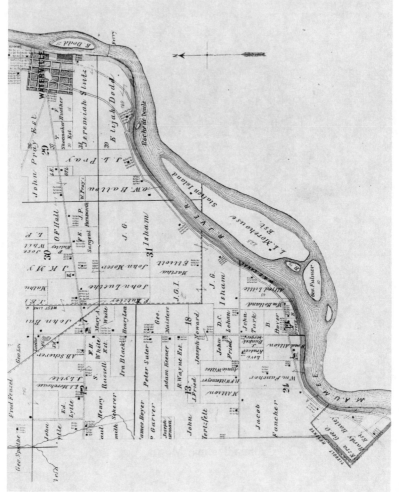

Map of the Maumee River

The Hurons of Detroit had gone to Niagara, where a huge congress was being held with Sir William Johnson. From the British point of view it was of little value, because only these Hurons and the Senecas attended out of all the tribes who had borne arms against the English. All the rest of the numerous delegations were from the Ottawas of L'Arbre Croche, the Chippewas of St. Mary's River, the Menominees, Sacs, Foxes, Sioux, and Crees of the Lake Superior region who resented Pontiac's war. They came to solicit the resumption of trade and to ask that traders be sent among them. Their complaint revealed another fatal weakness in Pontiac's grandiose vision: the Indians themselves were not willing to forego the white man's trade which their warfare ruined.

isle. On leaving this village going upstream, Morris passed that same day an island on which Pontiac's village was located. The Maumee River widens just above Roche de Bout and is divided by two large islands. The first is Indianola Island, variously known as Missionary Island and Station Island. It contains 315 acres and is the largest island in the river. Off its south end is tiny Grave Island, so called because of the Indian graves found on it. The island next above Indianola and separated from it only by a narrow channel is Indian Island or Vollmar's Island, of 40 acres. The channel is a recent development, cut by an ice jam. Off the northwest side of Vollmar's Island is small Butler Island, possibly connected at one time, which is now known as Legion Island because a Toledo American Legion post owns it. It seems obvious that when the two larger islands were one, totalling 355 acres or more, they were the site of Pontiac's island village. Fred Vollmar informed me that arrowheads, stone pipes, silver brooches, skinning stones, and similar relics were found on Indianola Island and on Indian Island. C. E. Slocum, *History of the Maumee River Basin*, p. 122, believed that the Ottawa village on the north bank was on the site of the town of Providence, about eight miles up the river from these islands; at least some Ottawas lived there about 1800, but villages were frequently moved. For much of the foregoing information I am deeply indebted to Dr. Leonard Nippe, of Toledo, who interviewed local residents, measured the islands for me, and photographed them from the air.

Beyond this one congress, the British exerted little effort in the realm of diplomacy, partly because their ablest exponent in the West, George Croghan, was absent in England, partly because their policy was confused, but mostly because they were not yet through fighting.

Desperate to maintain his leadership and prosecute his ends, Pontiac began spreading lies. In this effort he was ably seconded by young Alexis Cuillerier, who had taken a letter from a French courier bound from Illinois to Detroit. What the letter actually said is not known, but Cuillerier told Pontiac that it was from the French king warning the English to leave Detroit because he was coming with a great army of soldiers and Indians to retake it. Possibly Pontiac believed this ancient fiction, despite the cool treatment he had received at Fort de Chartres; if not, he hoped to use it.

He succeeded in impressing Sekahos, his old Chippewa ally from the Thames River. That chief expressed a canny willingness to take up the hatchet again as soon as the French army should arrive. Pontiac also sent wampum belts to the Shawnees and Delawares with his message about the coming of reinforcements from France. Although some deputies from these two nations appeared at Detroit seeking peace, which Gladwin did not feel empowered to grant, the majority had no thought of giving up the war, but were anxious to raise new allies to resume it. Growing bolder, Pontiac also threatened the lives of the Ottawas who had been seeking peace with Gladwin at Detroit.

But summer was waning, the siege of Fort Detroit was not renewed, and no further word was heard of French troops. There was an army marching into the Indian country, but it was British.

The punitive expedition which General Amherst had been unable to set in motion in 1763 was launched in the summer of 1764 by General Gage with two spearheads. One point was to be driven through the Delaware and Shawnee villages in the Ohio country by Colonel Bouquet from Fort Pitt. The other point was to penetrate from Niagara across Lake Erie to Detroit, pricking the Delawares and Shawnees in passing. Col. John Bradstreet directed this push. Three new ships also were available for western traffic. Built at Niagara during the winter and spring, they were the schooners *Boston* and *Gladwin*, and the sloop *Charlotte*.

Bad luck still stalked the British, this time because Bradstreet misconstrued his instructions. General Gage allowed him to use his discretion after arriving at Detroit in attacking the Indians there or in sending them to Johnson to make peace. But he was not permitted any latitude with the Shawnees and Delawares; he must attack them en route in conjunction with Bouquet's moves. He was also to relieve Gladwin and reestablish the garrison at Fort Michilimackinac. As for the smaller posts, Gage did not think it worthwhile to reoccupy any of them.

Bradstreet embarked from Niagara with 1,200 men early in August, after assisting Johnson with the Indian congress. He landed first near the fallen Fort Presqu'Isle and was met by ten Indians who claimed to be deputies from the Delawares and Shawnees desiring peace. Unfamiliar with Indian wiles, Bradstreet believed them and called off his projected attack in that direction. Then, instead of sending them on to Johnson, the only person authorized to conclude formal peace, Bradstreet proceeded on August 12 to draw up a treaty with them himself and to notify Bouquet that it would not be necessary for him to chastise these two nations! They were to meet Bradstreet again at Sandusky and deliver up their white prisoners.

⟨ 255 ⟩

Gage was in a frenzy after he received the news of Bradstreet's presumption and stupid innocence, for with it he heard from Bouquet that the Delawares and Shawnees were again murdering frontiersmen. One party struck an isolated schoolhouse in Pennsylvania and massacred the teacher and all the pupils save one, who recovered from his scalping. Although it was too late, Gage penned a blistering reply to Bradstreet, declaring that he would not recognize such a treaty. "They have negotiated with you on Lake Erie and cut our throats upon the frontiers."[5]

Resuming his voyage, Bradstreet grew more confident as he proceeded across the lake. He decided to dispatch an officer to Fort de Chartres to inform the French and savages along the way of Johnson's congress at Niagara and of his own treaty with the Delawares and Shawnees, as well as to warn them not to oppose any movement of British troops. The officer was then to go down the Mississippi and advise the Indians there against attacking any other British expedition on that river. Thus all the enemy tribes in the West would be pacified by Bradstreet's exertions. The notion that the Indians should be warned and conciliated before British troops made their appearance among them was sound policy; but Bradstreet planned without knowing that the Shawnees and Delawares were on the warpath or that the nations along the Wabash and in Illinois were still under the sway of the uncompromising Pontiac.

Capt. Thomas Morris of the 17th Regiment was selected for this perilous mission. He was far from being a typical British officer, although he came from a military family. He could speak French, he had attended college before joining the army, and his tastes were always literary and scholarly. He left the service in 1775 and followed a career of writing songs, verses, essays, a biography, and a

[5] Gage Papers, Oct. 15, 1764.

romance. He kept a day-by-day diary of his journey up the Maumee River.[6]

Bradstreet's expedition stopped August 26 at "Cedar Point" long enough to start Morris across Maumee Bay. Accompanying him were two French guides, two servants, and nineteen Indians. One of the Frenchmen was Jacques Godfroy, whom Gladwin had sent to Niagara for trial over the capture of Fort Miamis. Bradstreet was returning him to Detroit on Gage's order and offered to pardon him if he would faithfully assist Captain Morris. The Indian escort was made up mostly of Iroquois, but included a Chippewa chief and Atawang, chief of the Ottawa village up the Maumee, who was to be Morris' first host.

At the rapids about eighteen miles up the river, the Ottawa chief sent to his village for horses, and the whole party rode to the settlement. As Morris drew near he found himself surrounded by a mob of savages who showed more antagonism than hospitality. Suddenly the crowd parted, and Morris was face to face with Pontiac. He "told me that the English were liars, that his father (the French king) was not crushed (rubbing one hand over the other) as they said, and presented me a letter to read directed to him, full of the most improbable falsehoods though beginning with a truth."

Morris stayed in Atawang's cabin that night and next day addressed a council of chiefs. He told them of Bradstreet's might and power, of the peaceful inclinations of

[6] Morris sent his diary to Lieut. Thomas Mante, Bradstreet's aide-de-camp, and asked him to take a copy of it for the colonel. Mante kept the original and evidently returned the copy to Morris. Bradstreet forwarded the original diary to General Gage, where it may be found among the latter's papers. Morris rewrote his diary in narrative form and published it in his *Miscellanies in Prose and Verse*, London, 1791, adding some details. The original diary was first published in the *Old Fort News*, VI, 1, Feb. 1941, a publication of the Allen County-Fort Wayne Historical Society, Indiana.

the Delawares and Shawnees, and advised them to go to Detroit to talk with Bradstreet. An Oneida chief, Thomas King, who had accompanied Morris for the purpose, spoke next, presenting the threat of the Iroquois if the western nations should not make peace with the English. The Ottawas were impressed and declared their friendly intentions. Atawang and Shamandawa were delegated to go to Detroit and treat with Bradstreet. A visiting Miami chief, Naranea, offered to accompany them as an observer.

Pontiac did not welcome Morris' appearance and he did not want the tribes from there to the Illinois reconciled to the English. Moreover, a delegation of fifteen Shawnees and Delawares had just passed up the river boasting of how they had deceived Bradstreet and carrying war belts from themselves and the deceitful Senecas which declared their unchanging enmity toward the English. The deputies said they would send a hatchet, a sign to begin war, in about a month.

Pontiac talked privately with Chief Thomas King and revealed to him the visit of the Shawnees and Delawares. The Senecas had gone so far in their message as to assert that all the six nations of Iroquois were going to continue the war, yet here was the Oneida chief calling for peace. Pontiac acknowledged that the Senecas were trying to deceive him. Possibly he suspected the Shawnee-Delaware envoys as well.

Whatever the reason, Pontiac abruptly showed a change of face. He permitted Morris to continue his journey up the river and gave him his protection. That is, to accompany Morris he sent along his nephew and a local French trader named St. Vincent with a huge wampum belt describing 180 villages on it. By this belt Pontiac said the road ahead would be opened up for the party. Pleasantly surprised and easily impressed, Morris reported that Pontiac had grown tractable and that his power was still absolute, neither of which was true.

Morris stayed three days with the Ottawas, and the most remarkable occurrence was that Atawang sold him, for a little powder, a volume of Shakespeare! How he came by it affords interesting speculation.

Now numbering twenty-four, Morris' party proceeded up the river mostly on horseback because of the stream's shallowness. They were in a rich game country and one day the party consumed two deer, ten turkeys, ducks, raccoons, Indian corn, etc. Morris limited himself to observing: "I never saw such hearty eating before."

On September 7 the embassy came within sight of Fort Miamis and was met by almost the whole village of Miamies armed with spears, arrows and bows, and tomahawks. While his Indians advanced to pacify the crowd, Morris stayed in a canoe in midstream reading *Romeo and Juliet*—or so he said. The hostility evinced by the Miamies was owing, of course, to the recent visit of the Shawnees and Delawares. The embassy had just left after stirring up fresh hatred of the English, seven to return to the Ohio country, five to go on to Fort Ouiatenon, and three to Fort St. Joseph. Although this was the first news Morris had had of the Shawnee-Delaware war party, he recognized its significance at once. He realized that the two nations had duped Bradstreet into a treaty which saved them from chastisement, but which they had no intention of observing.

The Miamies let Morris land, but shortly they seized him, stripped off his clothes, and bound him in one of their cabins. Two Kickapoo chiefs in the village promised to kill him in their town on the Wabash if the Miamies should let him pass. The Miami village was in an uproar, and Pontiac's protection was going to be ignored. But the great belt was exhibited, Pontiac's nephew and Atawang's son spoke, St. Vincent and Godfroy made appeals, and finally Pacanne, the young Miami chief, untied Morris. The captain kept in hiding for two days awaiting the result of a Miami council, which decided that he must turn back. As the Shawnees and Delawares who had gone to St. Joseph were on their way back, Morris thought it prudent to leave as requested. On September 10 the party marched down the Maumee and struck off into the woods for the trail leading directly to Detroit. Morris did not see Pontiac again and reached Detroit on September 17.

Meanwhile, Bradstreet had been to Detroit, sent off a detachment under Capt. William Howard to garrison Fort Michilimackinac, and installed Lieut. Col. John Campbell of the 17th Regiment to relieve Gladwin. The doughty savior of Fort Detroit embarked on August 31. Having received word of the death of his father, of whose estate he had been made executor, he planned to go directly to England. He stopped long enough in New York to report to his old friend, General Gage, and to arrange his retirement from the army on half pay.

Sailing for home on October 12, Gladwin married within the next few years and settled down to the life of a country gentleman at Stubbing, Derbyshire. He achieved the rank of a major general on the retired list, and died on June 22, 1791. The *Gentleman's Magazine*, which did not know where Detroit was in 1763, ignored that eminent aspect of Gladwin's career in its obituary notice of him. His monument in Wingerworth Church, however, makes conspicuous mention of his defense of Fort Detroit.[7]

[7] Charles Moore's statement that Gladwin was married during a quick visit to England in 1762 was evidently based on incorrect information furnished him. See "Gladwin Manuscripts," *Mich. P. & H. Coll.*, xxvii, 609. Gladwin left England with General Braddock late in 1754 and did not return home again

Bradstreet held a conference in Detroit with the Ottawas, Hurons, Chippewas, and Potawatomies from September 5 to 7. The Chippewas were represented by Wasson, the only chief present who had taken a prominent part against the English the year before. The Ottawas of the Maumee sent Atawang and Shamandawa, as we have seen, and Manitou no doubt represented the local band. The Potawatomies delegated Kiouqua and Nanequoba, not Ninivois or Washee. The Miamies were represented unofficially by Naranea, and the Huron chiefs were not named.

Bradstreet had intended to demand that Pontiac "be given up to be sent down the country and maintained at His Majesty's expence the remainder of his days."[8] But at the council he did not do so. Perhaps he realized that the Ottawas of Detroit could not deliver Pontiac, who was living on the Maumee, or that he was committing the Crown to an annual expense without authorization. Nevertheless, Bradstreet's intention was noised around Detroit, and the local Indians envied Pontiac his promised pension.

As principal speaker of the conference, Wasson blandly passed off the war by saying: "Last year God forsook us; God has now opened our eyes and we desire to be heard. 'Tis God's will our hearts are altered."[9] Anxious to escape punishment, he was fawning in his assurances of submission. Shamandawa then declared to Bradstreet that

until the end of 1764. His movements in 1762 are easily accounted for in the Gage Papers. He was not married in 1754 when he left England, as the girl he wedded was born in 1743. Her name was Frances Beridge, daughter of the Rev. John Beridge. She married Gladwin sometime between 1765 and 1775, possibly 1772. They had seven children, two dying in infancy.

[8] Bradstreet to Gage, Aug. 28, 1764, Gage Papers.

[9] "Transactions of a Congress held with the Chiefs of the Ottawas and Chippewaw Nations" in Bradstreet's letter to Gage, Sept. 12, 1764, Gage Papers.

Pontiac, too, was remorseful and would be thankful to be forgiven. That Pontiac had authorized any such plea is extremely doubtful, although it was smart policy on the part of the Maumee Ottawas so to represent him.

Bradstreet promptly granted them a peace treaty, requiring only that they acknowledge themselves subjects of King George and turn in all their captives. Wabbicomigot, the Mississaugi-Chippewa chief, arrived two days later from Toronto and desired to be included in the general treaty, which Bradstreet permitted.

While the colonel was still congratulating himself on his bloodless "conquest" of the western nations, some Indian couriers arrived, September 13, with the news that the Shawnees and Delawares were on the warpath and swearing that they would never make peace. Bradstreet knew then that he had been hoodwinked. He gathered his forces and left Detroit next day for Sandusky, where he originally had arranged to receive prisoners from the two tribes. From Captain Morris he soon got confirmation of the Shawnee-Delaware double dealing, but there was nothing he could do now except ask the Iroquois and the other western nations to go to war against them. He was only partially successful. Luckily for the English, Colonel Bouquet was taking care of the miscreants.

Delayed by the necessity of employing Pennsylvania militia, Bouquet did not leave Fort Pitt until October 1. Fifteen hundred strong, the force marched westward into the valley of the upper Muskingum River, the heart of the Delaware country. More resolute than Bradstreet and itching to attack the savages at the slightest provocation, Bouquet took no nonsense from the delegations that hastened to meet him in order to save their villages from destruction. He demanded sincere protestations of submission, all the prisoners they held, and hostages to keep while their chiefs repaired to Sir William Johnson's to sign a treaty. The Shawnees, Delawares, Mingoes, and Sandusky Hurons respected this display of power and capitulated wherever he went. Having accomplished his purposes, Bouquet turned back at the forks of the Muskingum and reached Fort Pitt again on November 28 with more than 200 captives and another 100 promised. The British insistence on having all prisoners turned in, including those youngsters who had been living with the Indians so long they remembered no other life and even the half-breeds born of prisoners, seems foolishly cruel today although it was a point of honor then.

Bouquet's crowning act was to send a Delaware and a Shawnee to the nations on the Maumee and the Wabash to advertise their submission. He hoped it would counteract the belligerency of the earlier deputies and undermine any hostile plans that Pontiac might lay in that region. It was an effective stroke, demonstrating to Pontiac that his allies were deserting him. He must now look along the Illinois and Mississippi Rivers for future support against the English.

General Gage complimented Bouquet on his thoroughness and added: "It were to be wished that Col. Bradstreet had given you full information of every thing that had passed on his side. There was a sort of peace made with Pondiac's tribe, and it was believed that he had lost his influence, in so much that his own belt was cut in pieces. But Capt. Morris found he had as much influence as ever, and he was not come into us, afraid to trust himself. He should, if possible, be gained to our interest; the Miamies, or Twightwees, Indians of the Ouabache, and the Illinois, tho' not openly in arms against us, are greatly averse to us, and Pondiac can manage them as he pleases. The peace lately made may possibly soften all these nations, and if a particular belt was sent to Pondiac to notify the peace, and to take him into favor, it may greatly advance the service. If he could be got to Fort Pitt or the Detroit, he might be made usefull, and as an earnest of his sincerity would be anxious to shew us his readiness to do us some notable service."[10]

The two expeditions under Bradstreet and Bouquet had accomplished something in recovering prisoners and in reducing Pontiac's potential strength. Yet the two objectives uppermost in General Amherst's mind when he planned this movement in 1763 had not been achieved. There had been no military defeat and punishment of the Indians in reprisal for their numerous victories, and the chief who had started the widespread uprising had not been molested or even brought into a treaty council. Gage was especially sensitive to this latter failure.

Safe and unobligated in his pleasant retreat on the Maumee, Pontiac may have smiled to himself.

[10] Gage Papers, Dec. 7, 1764.

19

Reluctant Submission

So far was Pontiac from submitting to the British that he was again plotting against them, although his movements in the fall of 1764 and winter of 1765 are obscured in vague rumors. One circumstantial account relates that St. Vincent, a French resident of the Ottawa village on the Maumee, had written a letter in the name of Pontiac to "the Gross Beast," a Miami chief (probably Le Gris), advising him not to permit any Frenchmen with "English hearts" to pass through his nation.[1]

Again circumstantial evidence suggests that Pontiac sent a message to *Le Grand Saulteur*, or Minavavana, the great chief of the Chippewas, to meet him in the Illinois country that fall. They met there with some of the French inhabitants, but apparently not with Captain St. Ange. The French were hoping to delay British occupation by any means. They reputedly told the two chiefs that if the Indians would keep the British out of the Illinois country next summer, the French king would send over an army, and the Spanish king would help, by the spring of 1766. They assured the chiefs that if the British took possession of Illinois they would set the southern tribes against the northern. This last threat was actually true: General Gage had indeed suggested such a stratagem to Major Farmar at Mobile, after the failure of the expedition up the Mississippi.

Captain St. Ange at Fort de Chartres had heard by

[1] Jean Baptiste Beaubien's testimony in Gage Papers, printed in Johnson Papers, iv, 676.

early November that Pontiac had sent to all the nations a belt six feet long and four inches wide on which were indicated the tribes under his influence. By it he invited them to join him against the English and threatened them if they didn't. He pictured the English as cruel and unreliable in their treaties. St. Ange did not report that he sent Pontiac some clothes, a hat, and some vermilion, and advised him to remain quiet.[2]

John Stuart, the superintendent of Indian affairs in the South, and Governor George Johnstone of West Florida were both of the opinion that Pontiac was scheming in October with The Mortar, an Upper Creek chief, and Alabama Mingo, a Choctaw chief, for a general and concerted attack on the English. According to Stuart and Johnstone, the three chiefs were preaching the doctrine that the English intended to surround the Indian nations and then wipe them out by cutting off their supplies. Therefore the northern and southern tribes, old enemies though they were, must unite and fight the English as their common enemy.[3] Even so, the two British officials believed that the French were at the bottom of the plot. A wild rumor reached George Croghan, just returned to America, that a confederation of eighteen tribes was being formed.

The report from the South must be read with great caution. Stuart and Johnstone may well have exaggerated some tale they had heard in order to justify the heavy expenditures they were making on Indian congresses. Moreover, it is hard to believe that the southern Indians would object to seeing the English wipe out their northern brethren. If Pontiac persuaded them of the need for unity against the common danger in retaliation against General Gage's suggestion that the southern tribes be set

[2] *Ill. Hist. Coll.*, x, 354-359.
[3] *Miss. Prov. Arch., Eng. Dominions*, 1, 184.

against the northern, he achieved a masterpiece of diplomacy. Be that as it may, nothing came of the supposed cooperation.

More certain is the fact that Pontiac sent war belts to the Arkansaws, who lived half way down the Mississippi, urging them to attack the British when they should ascend the river again.[4] Governor d'Abbadie of Louisiana sought to counteract this message as soon as he learned of it, for he stood ready to accommodate the British in accordance with his orders.

Pontiac was still not alone in his hostility toward the English. His friend, Charlot Kaské, the Shawnee chief, was fervently soliciting aid in the West to continue the war. He was a half-breed whose German father had taught him to hate the English, and he was married to an English woman who had been taken prisoner as a girl. Before Bouquet forced the Shawnees to terms, a group of 60 of them under Kaské had gone to Illinois to seek help for another outbreak. They had arrived at Fort de Chartres on August 27, 1764. Although St. Ange refused to aid them, the *habitants* promised them supplies and offered to send traders to their towns in Ohio. The delegation also held a council with representatives of nine tribes on the Wabash and in Illinois who agreed to support them if they renewed the war. With the exception of Kaské, the Shawnees then returned to Ohio, where they found that the rest of their nation had submitted to the exactions of Bouquet's expedition. The late arrivals acquiesced in the agreement and laid aside their plans for war.[5]

Not so Charlot Kaské. Uninformed of Bouquet's success, he determined to appeal over St. Ange's head to the governor of Louisiana. Taking passage on a boat early in

[4] *Ill. Hist. Coll.*, x, 456.
[5] Chief Kyashuta's testimony to Croghan, May 9, 1765, Gage Papers; *Ill. Hist. Coll.*, xi, 1.

November, he arrived in the Warm Town (that is, New Orleans) the next month. In an audience with Governor d'Abbadie on December 20, he displayed a belt containing symbols for forty-seven villages that wished to die attached to the French. He said they sought help to make war. The governor was touched, but refused to help him and urged him to live in peace with the English.

Kaské stayed in New Orleans, however, and was soon joined by an Illinois chief named Levacher, bent on the same mission. They were also uneasy about the prospective disappearance from the continent of all French authority because of the cession to Spain of New Orleans and the French claims on the west side of the Mississippi. The Spaniards were daily expected to come and assume possession.

Governor d'Abbadie died on February 4, 1765, and the two chiefs held a council with his successor, Governor Aubry, but were again refused assistance. They were reminded that they must reconcile themselves to British occupation. Disappointed, the chiefs prepared to return northward.[6]

Probably influenced by the steps taken by Kaské and Levacher, possibly urged by Pontiac himself, a Kaskaskia war chief named Chacoretony took a fellow warrior and left the Illinois country on February 19 in the bateau of Mons. Vallée for New Orleans. He, too, was going

[6] The two conferences held with Kaské and Levacher were reported in Aubry's letter to the minister, March 1, 1765, Parkman Papers, vol. 27A; printed in *Ill. Hist. Coll.*, x, 448 and 455, under date of Feb. 25. In his book (end of chapter 29) Parkman describes these conferences and gives as his source apparently the same letter and its inclosures. But he designates these records as "Ms. Report of a Conference with the Shawanoe and Miami delegates from Pontiac, held at New Orleans, March, 1765. Paris Documents." The "Miami" is apparently an error for the Illinois chief, and the statement that the chiefs were "delegates from Pontiac" is an unwarranted assumption.

to Governor d'Abbadie, not knowing of his death. He was also carrying war belts to the tribes on the lower Mississippi.

In the meantime Maj. Robert Farmar, who commanded at Mobile, had dispatched Lieut. John Ross overland to Fort de Chartres accompanied by Hugh Crawford, the trader seized on the Wabash in 1763 and exchanged at Detroit, and three others. Their task was to persuade the tribes in Illinois to accept peaceably the coming of a British garrison. They reached Fort de Chartres on February 18, 1765, but their arrival was not known to Chacoretony before he set out down the Mississippi. Ross immediately advised Major Farmar to seize the chief as he "is one of our greatest enemies."

Ross could do nothing until the Illinois tribes came in from hunting, and then St. Ange assisted him in calling a council for April 4. When the Kaskaskias, Peorias, Cahokias, Michigameas, joined by the Osages and Missouries from across the river, assembled, they heard Ross's plea for friendship. Tamarois, the spokesman for the Illinois Confederation, replied that they did not want to see the English in Illinois; indeed, they favored continuing the war and he warned Ross to leave the country. One of the Osages admitted that they had promised Pontiac to attack the English. Since the Ottawa chief was expected daily, St. Ange advised Ross to leave before the savages got out of hand. Seeing that he could accomplish nothing further, Ross set off down the river on April 7—one day before Pontiac arrived at Fort de Chartres.[7]

No doubt Pontiac was gratified by the resoluteness of his allies. He had brought with him a number of Ottawa warriors and was soon followed by some Potawatomi and Chippewa chiefs. The Potawatomies were in trouble again at Detroit, some of their braves having killed and

[7] Ross's letter to Farmar, May 25, 1765, Gage Papers.

scalped two soldiers outside of the fort. If Pontiac was disappointed not to encounter Lieutenant Ross, he had not long to wait before another British officer hailed Fort de Chartres.

George Croghan had been ordered by Sir William Johnson and General Gage to proceed to Illinois and prepare the Indians for British occupation. Gage commissioned Lieut. Alexander Fraser, a reduced officer of the 77th Regiment who could speak French, to accompany Croghan and even supplied him a cipher for secret correspondence. At Fort Pitt, Croghan was held up in his efforts to procure a proper delegation of Iroquois, Delaware, and Shawnee chiefs to accompany them. The impatient Lieutenant Fraser obtained a boat and set off down the Ohio with only the crew and a few Indians on March 22. He turned up at Fort de Chartres on April 17.

St. Ange greeted him with trepidation, having just got Lieutenant Ross off his hands. At supper that night, he entertained Fraser and the village curate. They discussed holding another Indian council. The party was suddenly interrupted when Pontiac and eight of his followers burst into the room and demanded Fraser as a prisoner. Pontiac said he had sent a letter by Major de Villiers to the French king to learn directly from the Great Father whether peace had been made with the English in Illinois. Meanwhile, he regarded Fraser as an enemy trespasser. St. Ange got rid of Pontiac only by promising to give up Fraser in the morning. The Illinois savages, however, seized two of Fraser's boatmen and held them at Kaskaskia, a French town eighteen miles below the fort.

As Pontiac did not return next morning, Fraser called the Illinois chiefs together and talked sharply to them. He assured them that the Delawares and Shawnees and Senecas had already made peace with the English, as his Indian companions would testify. Therefore the Illinois tribes were alone in their stubborn hostility. Moreover, George Croghan was on his way, twelve days behind Fraser, and would stop at the mouth of the Wabash until he had received an answer from the Indians. Finally, Fraser expressed surprise that they should have seized two British soldiers who were part of his embassy at the behest of a man who belonged to another nation. He was referring to Pontiac, of course, hoping to weaken his authority.

Dismissing them, Fraser next called Pontiac for a private council. He began by saying that the English looked upon the chief now as their brother, because the Ottawas had made peace at Detroit with Colonel Bradstreet. Fraser added the news of Croghan's coming and declared that the agent was bringing along certain chiefs of the Shawnees, Delawares, and Iroquois who would prove to Pontiac in person that their nations were at peace with the English.

The two reasons for Pontiac's continued hostility now were uncovered. He did not believe the Shawnees had submitted to the English because he had seen several of them during the winter and they had not mentioned any peace. Secondly, he would not believe that the French king had concluded a peace treaty with the British which applied to Illinois.

In the afternoon Fraser and St. Ange spoke to the assembled tribes, numbering more than 500 savages. St. Ange opened the congress by emphasizing that the French were indeed at peace with the English everywhere—Canada, Louisiana, and Illinois—and wished ardently that the Indians would be too. This authoritative and brusque speech impressed the Indians. Fraser then stood up to repeat much of what he had said that morning and urged them to send deputies to meet Croghan. Tamarois replied for the Illinois chiefs that they would be ruled by the decision of their "older brothers," the Ottawas.

Peace or renewed warfare suddenly centered on the inclination of one man. Evidently doubts had entered his mind in thinking over Fraser's conversation. Since the collapse of the siege of Fort Detroit, he had relied on the Shawnees and Delawares to continue hostilities until he could persuade the Illinois Confederation to join them. Thus, though the Lakes might be lost to the British, the Ohio Valley and Illinois country would remain in Indian and French hands. But if the Shawnees had made peace, and if St. Ange spoke the truth. . . . Perhaps it would be prudent to hear what George Croghan had to offer.

All eyes on him, Pontiac rose to reply.

"This same war that I have waged against the English was undertaken solely on repeated invitations made me by the Delawares, Iroquois, and Shawnees," he began, shifting the blame in best Indian fashion. "They were almost two years urging me to take up arms against you, and I let myself be won over and adopted their sentiments. I am surprised that they have not advised us of their intentions and that they have not come themselves to give us word of it. However, my father, you urge me so much to make peace that I can no longer refuse you, and I submit to the wish of the king, my father. I do not desire to oppose him longer and consider from this moment that you have restored peace to all these children; for the future we will regard the English as brothers, since you wish to make us all one."[8]

It was as simple as that in the end. But the chief was not through.

"As for the meeting place that our English brother asks us to appoint, it is up to the Illinois to fix it, because they are on their own land. Tomorrow we will render you a reply to the above. As all our warriors may still have some bad intent in their heart, it will be good, my father, to

[8] Minutes of council enclosed in St. Ange's letter to Gage, Apr. 28, 1765, Gage Papers; my translation.

give them a cup of your milk to wash their hearts and drive out all resentment."

In other words, how about some brandy? Referring to his attempted seizure of Fraser the night before, Pontiac explained: "The attempt I made yesterday was not to be viewed as you have supposed. I did it with a good motive. It was to protect this officer from any accident, because being with me he would be insulted by no one."

Fraser reported some additional remarks of Pontiac, possibly made later. The chief expressed the hope that the British might now be more sincere in their promises than they had been. As a further dig, he observed that he was glad Croghan was coming to speak to him, as he could not believe the agent would be imprudent enough to tell the Indians more lies since they had detected him before in so many.

At the conclusion of the council the Illinois tribes released the two British soldiers, and Fraser bought them 130 pots of French brandy and a bullock to barbecue. A delegation of chiefs prepared to set out on April 24 to meet Croghan.

Fraser found himself still despised as an Englishman, however. The French inhabitants continued to whisper lies about the cowardice of British troops in the hope of inciting the Indians to resist. Pontiac and his followers drank a good deal, and in an effort to scare Fraser off and ingratiate themselves with the French, threatened to scalp or burn him. Still, everything would have worked itself out smoothly but for a succession of external occurrences.

The Chippewas and Potawatomies from St. Joseph, followed by some Kickapoos and Mascoutens of the Wabash, arrived on April 28 in an angry mood. They demanded brandy. Whether they got drunk, or were enraged by St. Ange's refusal to give them liquor, they took offense at Fraser's presence and asked that he be turned over to them. St. Ange hid him, but the Indians seized his soldiers and took them to their camp. There they got drunk for certain and threatened to massacre the soldiers if the officer was not delivered up. Fraser then gave himself up in the hope of saving his men. Next day the chiefs apologized, blaming the incident on their young men, and liberated the soldiers. Fraser and St. Ange even talked them into going to meet Croghan.

Then an Illinois warrior arrived with a wild tale that fourteen of his people had been killed down the river by a party of British and Cherokees who were lying in ambush for an expected convoy of French trade goods. The Illinois tribes flew to their arms and rushed to Fraser's quarters to kill him in revenge. Luckily Pontiac was there and threatened them with death if they harmed any of the Englishmen. So great was his power that with only a handful of Ottawas he stood off several hundred enraged Illinois. In a few days the bubble burst when the Indians who were supposed to have been killed walked into Kaskaskia.

Everything was easy again, and the Indians moved down to Kaskaskia to make peace wampum to deliver to Croghan. Kaskaskia was the largest French settlement in the Illinois area, including eighty houses well built, mainly of stone, and set on lots large enough to contain a garden as well. The town was situated on the river of the same name about six miles east of the Mississippi.

Fraser went there with the savages in order to keep himself under Pontiac's protection. Then the French convoy arrived from New Orleans. These goods had been shipped to avoid any regulations the Spaniards might impose for their own advantage. Among the supplies was a great quantity of powder. Returning with the boats was Charlot Kaské, the Shawnee chief. Despite his rebuffs in New Orleans, he now broadcast a monstrous falsehood, announcing that Governor Aubry had sent a war belt by him to all the nations to strike the English, that the king of France was going to declare war on England within a month, and that he was sending these traders to them with ammunition. The traders, indeed, may have been responsible for Kaské's declaration.

This fictitious news undid all of Fraser's work. Because the Indians wanted to believe such a story, they would listen to no contradictions. They did not doubt Kaské's word about the war belt, and the kegs of powder were visible. The French of Illinois were not loath to second Kaské's story, and St. Ange did not, in spite of Fraser's frantic request, disabuse the Indians. Oddly enough, only Pontiac remained sceptical of Kaské's inflammatory report. Having perpetrated similar lies in the past himself, he may have recognized the imaginative product of a fellow chief.

Fraser's party was seized again; he was beaten, abused, and threatened with death. The lieutenant was released, however, by some Arkansaws who had also come up with the convoy, because Lieutenant Ross had won their friendship on his way down the river. The Illinois Indians finally decided to ship Fraser and his men down the Mississippi before they began war anew. At this juncture the chiefs who had gone to the mouth of the Wabash to meet Croghan returned on May 18 without having seen him or heard anything from him. They accused Fraser of having misled them. They were going to their village to plant corn; peace with the English could wait—which meant that they probably would be persuaded to participate in the war Kaské was fomenting.

To save his men Fraser sent them off down the river secretly on May 19. He prevailed on Pontiac, whom he had grown to admire, to stay another ten or twelve days for word from Croghan, who seemed to be unaccountably delayed. For a white man and especially a British army officer, Fraser had unusual respect for the chief. "He is the person who seems most inclined to peace of any amongst them, and it is much to be wishd he may be prevaild on to make peace, as it will probably be of a longer duration than any made without him. He is in a manner ador'd by all the nations hereabouts, and he is more remarkable for his integrity & humanity than either Frenchman or Indian in the colony. He has always been as careful of the lives of my men as well as my own as if he had been our father."[9]

Perhaps Pontiac, having at last become acquainted with a likable Englishman, was beginning to lose his contempt for Englishmen generally. Certainly he had emerged as the only person who could stem the tide of war, and thus by a strange transition the Ottawa chief had become the bulwark of the British for peace in the West! He was for the moment more powerful than Johnson or Gage. Yet even he would fail unless he was convinced by Croghan's arrival of the sincerity of the British.

One night the traders got Pontiac and some of his braves drunk and reproached them for having allowed Fraser's men to escape. In his liquor Pontiac seized Fraser and declared him a prisoner. Some of the Ottawas wanted to kill him, but the chief would not go that far. Next day, when Pontiac was sober, Fraser told him he expected better treatment after staying behind his men on purpose to establish peace between him and the English. Pontiac was contrite and promised that Fraser should suffer no more, regardless of what any of the French said.

"I see you have not profited by any of the late opportunities of going away," he said, "I am persuaded that what you say is right and I will believe none who will tell

[9] Fraser's adventures are recounted in his lengthy reports to Gage, Apr. 27, May 15, 18, and 26, 1765, Gage Papers.

me the contrary hereafter. I believe that the nations on the Ohio have made a peace and that they come with Croghan. As soon as I see them or I am informed by them that they made peace, I will do the same, and you may be assured that as soon as my hatchet is buried all others in this quarter will."[10]

Pontiac added that he must return to his village, where he would be glad to hold a council with Croghan, and that he had bidden the other chiefs to meet them there. As for Fraser, Pontiac advised him either to accompany him to the Ottawa village or to set off down the river to New Orleans, as the chief could not guarantee the officer's safety after he should depart. Fraser chose the latter course in order to inform Major Farmar of the situation in Illinois. He provided Pontiac with letters to Croghan and to Lieutenant Colonel Campbell at Detroit. With a last warning to St. Ange not to permit any trade goods to be sold to hostile Indians, Fraser set off on May 29.

The treatment Fraser had received during his six weeks' stay did not endear the Illinois country to him. A second visit a year later did not alter his outlook. Biased though he was, his report on the inhabitants is amusing by its very violence: "The Indians are cruel, treacherous, and cowardly unless they can surprise their enemy without probability of suffering any loss themselves, but in that case they attack often ten times their own number. . . . Nothing can equal their passion for drunkenness, but that of the French inhabitants, who are for the greatest part drunk every day while they can get drink to buy in the Colony. They import more of this article from New Orleans than they do of any other, and they never fail to meet a speedy and good market for it. They have a good many Negroes, who are obliged to labour very hard to support their masters, in their extravagant debaucheries. Any

[10] Fraser to Gage, May 26, 1765, Gage Papers.

one that has had dealings with them must plainly see they are for the most part transported convicts, or people who have fled for some crimes. Those who have not done it themselves are the offspring of such as those I just mentioned, inheriting their forefathers' vices. They are cruel and treacherous to each other and consequently so to strangers. They are dishonest in every kind of business and lay themselves out to overreach strangers, which they often do by a low cunning peculiar to themselves, and their artful flatteries with extravagant entertainments (in which they affect the greatest hospitality) generally favour their schemes."[11]

Pontiac remained in Kaskaskia longer than he had anticipated. Early in June, Pierce Acton Sinnott, John Stuart's deputy in the southern Indian department, and Capt. Harpain de La Gauterais, a French militia officer, arrived there. They constituted another pacifying mission from Major Farmar, since his first under Lieutenant Ross had failed and he did not yet know of Fraser's success. Sinnott was provided with gifts for the Indians. Pontiac and the other chiefs accepted the presents, but the distrust which had been rising when Fraser left was ably fanned by the local Frenchmen and caused the chiefs to deliberate for five days on Sinnott's demand that the coming British garrison be allowed peaceable possession.

Ill with fever and apprehensive over his cool reception, Sinnott received word on June 14 that George Croghan at last was coming. The two Indians who brought the letter informed the Illinois chiefs of the peace made at Fort Pitt by the Shawnees, Delawares, and Senecas. This news ended the long deliberation of the chiefs and they returned a favorable answer to Sinnott. Then several days passed and Croghan did not appear. The French improved on the delay by spreading a new lie that the British wanted

[11] Ind. Hist. Soc. *Publications*, II, 11, pp. 411 and 415.

to gain possession of the country only in order to oust the Illinois Confederation and settle the hated Cherokees there. Even Pontiac seems to have been taken in by this falsehood, and the inevitable result was that Sinnott and La Gauterais were forced to flee in the night, their gifts wasted, their mission unsuccessful.

George Croghan, whose delay and non-appearance had twice caused a change of heart among the Indians, had been held up at Fort Pitt by the necessity of conducting a congress with the Indians and receiving the last of their captives. Not until May 7 did all the Indians arrive, and then more than 500 chiefs and braves had gathered, with their wives and children. Croghan reminded them that they had not yet sent deputies to Johnson to make formal peace and that no trade would be opened with them until they had done so. Actually, Colonel Bouquet had promised them a resumption of trade as soon as they should bring in the last of their prisoners, and Croghan had ordered gifts and trade goods sent to Fort Pitt for that purpose. But ruffians in Cumberland County, known as the Black Boys, incensed by this official decision to supply the savages who had ravaged the frontier, attacked the convoy at Sideling Hill and destroyed or captured the goods.

Croghan then asked for a delegation to accompany him to Illinois to tell the tribes there of their submission. Kyashuta, the old Seneca mischief maker, made his peace at last, and the other chiefs declared their sincere humility. A number of them agreed to accompany Croghan on his westward journey. They set out on May 15.

Their passage down the Ohio was largely uneventful until they passed the mouth of the Wabash on June 7. From their next camp (on the site of Shawneetown, Illinois) Croghan dispatched two Indians overland to Fort de Chartres with a letter to Fraser which Sinnott opened, as we have seen. Early next morning, however, the camp was attacked by a party of eighty Kickapoos and Mascoutens. Two white men and three Shawnees were killed, and all the rest of the mission except three were wounded.

"I got the Stroke of a hatchett on the Head," Croghan reported in his original orthography, "but my Scull being pretty thick the hatchett wou'd not enter, so you may see a thick Scull is of Service on some Occasions."[12]

The attackers knew their white victims were English, but they had been told by some Frenchmen that the Indians with them were Cherokees. This error of identification turned out to be the luckiest break for the English and the worst possible blow for the rascally French and recalcitrant Illinois who hoped to keep up hostilities.

As soon as the Shawnees, Delawares, and Senecas had identified themselves, the Kickapoos and Mascoutens were apologetic and fearful of the revenge that would be visited upon them. They released the Indian deputies, who apparently struck off for Fort de Chartres at Croghan's bidding. With the Englishmen still prisoners, however, the marauders hurried up the Wabash to Vincennes. Captain St. Ange had left two residents as civil and military leaders of the settlement.

"I found," Croghan wrote, and his report is here edited, "a village of about 80 or 90 French families settled on the east side of this river, being one of the finest situations that can be found. The country is level and clear, and soil very rich, producing wheat and tobacco. I think the latter preferable to that of Maryland or Virginia. The French inhabitants hereabouts are an idle lazy people, a parcel of renegades from Canada, and are much worse than Indians. They took a secret pleasure at our misfortunes and the moment we arrived they came to the Indians, exchanging trifles for their valuable plunder. As the savages

[12] Croghan's letter to Murray, July 12, 1765, Gage Papers.

took from me a considerable quantity of gold and silver in specie, the French traders extorted 10 half-Johannas [worth nearly nine dollars] from them for one pound of vermillion. There is likewise an Indian village of the Piankeshaws, who were very much displeased with the party that took me, telling them: 'Our and your chiefs are gone to make peace, and you have begun a war for which our women and children will have reason to cry.' "[13]

The attackers replied that since their father (the French king) had given them the hatchet to strike the English, they would not release Croghan until they heard from their chiefs. Accordingly they continued their journey up the river to their own village near Fort Ouiatenon. About fourteen French families lived in the abandoned fort, and the Weas also had a settlement there. The latter were indignant over the assault. On June 30 the Kickapoo and Mascouten chiefs returned from Illinois and expressed their disapproval of the capture. Next day Croghan and his party were set at liberty.

Croghan counselled with the Wabash tribes and obtained their consent to British possession of posts in their country. He discovered that these nations now were so fearful of Shawnee revenge that they were glad to secure the protection of British soldiers. The Miamies also sent their chiefs to make peace. Thus, the last of Pontiac's supporters were won away from him. Croghan then heard of Sinnott's difficulties in Illinois, but also received a message from Pontiac that he would be glad to see Croghan and was starting out to meet him. Croghan therefore struck out westward on July 18 to complete his mission.

Pontiac left Kaskaskia with deputies from the four Illinois nations, and the Seneca, Delaware, and Shawnee deputies. Just below modern Allerton, Illinois, he met Croghan and his party. Together they returned to Ouia-

[13] *Ill. Hist. Coll.*, XI, 31-32.

tenon, where Croghan held a formal council with Pontiac and the others. This was the first time that Pontiac had submitted directly to a deputy of Sir William Johnson, the Crown's agent, and bound himself to maintain peace. Although the treaty he made on this occasion was considered official, it was not yet final, for Croghan had been instructed to send Pontiac to Johnson for the conclusive ceremony.

Pontiac insisted upon one shrewd condition in his treaty: the British were not to regard their possession of the former French forts as giving them title to the country for Englishmen to settle, because the French had been there only as tenants, not as owners. When this condition was reported to General Gage, he would not admit it, because he was under the erroneous impression that the French had settled the Illinois country before the Indians did. Croghan, of course, never intended to respect the condition. He had the white man's contempt for the savages, recognizing them neither as human beings nor as nations endowed with rights and possessions. He often understood their feelings better than his policy-making superiors, but that understanding did not prevent him from taking advantage of the Indians when he could safely do so. He perceived Pontiac's abilities, just as Fraser had, but he had no interest in what Pontiac was fighting for. He sought only to use Pontiac for British ends.

"Pondiac is a shrewd sensible Indian of few words, and commands more respect amongst these nations than any Indian I ever saw could do amongst his own tribe," Croghan reported to Johnson. "He and all the principal men of those [Illinois] nations seem at present to be convinced that the French had a view of interest in stirring up the differance between His Majesty's subjects and them and call it a Beaver War."[14] But at the same time

[14] ibid., p. 53.

Croghan wrote to his assistant at Fort Pitt: "Pondiac and I is on extreame good terms and I am mistaken if I don't ruin his influence with his own people before I part with him."[15]

His mission successful, Croghan notified General Gage that a detachment could be safely dispatched from Fort Pitt to garrison Fort de Chartres. Making no further attempt to pursue his way to Illinois, he started for Detroit on July 25, accompanied by Pontiac and several other chiefs. Along his way Croghan picked up the remaining white prisoners among the Miamies and Ottawas on the Maumee. The party reached Fort Detroit on August 17, where a large body of Ottawas, Chippewas, Hurons, and Potawatomies were congregating in response to the invitation issued by Bradstreet a year ago. This was Pontiac's first entrance into the fort since May 8, 1763.

In company with Lieutenant Colonel Campbell, Croghan first held meetings with deputies of the Miamies, Weas, Piankashaws, Kickapoos, and Mascoutens. The latter were sorry for their recent misbehavior and all expressed satisfaction that terms had been made between the English and their neighboring nations. Each exhorted the other to behave himself and then asked for some clothing and rum. Finally Croghan got around on August 27 to meeting with Pontiac and the Ottawas, Chippewas, Hurons, and Potawatomies. In highly metaphorical language he painted the blessings of peace and urged the tribes to sustain it. He implied that he would like to see the Maumee Ottawas settle again on the Detroit River, where, of course, the fort commandant could keep tab on them.

The meeting broke up for that day to reconvene on the next. When all were assembled again, Pontiac replied:

"Father, we have all smoked out of the pipe of peace.

[15] Croghan to McKee, Aug. 3, 1765, Gage Papers.

It's your children's pipe, and as the war is all over and the Great Spirit and giver of light, who has made the earth and everything therein, has brought us all together this day for our mutual good to promote the good works of peace. I declare to all nations that I had settled my peace with you before I came here and now deliver my pipe to be sent to Sir William Johnson, that he may know I have made peace and taken the king of England for my father, in the presence of all the nations now assembled; and whenever any of those nations go to visit him they may smoke out of it with him in peace.

"Father, we are obliged to you for lighting up our old council fire for us and desiring us to return to it, but we are now settled on the Maumee River, not far from hence. Whenever you want us you will find us there ready to wait on you. The reason I chose to stay where we are now settled is that we love liquor, and did we live here as formerly, our people would be always drunk, which might occasion some quarrels between the soldiers and them. This, father, is all the reason I have for not returning to our old settlements, and since we live so nigh this place when we want to drink we can easily come for it."

Here he passed over a large pipe with a belt of wampum tied to it.

"Father, be strong and take pity on us, your children, as our former father did. 'Tis just the hunting season of your children. Our fathers, the French, formerly used to credit his children for powder and lead to hunt with. I request in behalf of all the nations present that you will speak to the traders now here to do the same. My father, once more I request you will take pity on us and tell your traders to give your children credit for a little powder and lead, as the support of our families depend upon it. We have told you where we live, that whenever you want us and let us know it, we will come directly to you."

He presented another wampum belt.

"Father, you stopped up the rum barrel when we came here, till the business of this meeting was over. As it is now finished, we request you may open the barrel that your children may drink and be merry."[16]

Croghan "unstopped" the rum barrels as requested, to satisfy the Indians. The chiefs of the Wabash tribes returned in a few days to repeat a sly warning to Croghan that the French had never conquered them or purchased a foot of their land. Hence, the French could not deed it to the English. The Indians had given the French liberty to settle in their country and in consequence "they always regarded us and treated us with great civility." Frankly, "we expect to have proper returns from you."

This concept spread rapidly among the nations at Detroit. The Hurons returned with a similar speech. On September 4 Pontiac and several chiefs of the Ottawas, Chippewas, and Potawatomies complained that the French had settled parts of their country without buying any tracts. They hoped that the English would consider this fact and make proper satisfaction for it, since the French occupants had now become British subjects. Pontiac explained that since their country was large, they were willing to give up parts of it to the English for forts and trading posts, provided the Indians were paid and their hunting grounds were left undisturbed.

The savages were clearly in the right. The French were tenants and maintained themselves in peaceful occupancy by frequently making presents to the Indians. The British government, however, professed to be governed in such transactions by international law, which as we have seen was not universal law. Indian nations not being regarded as members of the "family of nations" had no rights at the bar of international justice. As far as Britain was con-

[16] *Ill. Hist. Coll.*, XI, 46-47.

cerned, France and France alone owned Canada and Louisiana by right of exploration and settlement. France alone had the power to cede those provinces to someone else, in this case her conqueror. The Indians had no more rights than the wild animals that roved over the land— except that they were more troublesome and had to be mollified with gifts, payments, deeds, treaties, and other instruments by which the white man salved his own conscience and recognized their ownership of the land but not their sovereignty.

No doubt Croghan assured Pontiac that his wishes would be respected, although he knew that his British superiors would never recognize such limitations on the domain they had wrested from France with bloodshed. If Pontiac could have carried his point, he would have won his war despite the fact of defeat at arms. But he was opposing a conception of land tenure, of sovereignty, and of war as old as Europe and as fundamental as life itself to the European.

The net result of all these protests by Pontiac and the other chiefs was simply that some of the French residents at Detroit and some of the English traders and officers who wanted to secure land there sought deeds from the Indians to strengthen their claims or purchases. Several such deeds signed by Pontiac in September survive.[17] Pontiac's mark was simply a spiral, such as a child might draw, and never twice alike.

[17] On Sept. 8, 1765, Pontiac deeded a parcel of land on the south side of the river to Dr. George C. Anthon. On Sept. 17 he signed two deeds: one to Lieut. Edward Abbott for a tract on the south side of the river (Sandwich township, Essex County, Ontario), four acres in width on the waterfront and extending back from the shore eighty acres in length; and one to Mini Chesne on the north side of the river. The next day Pontiac deeded the tract lying just east of Lieut. Abbott's grant and of the same size to Alexis Maisonville. The deeds were drawn up in the presence of Croghan.

Croghan left Detroit on September 26 for Niagara to report to Johnson and Gage on Indian affairs in the West. British troops under Capt. Thomas Stirling reached Fort de Chartres on October 9 and took possession. Captain St. Ange removed his garrison across the river and northward to the new settlement of St. Louis, there to await the coming of the Spaniards. He was followed by many of the French and savages of the Illinois Confederation. The British consequently found themselves in possession of a half-abandoned district. They renamed the fort Cavendish, but the old name stuck in most minds.

Croghan's boast that he would ruin Pontiac as an Indian leader apparently was not fulfilled. The wily agent did something, however, which aroused the jealousy of the other tribes toward Pontiac. Perhaps it was as subtle as paying excessive attention to the Ottawa chief and showing him great deference. A letter mentioning that jealousy, which showed itself immediately after Croghan departed, alludes also to "Pontiac's sickness." His illness must have occurred late in September or early in October. Unfortunately for the completeness of this narrative the letter, written by Lieutenant Hay on October 5 to Johnson, was destroyed by fire, and only the briefest statement of its contents survives.

Doubtless Pontiac returned to his village on the Maumee in October and under the necessity of hunting may have moved farther south. Nothing was heard from him at the forts during the winter. He was under promise, though, to go to Sir William Johnson in the spring.

20

Formal Treaty Negotiations

To escort the western Indian chiefs safely to Fort Ontario at Oswego, New York, to meet Johnson, George Croghan sent Hugh Crawford to Detroit in the spring of 1766. Crawford was the Pennsylvania trader who had accompanied Lieutenant Ross to Fort de Chartres the year before. He arrived in Detroit on May 6 and set about calling in the principal chiefs of the Ottawas, Chippewas, Potawatomies, and Hurons who were delegated to attend the congress. Although Lieutenant Colonel Campbell was not impressed by his abilities and thought him extravagant, he discharged his mission carefully and won the friendship of all the Indians he accompanied.

Pontiac arrived in Detroit early in June and waited there until the party was ready to sail. As the other chiefs gathered, their old jealousy of Pontiac cropped out again. For one thing, the story of the pension offered by Bradstreet was revived, and some of the Indians thought that Pontiac would begin collecting his enviable annuity from Johnson. It was rumored that the chief would be paid ten shillings a day by the crown—a sum equal to the pay of an army captain![1]

The Ottawa chief also became involved in a fight that may have had some bearing on his fate three years later. Three Illinois Indians, a chief and two others, reached Detroit on their way to the Oswego council. In some sort

[1] Evidence of a trader named Young, in Benjamin Roberts' letter to Sir William Johnson, June 3, 1766, *Johnson Papers*, v, 279; McLeod to Johnson, Aug. 4, 1766, Stone's *Johnson*, II, 279.

of quarrel or drunken fight, Pontiac stabbed the chief. The wound was so serious that the three Illinois savages did not continue their journey.[2] No further mention of the incident was made, not even by Johnson at the congress. If the stabbing took place during a drunken frolic, the Illinois chief probably bore Pontiac no malice, as Indians did not hold one another accountable for their conduct while drunk. But if it was a sober assault, the reception which Pontiac met in Illinois in 1769 perhaps may have had its inception in this encounter.

Crawford, Lieut. Jehu Hay, newly appointed commissary for Indian affairs at Detroit, Elleopolle Chesne, interpreter, Pontiac, and the other chiefs, composing a party of perhaps forty, left Detroit shortly after June 20 and were at Fort Erie (Fort Erie, Ontario) by June 27. The story is related that shortly after arriving, Pontiac heard several muskets discharged. He showed great fear, thinking that he might be in a trap. The firing, it turned out, was caused only by some soldiers shooting at a flock of pigeons. The travelers stayed at the fort long enough for the commandant, Lieut. John Carden, to obtain a deed of land at Detroit from Pontiac, and for the chief to talk with Maj. Robert Rogers, who was on his way to command Fort Michilimackinac.

On July 1 the party was at Fort Niagara, where Benjamin Roberts, the Indian commissary, made them welcome with a little tobacco and rum. Pontiac probably renewed his acquaintance with Capt. Thomas Morris, who was now commanding Fort Niagara. Next morning the chiefs and their escort went aboard another vessel on Lake Ontario. Roberts sailed with them on this final stretch, but returned at once to his duties at Niagara. In two days they landed at Fort Ontario, at the mouth of the Onondaga River.

[2] Johnson Papers, v, 279, 289.

The fort was commanded by Capt. Jonathan Rogers of the 17th Regiment, but the Indian commissary there, Norman McLeod, took charge of the visitors. Johnson had not yet arrived; indeed, he had not been informed that the Indians were on their way. After a short-lived attempt to send the negotiators on to Johnson Hall, the Indians camped across the river from the fort and waited. Some Iroquois chiefs put in an early appearance and were followed about July 22 by Johnson himself. In his party were his sons-in-law, Daniel Claus and Guy Johnson, both in the Indian service, and Capt. John Butler, an officer in the late war, a friend and neighbor of Johnson now assisting him.

The congress opened on Tuesday morning, July 23, 1766. A bower or arbor to keep off the sun had been constructed, probably just outside the fort. There Johnson took his seat, flanked by Claus and Butler, with Guy Johnson acting as clerk. Hay and McLeod, Captain Rogers, Lieutenant Shalke, and Ensign Banks from the fort completed the British representation. Facing them were all the Indian chiefs assembled to listen and reply.

Johnson convened the first meeting with the usual ceremonies of welcoming the chiefs and begging them to be open-minded and attentive. He also condoled with the Hurons for the recent death of their chief Aughstaghregi and figuratively covered his grave with a belt of black wampum. After these formalities the meeting was adjourned, and Johnson spent the rest of the day in private conferences with the various chiefs.

As in modern conventions, most of the real diplomacy and bargaining was accomplished in these conversations with individual chiefs. Unfortunately, Johnson left no record of what occurred at those interviews, nor did he leave a note of his impressions on first meeting Pontiac. A guess may be hazarded that Johnson deliberately played up to the chief with Croghan's motive of undermining his standing among the western tribes by stirring their jealousy. The congress continued next day with everyone assembled as before. Tactfully Johnson lighted the pipe that Pontiac had sent to him by Croghan the previous fall and handed it around. Then he addressed them at some length.

Thanking them for their reception in the previous year of Croghan, whom he had sent again to Illinois this year, Johnson urged them to remember and abide by the promises they gave then. He reminded them of the benefits of peace: traders at the posts, interpreters, gunsmiths, surgeons, and commissaries. Hunting and trapping therefore were now easier and more profitable. Referring to some recent crimes committed both by the Indians and by some frontiersmen on the savages, Johnson asked that they punish their guilty ones and assured them that the white murderers would be prosecuted. Finally he exhorted them to hold fast to "the chain of friendship" and to listen no more to "bad birds who come with false stories to lead you astray."[3]

Pontiac responded with a brief acknowledgment. "Father, your children heartily thank you for what you have said to them today, and have heard with pleasure as everything is good and will give an answer to every article of it tomorrow. If we should forget anything [I] beg you will remind us of our omission, as we would be sorry to forget any part of it."

Teata, the Huron chief who had reluctantly taken part in the war for a short time, spoke first next day. He responded properly to all of Johnson's points. Then Pontiac addressed the congress:

[3] Guy Johnson's minutes of the congress in the Gage Papers, vol. 57; also printed in Docs. Rel. Col. Hist. N.Y., vii, 854-867.

"Father, I beg you will attend to what I have to say and that you will make allowance for my want of understanding. Father, we heartily thank the Great Spirit for affording us so fine a day to meet upon such good affairs. I speak in the name of all the nations to the westward whom I command. It is the will of the Great Spirit that we should meet here today, and before Him and all present I take you by the hand and never will part with it, and I call Him to witness that what I now say I shall steadfastly perform, for since I took Col. Croghan, whom you sent to us last year, by the hand I have not let it slip. From this day I am resolved to hold your hand faster than ever, for I perceive that the Great Spirit who has made all these lands about us will have it so. Father, while my father of France was in this country, I held him by the hand and never did any bad action. Now he is gone, I this day take you by the hand in the name of all the nations, of which I will acquaint those at home, and promise as long as I live no evil shall ever happen about Detroit, if in my power to prevent it."

He handed Johnson a wampum belt of seven rows of beads.

"Father, you told us yesterday to have sense and to avoid those bad people who delight in doing mischief and disturbing the public tranquility, and you may be assured we shall observe what you said. You likewise advised us of Mr. Croghan's journey to the Illinois and desired that we would take care that he returned safe. Father, be assured he shall meet with no insult, for on my arrival at my village I'll send some of my warriors to conduct him back in safety. You had no reason, father, to be angry at the disasters of last year; the conduct of the Indians there was without my knowledge and contrary to my inclinations and advice, which was to behave in the most friendly manner to all the English they met with, but their minds were afterwards poisoned by some other people which has since given me great concern."

Here he offered a belt of nine rows of beads.

"Father, this day you have conferred a signal favor on us by releasing the Potawatomies [two prisoners held at Detroit], for which we all heartily thank you, and that nation in particular. Father, it was contrary to my advice that the Potawatomies acted this bad part, for I charged them the day I took your deputy, Mr. Croghan, by the hand to lay aside all their hatred to the English, but they have not observed my advice. Father, you told us yesterday that when the Potawatomies were delivered up to us, we should bring in every person belonging to you amongst us, and you may be assured as soon as I return I'll make a search among the several nations and should any yet remain amongst us, they shall all be delivered up to the commissary."

Two belts of five rows and one of six were given.

"Father, we thank you for the goodness you have for us in sending plenty of merchandise to Detroit. This will be a great means of promoting a good understanding between us, as it will enable us to clothe our children well. We likewise heartily thank you for not letting the traders straggle through the woods to our villages, but to trade only at the posts under the inspection of the commissaries. It was not prudent to let them ramble where they pleased, but as you have settled it, there will be no danger along the waters to the forts and then we shall be justly dealt with."

A belt of six rows.

"Father, though you address me, yet it is the same as if you address all the different nations. Father, this belt is to cover and strengthen your chain of friendship, and I lay it over yours to show you that if any nation attacks you or would trouble the earth, we shall feel it first and resent it. Father, yesterday you told us to turn our eyes towards the sun rising; I do and when I get home I shall desire all the nations to do the same, and there they will always see their father and by stretching out their hands they can always take hold of his."

A belt of ten rows.

"Father, we thank you for having appointed Mr. Hay our commissary, as he is a man we know and esteem. Father, here's a man"—pointing to Hugh Crawford—"who has made a friendship with me and for whom I have a great regard, who brought me here, and who knows our customs and affairs. I beg therefore that as Detroit is a place where much business is transacted, you'll appoint Mr. Crawford to be assistant to Mr. Hay; at any rate we expect you'll permit him to return with us."

The conceit in this speech may not have been well received by the other chiefs. No doubt Pontiac had been selected to make the speech in behalf of the western nations, but they hardly authorized him to say that he commanded them—if we may credit the interpreter that he really said this. His general tone was unmistakably paternalistic toward the Great Lakes and Wabash tribes. He was not the defeated, cringing Indian pleading for his fellows, but a recent adversary of first rank dealing with the Crown's agent on terms of equality.

Bad weather delayed the second round of speeches for two days; then Johnson addressed the savages again. The only new topic he introduced concerned the belts of war wampum still outstanding. He asked that the tribes recall those they had sent out and return those they had received. When he had finished, Pontiac replied:

"Father, I thank you for everything you have said, it being all very good and true and meant for our interest and welfare. I think with you it's very necessary that all the belts you mentioned should be withdrawn and thank you sincerely for your advice. We shall now take everything you said into consideration and tomorrow morning answer you fully thereupon."

Presumably the chiefs conferred again and discussed their reply. Again Pontiac was chosen to answer or insisted upon speaking. Accordingly he addressed Johnson the next day.

"Father, we thank you for the good advice you have given us, since we have been here, as it is all good and for our benefit. Father, you may be assured we shall do everything you have desired of us; we shall do nothing but what is good and reject everything bad, not only me but all the nations of whom I am master to the northward. You may be sure by this string I shall fulfill my promise."

He handed over a wampum string of four branches.

"Father, yesterday you told me that the traders should all remain at the posts, which gives me pleasure, as it is agreeable to the great king our father's orders, but we hope that the trader who is at present at Fort Erie, called Male, may be continued, as it will prevent the trouble we shall have in going over the carrying place to Fort Niagara. That is all I have now to say or ask."

Offering a final string of wampum, Pontiac sat down. The Huron chief, Teata, followed him with a brief speech, and then the Onondaga speaker answered for the Iroquois about the war wampum. He said that the belt Pontiac had sent to them must be among the Senecas, who had not told them of it. The only other belt the Iroquois admitted having was one from the Miamies given them as a warning of danger from tribes farther west. The Iroquois would be glad to return it now with thanks.

"I shall return this belt to the Miamies myself," said Pontiac, "and tell them your sentiments."

At the next session of the congress, Johnson delivered his final speech winding up the proceedings. He then announced that he had presents for the conferees which would be distributed tomorrow. Pontiac gave the valedictory.

"Father, you may be sure that all my brothers to the westward shall hear everything that has so happily passed here, and that I will as long as I live do nothing but shall be agreeable to my father, and that all the nations over whom I have any influence shall do the same. I shall at all times do everything in my power to assist you to preserve the public tranquility from being disturbed. Father, all our brethren here present have heard your good advice and are of the same opinion with me and promise that since you have been so good as to bury everything that was or might be disagreeable to us, we shall reject everything that tends to evil and strive with each other who shall be of the most service in keeping up that friendship that is so happily established between us. Father, it will take some time before I can make known to all the nations what has passed here, but I will do it even from the rising of the sun to the setting and from north to south.

"Father, we heartily thank you for your present and are well convinced thereby of the goodness of the great king, our father, and shall follow your advice in conserving it in the manner you mention. Father, we acquiesce in everything you have said, both as to trade and everything else, being convinced you do everything for our good. We heartily wish all the English may continue to us their promised friendship, and we hope to convince you by our future conduct that we are thankful for the good advice we have received and determined to fulfill our engagements."

The gifts were distributed to the Indians next day and were warmly received. Among other parcels each chief received a silver medal bearing the inscription: "A pledge of peace and friendship with Great Britain, confirmed in

1766." Johnson took leave of the western chiefs on July 31, and Pontiac said they proposed to visit him at his home next spring. Johnson departed that same day, well pleased with the congress. Pontiac likewise was satisfied and flattered. He had been addressed and had spoken as the leader of all the western nations, and the king's agent had sought his friendship. The spotlight had been focused on him for the past several days, but this climactic appearance on the stage of Indian diplomacy was his last role of consequence. Once returned home he was destined to lose influence steadily.

Perhaps he overplayed his part at Fort Ontario; perhaps Johnson cunningly kept him in the limelight. Whatever the cause, the respect and honors shown him did not sit well with the other chiefs. McLeod reported to Johnson after the congress that a French trader from Detroit "offered to lay me a bet that Pontiac would be killed in less than a year, if the English took so much notice of him."[4]

[4] Stone, *Johnson*, II, 279. The printing of part of this letter is not mentioned in the *Johnson Papers*, V, 340, where it is said to have been burned and is only summarized from the description in the calendar.

〈〈〈〈◊〉〉〉〉

21

Peace—and Persecution

PONTIAC LEFT OSWEGO ON JULY 31, 1766, in company
with Hugh Crawford, Teata, and some other Indian
chiefs. The return journey was by way of Niagara and Fort
Erie to Detroit, where they arrived on August 31. Pontiac
does not appear to have stayed any time in Detroit, but
continued on his way to his village on Indianola Island in
the Maumee.

With the memory of the deference shown him by Sir
William Johnson still fresh in his mind and with the presents he had received not yet used up, Pontiac's new-found
ardor for the English burned warmly during the autumn.
Whether he fulfilled his promise of sending warriors to
escort George Croghan back from Illinois is not known;
Croghan did not return eastward overland, but sailed
down the Mississippi and reached New York by ship.
Pontiac did make an effort to round up the remaining
English prisoners among his neighbors, and by means of
his couriers probably publicized the council, as he had
promised Johnson he would.

He had not been back in his village long before he was
visited by a Wea chief called the Goose, who had accompanied Croghan and Pontiac to Detroit in 1765, and some
Miamies. They offered him two belts of war wampum.
One had originated with the French officers across the
Mississippi, the other with the Arkansaws, a branch of the
Siouan nation. The message of both belts was an inquiry
why Pontiac had buried the hatchet and a request that he
take it up and "keep it bright till spring, when it should

be used with more vigor than ever."[1] Pontiac refused to accept the belts and warned the people of his village not to listen to such arguments, as he was resolved henceforth to believe only what he heard from the English. Then he sent his nephew to Detroit to notify Lieutenant Hay and Capt. George Turnbull, the new commandant, of his demonstration of loyalty.

Pontiac's indifference to this proposal did not prevent the conspiratorial French on the Spanish side of the Mississippi from approaching his former allies at the same time. An Indian deputy appeared at Fort St. Joseph with seven belts of wampum which he said he had received from Captain St. Ange at St. Louis with directions to carry them to Wasson, the Chippewa chief at Saginaw Bay, for distribution among the tribes between Detroit and Michilimackinac. The purport of these belts was the old lie that the king of France was sending another army up the Mississippi under a Spanish officer and that the Indians should hold themselves ready to strike the English when the word was given. Maj. Robert Rogers at Michilimackinac and Lieutenant Hay at Detroit were sure the army was fiction, but tried nonetheless to have the Indians surrender the belts as evidence of good faith.

Toward the end of the year Pontiac sent word to Johnson that he would bring several western chiefs with him when he should make the journey to Johnson Hall in the spring. Then the winter swallowed him up. The ever-present necessity of providing food for his family doubtless took him to his winter hunting grounds, probably on the Wabash or the White River.

Word reached Captain Turnbull early in May 1767, that Pontiac would arrive in a few days with three English prisoners, two from the Potawatomies at St. Joseph and one from his own nation on the Maumee. Pontiac

[1] Turnbull's letter to Gage, Oct. 19, 1766, Gage Papers.

⟨ 299 ⟩

did reach Detroit late in May in company with a band of Kickapoos, with whom he may have spent the winter. To the joy of the traders they brought with them more than a hundred packs of peltry, but not the three prisoners. Pontiac did his trading and stayed on at the fort. Apparently he had lost a child by death since his last visit to Detroit, for Lieutenant Hay gave him some appropriate present to "cover" the child's grave, according to Indian custom. Pontiac was still there on June 6, but seems to have returned to his village sometime during the month. For some reason he did not go east as planned; indeed, he never saw Sir William Johnson again.

Summer passed without further word from him. Meanwhile, trouble was fomenting in the Shawnee country. The determined encroachment of white settlers over the Alleghenies on lands recognized as belonging to the Indians, and the insufficient effort of troops at Fort Pitt to dispossess them provoked the Delawares and Shawnees to call a general council of the western tribes. Each was asked to send deputies for the purpose of making a united appeal to Captain St. Ange at St. Louis for ammunition and assistance in resisting the English. Johnson was gravely disturbed when he learned of this proposed council, and he dispatched Croghan to attend it and then go on to Detroit to allay ill feeling there. In addition, a murder had been committed by two Chippewas at Detroit, and a party of Ottawas and Chippewas from Saginaw Bay, led by Pontiac's nephew, had recently killed eleven traders on the Ohio River.

About the middle of August, Pontiac sent word to Lieutenant Hay that he had no corn and was therefore going hunting. Whether bad weather had ruined his corn, or his village had failed to plant a proper crop, he did not say. He alluded to his failure to visit Johnson Hall and said he would make the trip next spring. He assured Hay that he had no bad design in leaving his village so early in the season; on the contrary he was still recommending friendship with the English wherever he went and "was not one of those who, like dogs, did nothing but try to bite wherever they could."[2]

His continued allegiance to the English was undermining his influence, for it became known that he now had a strong faction against him in his own nation. The situation was just the reverse of that in 1763, when his stubborn hostility to the English raised a faction under Manitou favoring peace.

Pontiac's message crossed a summons Hay was sending to the chief, asking him to appear in Detroit as a witness in a criminal case. Captain Turnbull had just arrested Alexis Cuillerier, who had fled Detroit in 1763 because of his part in the war, for murder on the sworn accusation of one John Maiet. Young Cuillerier was accused of having deliberately drowned Betty Fisher, seven-year-old daughter of Mr. and Mrs. James Fisher, themselves among the first victims of Pontiac's war. The crime had taken place at the Ottawa village on the Maumee in 1764 where the girl was held prisoner. The accused's relatives were trying desperately to clear him and had asked to have Pontiac's testimony. The examination of Cuillerier was abruptly prevented by his escape from custody on August 17, before Pontiac arrived.

In response to Hay's urgent message, Pontiac postponed his hunting trip and reached Detroit on August 29. He expressed great regret about the behavior of the Saginaw Bay Indians and said he wished his treacherous nephew were dead. He readily detailed the manner in which the little Fisher girl was killed. She had been sick for some time with a "flux," or dysentery, and in a moment of rage over her soiling some of his clothes, Pontiac

[2] *Johnson Papers*, v, 637.

picked her up and threw her in the Maumee River. Young Cuillerier, or Muchet as he was called by the Indians, then waded into the stream and held the unfortunate child under water until she drowned. He also carried her out and buried her.

In his accusation John Maiet had related that Pontiac was angered by the girl's attempt to stay near his fire while her soiled clothes were drying. After throwing her into the river, Pontiac called to "Mushett Cuerié" to go drown the child. "You bragged of your courage. Show me now if you are a man or not." Cuillerier took no notice until Pontiac spoke a second time, and then he committed the revolting murder. Maiet helped him bury the child.[3]

Pontiac's story was not what Cuillerier's relatives expected or wished him to relate, and as soon as they learned what he had said they went to him and persuaded him to change his testimony. Knowing that Pontiac himself would escape punishment for such a crime and playing on his affection for the French and the Cuillerier family in particular, they urged him to assume all blame for the murder. In company with the relatives, Pontiac went back to see Hay and confessed that he had lied the first time and now wished to say that he himself had drowned the child.

In their anxiety the relatives went too far. They introduced certain local inhabitants who swore that Pontiac had told them of his guilt and that the interpreter must have misunderstood or twisted the confession. Hay at once suspected what had happened and put the interpreter, Elleopolle (Mini) Chesne, on oath. He swore that his rendering of Pontiac's testimony was correct the first time and that further Pontiac had told him once last winter of young Cuillerier's having drowned the child.

[3] Maiet's accusation, Aug. 4, 1767, was not sent to Gage by Turnbull until Apr. 25, 1768, Gage Papers.

As there were a number of other chiefs in Detroit at this time, Hay questioned two of them on the murder case. Oskkigoisin, Pontiac's brother-in-law, testified that Pontiac had thrown the child in the river, but that Cuillerier had plunged in and drowned her. Later Pontiac's nephew, who had come to defend himself over the murder of the English traders on the Ohio, asserted that he had seen the whole incident, and he related it just as Pontiac had the first time. This testimony was taken in the presence of Pontiac and he was somewhat chagrined at being discovered in his attempted lie. Hay then turned to the chief and tried to explain the law in the case. He added that everything which had happened during the late war was forgiven the Indians, and if anyone tried to make them believe the English conspired against them, he should be punished.

"Father," Pontiac answered, "no one has said anything to me upon this subject, and if they had I should not have listened to them. I should be glad this man [Cuillerier] could be pardoned if caught again. If I thought he would and could find him, I would bring him in myself. Nay, I would go to my father, Sir William Johnson, was it not so late, if I thought he would be pardoned."[4]

Hay explained that it was not in Johnson's power to pardon a Frenchman accused of crime. As Pontiac had put himself out to come to Detroit and had delayed his hunting, Hay promised him some clothes and ammunition when he should depart. Pontiac made one further request.

"Father, I shall repeat a few words that my father, Sir William Johnson, told me last year. He said, 'Child, here is Mini Chesne, who will go with you to your winter quarters and remain with you, and will be your ear to listen and report anything you have to say to Mr. Hay,

<hr />

[4] *Johnson Papers*, v, 673.

commissary at Detroit.' Accordingly, he went with me, and I hope you'll let him go with me now."[5]

Hay refused to let Chesne leave Detroit, however, as he was about to lose his own interpreter and needed Chesne for himself. Pontiac left Detroit about the middle of September 1767, probably on the 14th, and on the 15th Chesne ran off to the Maumee without Hay's permission. Toward the end of the month Hay dispatched a Frenchman to the Maumee with a present of ammunition for Pontiac and a letter to Chesne demanding his return to duty at Detroit. But Pontiac had already gone to the Wabash to hunt, and Chesne, although he received the message, had fallen in with a French trader and said he would not return. Captain Turnbull was of the opinion that Chesne had been threatened by Cuillerier's relatives.

As for the ominous and impending grand council to be held at the Lower Shawnee Town (near Chillicothe, Ohio), George Croghan reached Fort Pitt in October on his way to it and there learned that it had been postponed until spring. Nevertheless, he pressed on to Detroit to fulfill another part of his mission and in quest of the tribe which had originally called the meeting. He arrived in Detroit on November 15.

At a council with the chiefs of the Ottawas, Chippewas, and Hurons still in the vicinity, Croghan learned what had happened. The Iroquois, particularly the Senecas, claimed the land between the crest of the Alleghenies and the Ohio River which was being unlawfully settled. It was the old story: the white people not only tried to keep the Indians off this land in traveling, but they also drove out the game by their very presence. So the Senecas quietly had passed a belt to the Mississaugi-Chippewas of Toronto urging a general conference of the Iroquois and western nations in the fall at the Lower Shawnee Town.

[5] ibid., p. 673.

The Mississaugies carried the belt to their Chippewa relatives at Saginaw Bay. They in turn informed the tribes on the Wabash and Illinois, as well as the Shawnees and Delawares. For some reason, probably because of their loyalty to the English, the Hurons were not invited to attend. The Chippewa chiefs told Croghan that the meeting's only purpose was to iron out some disputes between the western and northern (Iroquois) nations and to talk over the conduct of the English. Croghan knew that such a negotiation was only preliminary to united action of a belligerent nature directed, without a doubt, against the English.

Whether Pontiac's refusal to participate in the congress disturbed the plans, or whether the trouble the Chippewas and Ottawas feared might result from the rash killing of the English traders on the Ohio dissuaded them, the Chippewas had broadcast a postponement of the meeting. The crisis was past for that year, but Croghan feared a renewal of activity in the spring. He pleaded the certainty of justice being done the Indians in regard to the illegal settlements, and to show the Chippewas how highly the English regarded them, he returned the two Chippewas who had been sent down to Johnson for killing a white man at Detroit. The gesture mollified the Chippewas, as Johnson anticipated it would.

To the Ottawas Croghan issued a warning that they must control their young men and that Johnson might yet demand the murderers of the English traders for punishment. Then he particularly thanked the Hurons for their uniformly good conduct toward the English. Although successful in averting a rupture with the western Indians that winter, Croghan was pessimistic over what the spring would bring. He warned both Johnson and General Gage that a great many gifts would be required to preserve peace if no other action were taken by the colonies.

Although Pontiac's allegiance to the English may not have been the principal factor in upsetting the grand conference, his attitude was steadily increasing the opposition to him in the village he nominally ruled. Captain Turnbull reported rumors that Pontiac had been given beatings by his tribe more than once and that his influence was waning. He spent the winter hunting in the Wabash region below Ouiatenon. In April 1768 Hay sent him a message asking him to come to Detroit when he returned to his village. With the secretarial help of a Frenchman at Ouiatenon, Pontiac dictated a reply to Hay on May 10 which revealed that he was virtually in exile.

"My father:

"I have no complaint whatever against the English. It is only my young men who have shamed me. This has obliged me to leave my village. It is solely against my own nation that I am offended, by the several insults they have made me, saying that I was never chief. I have replied to them, 'You are chiefs like me; make arrangements to command the village. As for me, I am leaving it.'

"I have spoken to Sir William Johnson. He had bound me to him, and I am still united with him.

"My father, it appears that you have sent to see me. I will go next spring. I am hunting at present in order to pay my debts. I am going to Illinois to find the brothers of my wife. On my return next spring, I repeat, I will go to Detroit.

"My father, I am loyal. I never listen to the bad birds and never pay any attention to those who speak against me.

"My father, if I go to the Illinois it is of my own free will. No one calls me there. It is only to get some shot. Do

⟨ 306 ⟩

not think I go there to complain. Sir William Johnson and I have put away all bad happenings.

"My father, I always hold fast to your hand, as you tell me to by your belt and twist of tobacco, which I have accepted and which is proof that I have never acted to perpetrate any bad affairs. I tell you goodbye until next spring and I hold you ever by the hand.

"Ouiatanon, 10 May 1768, in presence of Mr. Maisonville and several other Frenchmen."[6]

Pontiac went to Illinois as he stated. He paid his respects to the Indian commissary, Edward Cole, at Fort de Chartres and received some presents. There were several Indians with him. He told Cole that he had come to visit his brethren in that region and to learn their sentiments and dispositions. If he found any "bad reports amongst them" (*i.e.* hostility toward the English) he declared he would warn them to shut their ears against all bad birds. What else he said to Cole is unfortunately not known, as the rest of Cole's memorandum to Johnson was burned.

Pontiac had no trouble finding "bad birds" at first, for early in May a band of Potawatomies from St. Joseph, threatening to strike the English, had carried off a soldier and his wife from Cahokia. Kaskaskias and Michigameas had been dispatched in pursuit of the kidnappers, but lost their trail in heavy rains. The Potawatomies, however, brought back their two prisoners unharmed in June and begged forgiveness for their rash act. Some Chippewas, Ottawas, and Kickapoos were at St. Louis supposedly on their way south to attack the Cherokees, but they were expressing hostility toward the English, too. The simmering pot of ill-feeling among the western nations finally

[6] Enclosed in Turnbull's letter to Gage, June 14, 1768, Gage Papers.

boiled over late in June, when some Indians of Vincennes
—Piankashaws and their neighbors—killed nine English
traders on the Shawnee River (Cumberland River, Kentucky) and another Englishman out of a party of Virginia
hunters on the Green River (in Kentucky) early in July.

Pontiac was not connected with these events. Indeed,
neither his movements nor his speeches were referred to
again by the officers of Fort de Chartres. No doubt he
crossed the Mississippi and visited his French friends in
St. Louis. What else happened to him we are left to con-
jecture, but presumably he did have trouble with the
Illinois tribes before he left. Possibly it was a personal
slight or insult; possibly one or more of his Ottawa followers fought with or was killed by some Illinois. International jealousies may be ruled out, as both the Illinois
and Pontiac were on the friendliest terms with the
English in 1768. From subsequent events it seems apparent that Pontiac left the region in a hostile mood,
threatening to return in the spring with enough braves to
punish the Illinois for whatever they had done.

When Pontiac left the country we do not know, but
probably he went only as far as the Wabash to hunt. It is
not likely that he returned to his village on the Maumee,
since he had exiled himself from it and as Captain Turnbull in Detroit would have heard of his return had he done
so. Once a chief whose words and actions influenced
eighteen tribes from Lake Ontario to the Mississippi,
Pontiac was now a hunter without a tribe or even a village
—only a following of a handful of relatives and close
friends who still believed in his prowess and his judgment.

---------------------------- 〈〈〈〈◊〉〉〉〉 ----------------------------

22

Assassination—and Fame

IN THE FATEFUL SPRING OF 1769, Pontiac again descended to the Mississippi to trade and talk and drink. News of his intended visit swept ahead of him and, owing to unknown incidents of the previous year, disturbed the Illinois tribes who had just come in from their hunting. They were not aware of Pontiac's lack of power and inability to muster a force of warriors.

Captain St. Ange still commanded at St. Louis, waiting for the Spaniards to arrive, but there was a new British commandant at Fort de Chartres. He was John Wilkins, now lieutenant colonel of the 18th or Royal Irish Regiment, and true to its name the most quarrelsome regiment on the continent. This was the same inept Wilkins who at Fort Niagara in 1763 had failed so often to succour Detroit. He knew little about Indians then, and he had learned nothing since.

The Kaskaskias, who lived south of Fort de Chartres, asked Wilkins on March 29 for powder and lead to protect themselves from Pontiac, who, they had been told, was coming with 150 canoes of northern Indians to make war on the Illinois Confederation! Next day Wilkins learned that Pontiac had arrived on foot at Cahokia, forty-five miles north, with thirty warriors. Even that number may have been exaggerated. Pontiac had with him his two grown sons and a few other Indians. He said he came to trade in peace and he did just that. His quarrel with the Illinois he had seemingly forgotten. He also visited St. Ange across the river and stayed for a few days with Pierre Laclede, a trader and the founder of St. Louis.

Cahokia, the oldest French settlement in Illinois, stood (and still stands as a suburb of St. Louis) on the east bank of the Mississippi, eighteen miles below the mouth of the Missouri. It was screened from the main channel of the river by Cahokia Island. The village comprised a Catholic church; a store operated by an agent for Baynton, Wharton, and Morgan, Philadelphia merchants; a ruined fort; and forty-five houses strung out for three-quarters of a mile along the river.

Near Cahokia was a village of Peorias. They now came to a decision to remove the menace of Pontiac forever by killing him.[1] Their motive is still unknown, but must have arisen from something that occurred during Pontiac's visit the year before. Moreover, they had a reputation for ambush and assassination as a policy of foreign relations, with the bully's surprise and outraged cry when they were drubbed for their cowardly attacks. They even discussed Pontiac's assassination in council, approved it generally, and then entrusted the treacherous job to the nephew of Makatachinga, or Black Dog, their chief. This council occurred in April. The young Peoria thereupon

[1] Parkman got the story from Pierre Chouteau (1758-1849) through his son, Liguest, in 1846 that Pontiac was killed by a Cahokia Indian who was instigated to the deed by an Englishman named Williamson. J. N. Nicollet obtained essentially the same story from Pierre Chouteau and Pierre Menard six or seven years before Parkman's interview, except that Nicollet reported that Williamson bribed a Kaskaskia Indian to do the deed. The only Williamson in Illinois I could find was Alexander Williamson, who was engaged by George Morgan of Baynton, Wharton, and Morgan, to take a cargo of goods to Vincennes in 1768. He was to trade them to the Indians and French and was expected to stay in Vincennes all winter. As March and April would be his busiest months of trading, it is unlikely that he could return to Illinois by the middle of April. Chouteau's story may have been part of the propaganda started by the Peorias and spread by the French.

sought the company of Pontiac and waited a proper opportunity to execute his black design. The Ottawa remained unaware of his danger.

The 20th of April found Pontiac again in Cahokia transacting some trade in the store of Baynton, Wharton and Morgan near the center of the village. He was unarmed and alone, except for the seemingly friendly Peoria brave with him. Together they left the store. Just as they emerged into the street, Pontiac ahead, the Peoria raised his club and struck him on the back of the head. Stunned, Pontiac sank to the ground. The Peoria leaped on him and stabbed him fatally, then fled. The great chief expired almost at once.[2]

The hubbub in the small settlement can be imagined. Apprehension tinged excitement. This was a foul deed, not a fair fight or an act justified by war. It was no ordinary assassination: the great Pontiac had been killed. What repercussions would that bring? The news was rushed down to Fort de Chartres by courier, was carried across the river to St. Louis. Pontiac was dead! Pontiac had been killed by a Peoria!

[2] This account of Pontiac's death is taken from Daniel Bloüin's ms. "Mémoire," pp. 17-20, as presented to General Gage in 1771. A merchant in Kaskaskia in 1769, Bloüin left Illinois in Sept. 1770, to seek redress from Gage for grievances against Wilkins. His lengthy manuscript complaint reviews the events of Wilkins' command and is the most detailed contemporary account of Pontiac's assassination yet found. Father Meurin, writing from Cahokia on June 14, 1769, said, "Pontiac was assassinated in this village in the second week after Easter." (*Ill. Hist. Coll.*, xvi, 556.) As Easter fell on Mar. 26 in 1769, the second week thereafter was April 2-8. It is apparent that the missionary's memory of the date was not exact, and that he made an error of two weeks. Both Bloüin and Meurin agree that Pontiac was killed right in the village of Cahokia, and not in the adjoining forest, as Parkman stated. Lyman C. Draper tried to persuade Parkman that the chief was killed near Fort de Chartres, rather than near Cahokia.

The two sons of Pontiac and a handful of Ottawas heard the news in grim silence. They did not wail in grief or cry out for revenge. They did not take the body back to their village. Quietly they departed homeward. Their behavior struck the Peorias uneasily. Fears grew. They sensed that they would hear more from the Ottawas. The war song rolling out of their council would be picked up by the Miamies, the Weas, the Kickapoos, the Mascou-tens, the Piankashaws, the Sacs, the Foxes, the Chippewas, the Potawatomies, the Hurons, the Shawnees, the Dela-wares, the Mingoes, the Senecas—all powerful nations who knew Pontiac well, who recalled his greatness, who respected him yet. The full force of the revenge they faced terrorized the Peorias. How could they shift the blame?

They considered flight and crossed the river to put themselves under the protection of St. Ange. To him they told a story of being instigated by the English to commit the murder. Whether or not St. Ange believed it, he sent out messages to the northern tribes that the English had set on an Indian to kill their chief and champion. But the cautious commandant would not let the Peorias stay, as he did not want his settlement involved in the results of their crime. They returned to the east side of the river, but the transactions of their council planning Pontiac's murder becoming known, they fled down to Fort de Chartres to appeal to the British commandant.

Wilkins had heard the story the French were spread-ing soon after he was informed of Pontiac's death. Wisely he ordered "the trader" at Cahokia to see that Pontiac was properly interred in the Indian manner—thereby pre-cipitating another historical mystery as to the place of burial.[3]

The unidentified trader—it could have been Baynton,

[3] Wilkins' orders for Pontiac's burial are found in his ms. "Journal of Indian Transactions," Gage Papers.

Wharton, and Morgan's agent, or a prominent French-man—may have buried Pontiac right there at Cahokia, which seems to be what Wilkins expected. He issued his order to show how much the English respected Pontiac and thereby to counteract the French propaganda. However, he did not follow up his request, and other evidence implies that the trader permitted the body to be taken across the river by the French, thus nullifying Wilkins' purpose.

The persistent tradition in St. Louis is that Pontiac's remains were brought across the river at St. Ange's request and buried in that town. One account gives him a funeral with military honors. Even so, the exact location of his last resting place in St. Louis is disputed. He may have been buried in the town's only graveyard, the Catholic cemetery adjoining the old Cathedral (which faced on Second Street, between Walnut and Market). Father Meurin complained in June 1769 that the French buried all the dead, Christian and pagan, in this cemetery.[4] The Missouri Historical Society, believing rather that Pontiac was not placed in consecrated ground, once determined the exact spot as twenty feet east of Broadway and fifty feet south of Market—two blocks west of the old cemetery and behind the village as it was laid out in 1769.[5] On the other hand, the St. Louis chapter of the Daughters of the American Revolution placed a tablet in the corridor of the Southern Hotel (razed in 1934) reading in part: "Near this spot was buried by his friend, Acting Governor

[4] Meurin's letter, June 14, 1769, cited above; Stevens, *St. Louis the Fourth City, 1764-1909*, p. 383.

[5] Stevens, *op. cit.*, p. 383. Auguste Chouteau owned the land in the vicinity of the Market and Broadway intersection and when he sold parcels of it later he specified that no further burials were to be made on it. Information from the title records of McCune Gill in St. Louis, by Robert F. Britton.

St. Ange, Pontiac."[6] The hotel was bounded by Broadway, Walnut, and Fourth Streets, in the block south of the spot selected by the Missouri Historical Society.

A more substantial, yet more tantalizing, piece of evidence is found in a letter from Lieutenant Hay to Sir William Johnson, written in August 1769. Hay mentioned the arrival in Detroit of a French trader. "The above Frenchman is an inhabitant of St. Louis and the person that buried Pontiac, who was   at his house."[7] The blank is at a point where part of the letter was burned away. The inference is plainly that Pontiac was buried in St. Louis, and if the missing word was "visiting," then the Frenchman probably was Pierre Laclede. It is remotely possible that the missing word might be "interred" or "buried," suggesting that the chief was placed on someone's private property, perhaps that of Laclede, whose house faced Main Street between Walnut and Market.

These possible burial spots are not as scattered as they may seem. All of the suggested places in St. Louis lie within a rectangle 1,200 by 450 feet. If Laclede's property is excluded as being the least likely place, the area is reduced to 900 by 450 feet. The next least likely burial spot is the Catholic cemetery, and if that is eliminated, the area of probable interment is only 300 by 450 feet, or the

[6] Stevens, op. cit., p. 385, and information from Robert F. Britton, to whom I am also indebted for a map of old St. Louis and measurements of the streets.

[7] Johnson Papers, VII, 94. There is a wild tale found in Drake's Book of the Indian, Book v, 57, that Pontiac was killed in 1779 when he spoke against the British during the American Revolution! An equally unfounded story noted in the McDougall MSS says that Pontiac died opposite Detroit about the beginning of the American Revolution (Parkman Papers, 23, p. 313). A little known Detroit tradition, probably connected with the above stories, has Pontiac buried on Apple Island in the center of Orchard Lake, just southwest of Pontiac, Michigan.

square and a half lying south of Market Street between Broadway and Fourth.

When the Peorias requested permission to leave their village and come under the protection of Fort de Chartres, Lieutenant Colonel Wilkins refused them. Instead, he sent them powder, lead, and rum to fortify themselves. Had he only continued this policy of disapproval toward the Peorias, he would have cleared the English in the eyes of the Ottawas. But, relenting shortly, he allowed the Peorias to move up next to the fort and build an entrenched and stockaded camp. Worse than that, he made no effort whatever to obtain satisfaction from them for the crime or to determine whether any Englishman might have been accessory to the deed.

The Ottawas and their allies may well have concluded that the rumor of English instigation was true. Yet the bloody revenge which the Illinois Confederation feared did not materialize. Doubtless there was division among the Ottawas, some not being sorry to have Pontiac eliminated. Tracks of skulking parties were found around Fort de Chartres, and six Kaskaskias were reported scalped by a party of Sacs and Foxes. Black Dog, the Peoria chief, profited by these alarms to obtain plenty of ammunition from Wilkins.

The news of Pontiac's assassination traveled east slowly. General Gage learned of it from Wilkins early in August and informed Johnson on August 6. As Johnson had been traveling through the Iroquois country for a month, Gage's letter was apparently his first notice of the event. Yet in his reply he did not allude to Pontiac. An Indian courier took the news to Fort Pitt on July 13, and the *Pennsylvania Gazette* (Philadelphia) published it on August 17. The general ferment among the tribes at the moment eclipsed interest in this particular crime.

One chief heard the shocking news with regret and

deepening anger. That was Minavavana, *Le Grand Saul-teur*, the great chief of the Chippewas. He had been Pontiac's ally in 1763, had joined him in an appeal to the Illinois tribes in 1764. A favorite of the French and hostile to the English, he was sympathetic with Pontiac's efforts and admired the Ottawa chief enough to feel that his assassination called for personal revenge. In April of 1770, Minavavana arrived secretly at Cahokia with only two other warriors. He had heard a story of the crime which led him to suspect the company clerk, who had waited on Pontiac in the store just before his assassination. The three Chippewas were bent on kidnapping and torturing the clerk. Fortunately for him, the clerk was absent when they entered the store. Enraged by this frustration, they went out again and finding two servants of the company nearby promptly killed them. The savages then left the vicinity with the warning that they would not be satisfied until they had exterminated the Illinois tribes and the English.[8]

Apart from this act of vengeance, which was not followed up, Pontiac's death caused no intertribal warfare. Other and more immediate occurrences provided the usual number of savage broils, and the northern and southern nations continued their ancient fighting.

As for Pontiac's descendants, they are as shadowy as his family life. His widow, Kan-tuck-ee-gun, was reported living at the mouth of the Maumee in 1807 with her son, Otussa. She was still there in 1815. B. F. Stickney, one of Lewis Cass's agents, found at this Ottawa village in 1825 a chief named Tus-saw (who may have been the same person as Otussa), but Stickney then identified him as Pontiac's nephew. A few months later the same writer

[8] Bloüin's ms. "Mémoire," Gage Papers. Both Lewis Cass in 1829 and Parkman in 1851 believed that Pontiac's murder precipitated a great war of revenge in which the Peorias were wiped out. There is no truth in this yarn.

spoke of him as Pontiac's grandson. Whoever Tus-saw was, son, nephew, or grandson, he was engaged in dictating a biography of his celebrated ancestor to Stickney for Cass. The manuscript notes, evidently unfinished, have not been found.

How many children Pontiac had is not known, and no daughters are mentioned. The two sons Pontiac definitely had in 1769 are not named. One of them probably was Shegenaba, who gained some prominence in 1775 on restoring to his family Ezekiel Field, who had been captured in the Battle of Point Pleasant. The names of two alleged sons of Pontiac were supplied by Jim Pontiac, elderly resident of northern Michigan. This man claimed to be the great-grandson of Pontiac. He mentioned Kasahda, a son of Pontiac, who died childless, and Nebah-kohum, younger brother of Kasahda, from whom Jim Pontiac was descended. Another informant, Katherine Osawagin, of Hessel, Michigan, who claimed descent from Pontiac, said that he had but one son, named Njikwisena, and a daughter. She also stated that Pontiac's "real" name was Tcimjikwis.

The name Pontiac occurred later in history, but whether the persons bearing it were relatives we have no way of knowing. A deed was signed on the Detroit River in 1786 by Pondiac Assinowee, among others. John Askin, Detroit trader, wrote out a bill in 1796 "for a loaf to Pontiac."[9] The Indian treaty made by Lewis Cass at the Maumee Rapids in 1817 was signed by an Ottawa who called himself Pontiac.

Other descendants of Pontiac are known, although their line of relationship is not. A Michigan Indian, named Okemos (1775-1858), claimed to be a nephew of Pontiac. Shabonee (c. 1775-1859), an Ottawa who married the daughter of Chief Spatke of the Potawatomies

[9] John Askin's account book, Burton Historical Collection.

and succeeded his father-in-law as chief of that tribe, said he was a grand-nephew of Pontiac. Henry R. Schoolcraft in 1846 said he had known a few years earlier an Ottawa chief on the Maumee called Atoka, who was a descendant of Pontiac. George Henry Pontiac, late resident of New-berry, Michigan, believed he was some relation to the chief.

Pontiac's fame is preserved today in obvious forms and curious byways. A motorcar manufacturer has borrowed his name for its product, and a Detroit brewer even markets "Chief Pontiac Beer." Robert Rogers first put the Ottawa leader into a book in 1765 with an inflated and inaccurate account of his power, and first enshrined him in imaginative literature in a dramatic tragedy called *Ponteach*, published in 1766. But it was Francis Parkman who actually dramatized him and spread his fame through-out the English-speaking world. His classic *History of the Conspiracy of Pontiac*, first published in 1851, passed through ten editions and many reprints, being republished last in 1929. It is Parkman's incomplete and not altogether accurate picture of Pontiac that has fascinated later writers on Indian topics. Customary and enduring fame has been accorded Pontiac by the naming of seven towns after him: in Michigan, Ohio, Illinois, Kansas, Missouri, New York, and Rhode Island. Pontiac Lake is found in Oakland County, Michigan, and a lake and county in the Province of Quebec, Canada, bear his name.

23

Retrospect

PONTIAC PASSED FROM THE SCENE without disturbing it because his power had so far diminished that he lacked enough friends to precipitate a war. He had fought a losing war and made peace without attaining any of his objectives. His old friends and supporters, the French, were banished from the continent or turned into British subjects or Spanish hirelings. The weapons and forts of the British soldiers rendered them too strong to oppose. The time for military greatness among the Indians had passed. Postwar leadership should have encouraged unity for strength and education for self-dependence to prevent the red men from becoming indolent beggars on the British, and later on the American, doorstep. The role probably held little attraction for Pontiac, even if he had perceived its need in the new order.

As long as two European powers vied for supremacy in North America, the Indians were courted by both sides. But the defeat of the French, who had held the western tribes in economic dependence for generations, left the Indians at the mercy of the British, who regarded them as an expensive nuisance. Pontiac fought to restore the relative independence enjoyed by the western Indians and to force the British to change their fundamental policy toward peoples of inferior culture. His aims appear to us today just and ethical, even though his savage manner of warfare is revolting and his hope to maintain a primeval wilderness on the edge of civilization was impractical. He wanted primarily to have the tribes left alone as sovereign nations attached to the French. He did not seek isolation. The Indians had already given up much of their coastal land, and they might from time to time sell small tracts. They were willing to engage in a trade that was profitable to white men because it was beneficial to themselves. They were hospitable to Christian missionaries. They disliked being required to deliver up fellow tribesmen accused of crimes against white people for trial under English law, but they would probably comply. As for irresponsibility, it existed on both sides: youthful or drunken warriors killed soldiers and frontier families, and renegade whites debauched, swindled, and killed innocent Indians.

The old dream of an Indian wilderness on the border of civilization, nevertheless, died slowly among the red men. Once again, in 1776, they espoused the losing side of a white man's war. With their defeat the old treaty boundary was nullified by the new United States of America, and western migration swelled. Joseph Brant, an educated Mohawk, tried to unite the Indians and with British support negotiate a new northwestern boundary with Congress, but diplomacy failed. Little Turtle, a Miami chief, thought he could do what Pontiac had attempted and for a time he was successful in holding back the Americans by delivering two military defeats to Generals Harmar and St. Clair. Gen. Anthony Wayne shattered this dream in 1794 at Fallen Timbers in Ohio. Then Tecumseh, a Shawnee, revived the idea of an Indian empire, but a premature battle in 1811 at Tippecanoe in Indiana ruined his scheme. Black Hawk, a Sauk, tried to maintain his people east of the Mississippi, but in 1832 was defeated in battle in Wisconsin. Crazy Horse, an Oglala Sioux, tried to break up the infamous reservation system in 1876 and defeated Generals Crook and Custer, but he had to surrender himself the following

year in Nebraska. None of these chiefs could realize that
Pontiac's failure in 1763 had demonstrated the impos-
sibility of their succeeding at a later date. He had struck
too late himself.

Pontiac's failure exposed all the defects of British
Indian policy, yet very few changes were inaugurated. The
new United States of America fell heir to all the old
practices and attitudes. Visions of our destiny did not include a healthy place for the Indians. The passage of years
and the complete removal of the savage menace, along
with the disappearance of the frontier, have had the effect
of romanticizing both the westward movement and the
resistance of the Indians to it. Here were two races, two
civilizations, two aspects of human nature in inevitable
conflict. The differences between red and white cultures
were irreconcilable. Pontiac was vainly opposing an evo-
lutionary force that could not be stayed; he and his people
were the victims of it.

Ethically, the conflict is not so simply defined. The
Indian had some just claims to his land and his way of
life, and the shameful efforts by whites to exploit and then
eradicate the savages brought the vaunted superiority of
our moral conduct into question at times. Only of late
has American admiration for the underdog or losing
fighter stirred us to a sneaking respect for an Indian like
Pontiac, who dared draw his bow against the British
lion. It was no wanton gesture. He had a cause to defend,
a dream of life as it should be, and, gambling on the possibility of success, he struck in the manner he knew best.
When he made his peace he kept it and resigned himself
to living with the invaders he could not eject. Savage
though he was, he never degenerated into a whining beg-
gar. The advancing frontier produced many worse examples of manhood, both red and white.

Pontiac appeared at a moment when the Indians desperately needed a champion who could think clearly, speak forcefully, and act decisively. By his program he gave full expression to the many injustices long suffered by his race. He typified the Indian attitude and empowered it with dignity, force, and direction. He earned the respect of a few of his white enemies. Viewed in history's perspective he still deserves it. He stood in our path for a moment and thrust us back, revealing the tragedy of his people and the cost of human progress. Then we pushed him aside, and the uncomfortable revelation passed. We pressed on with determination to achieve the promises of the New World.

The significance of Pontiac in history is not alone that he was a warrior of heroic proportions who set in motion the most formidable Indian resistance the English-speaking people had yet faced, or ever would face, on this continent. What Pontiac was as a symbol exceeded the actual results he achieved. In Indian history he unknowingly put a period to one epoch and opened another. He proved that savages could not defeat civilized men or hold back their settlement of a rich land hunted on by aborigines. Henceforth, the Indians would have to live *with* the white man and adjust themselves to his way of life. From this date the real tragedy of the Indian begins, for he could neither perceive the meaning of Pontiac's defeat and thereby prepare for the inevitable change nor obtain an honest and sympathetic policy from the alien government. Indian independence was a lost cause, its banner snatched from Pontiac. The Indian way of life was doomed. Steadily and relentlessly they would be pushed from place to place, generation by generation.

Acknowledgments

I AM UNDER FOREMOST OBLIGATION to Dr. Milo M. Quaife, editor of the Burton Historical Collection, Detroit Public Library, and long a student of early Detroit and the Old Northwest, and to Professor Theodore C. Pease, chairman of the history department of the University of Illinois, a thorough scholar of the Old West and particularly of the Illinois country. Both of these men read the biography in manuscript and offered much helpful comment on my assembled facts. They are not to be held responsible, however, for the interpretations I have given those facts.

Calvin Goodrich and W. Vernon Kinietz of the University of Michigan Museums were kind enough to examine several chapters each and to give me the benefit of their studies of early Michigan history and Indian life.

I am indebted to the late Allyn B. Forbes, librarian, and the Massachusetts Historical Society for making easily available to me the papers of Francis Parkman. Robert F. Britton of St. Louis was most helpful in searching out information for me in that city. Julian P. Boyd, when librarian of the Historical Society of Pennsylvania, brought George Croghan's diary to my attention and allowed me to make a copy of it, thereby meriting my warm acknowledgments.

I have worked in the Manuscript Division of the Library of Congress, the Ayer Collection of the Newberry Library, the Burton Historical Collection of the Detroit Public Library, the library of the Western Reserve Historical Society, the Indiana Historical Society Library, the Windsor Public Library, the Toledo Public Library, the *Detroit News* Library, and the Grand Rapids Public Library, and I retain pleasant memories of the assistance I received from various staff members. By correspondence I have drawn on the resources of the New York State Library, the State Historical Society of Wisconsin, the Missouri Historical Society, the Canadian Archives, the Historical Society of Western Pennsylvania, and the Darlington Memorial Library. I have also covered the ground of Pontiac's activities in seven states and the province of Ontario.

Most of the new material on Pontiac I found is among the historical manuscripts in the William L. Clements Library of the University of Michigan. Fortunately for the progress of my research, my position was as curator of those manuscripts. The books, newspapers, and old maps in this library were also of great value to me. My colleague, Colton Storm, helped me locate obscure places and assisted in preparing materials for illustration.

To the many persons who have checked details or answered troublesome inquiries for me, I wish to extend my thanks: Glenn A. Black of the Indiana Historical Society, Hugh Flick of the New York State Library, Stella M. Drumm of the Missouri Historical Society, Mary A. Givens and B. R. Johnstone of the Historical Society of Pennsylvania, Richard G. Morgan of the Ohio State Museum, Harlow Lindley of the Ohio Archaeological and Historical Society, Dr. Leonard Nippe of Toledo, A. J. H. Richardson of the Canadian Archives, the late Louise Phelps Kellogg of the State Historical Society of Wisconsin, Lois Mulkearn of the Darlington Memorial Library, Susan E. Lyman of the New-York Historical Society, F. F. Holbrook of the Historical Society of Western Pennsylvania, Margaret Dempster of the Western Reserve Historical Society, Ruth Lapham Butler and Stanley Pargellis of the Newberry Library, John R. Alden formerly of Michigan State Normal College, Edward B. Ham of the University of Michigan, Ralph H. Brown of the University of Minnesota, Frances E. Curtis of the *Detroit News* Library, Elinor Barteau of the Windsor Public Library, Mildred Shepherst of the Toledo Public Library, John Francis McDermott of Washington University, Curtis W. Garrison formerly of The Hayes Memorial, Raymond McCoy of Bay City, Edward S. Bronson and Ralph W. Peters of Defiance, Mrs. Harry T. Watts of Vincennes, Erminie Voegelin of Indiana University and Mrs. Mills Van Valkenburgh of Cadillac.

Dorothy Riker and Gayle Thornbrough of the Indiana Historical Bureau gave me great assistance in reading proof.

Finally, I wish to record my thanks to the two men who reacted so enthusiastically to my first proposals of this study: my former department head, Randolph G. Adams, and my friend, Carl Van Doren. They encouraged me to undertake the biography. And without the steady interest of my wife, who endured many silent evenings, I probably should not have finished it.

Bibliography

PRIMARY SOURCES

MANUSCRIPTS

Sir Jeffery Amherst Papers, Public Record Office, London. War Office, 34, microfilm copy in University of Michigan General Library; 7 volumes of originals in the Clements Library.

George Croghan's diary, 1758-1763, in the John Cadwalader Papers, Historical Society of Pennsylvania.

General Thomas Gage Papers, 180 volumes, Clements Library.

Lieut. Jehu Hay's diary, 1763-1765, Clements Library.

Lieut. James MacDonald letters, 1763, Clements Library.

Capt. Thomas Morris' diary, 1764, in the Gage Papers.

Francis Parkman Papers, volumes 22 to 27d on Pontiac's War, Massachusetts Historical Society.

John Porteous Journals, Burton Historical Collection, Detroit Public Library.

James Sterling's letter book, Clements Library.

Col. Charles Whittlesey Papers, Western Reserve Historical Society.

MAPS

Boishébert, Louis D. H., *Carte du détroit Erie montent jusquau Lac Huron*, c. 1733. Service Hydrographique, Paris; photostat in Karpinski Collection, No. 698, Clements Library.

Delisle, Guillaume, *Carte de la Louisiane et du Cours du Mississipi* . . . Paris, Juin, 1718.

Hutchins, Thomas, *A Tour from Fort Cumberland North Westward round part of the Lakes Erie, Huron and Michigan* . . . 1762. Original in Henry E. Huntington Library; photostat in the Clements Library.

De Lery, J. G. Chaussegros, *La Riviere du Détroit* . . . [inset] *Plan du Fort du Détroit*, 1752 and 1749, in Bellin's *Petit Atlas Maritime*, Paris, 1764.

————, *Carte de La Riviere de Détroit* . . . 1752, as redrawn by C. E. Hickman, Ann Arbor, 1930. Clements Library.

BIBLIOGRAPHY

Montresor, John, *Plan of Detroit with its Environs*, 1763. Clements Library.

"Aspinwall Papers" in *Collections* of the Massachusetts Historical Society, 4th Series, Volume IX.
The Papers of Col. Henry Bouquet, edited by Sylvester K. Stevens and Donald H. Kent. Pennsylvania Historical Commission, 1940-1943. 17 volumes.
"Cadillac Papers" in *Michigan Pioneer and Historical Collections*, Volume XXXIV.
The Writings of John Forbes, edited by A. P. James. Pennsylvania Historical Commission, 1938.
"The Gladwin Manuscripts" edited by Charles Moore in *Michigan Pioneer and Historical Collections*, Volume XXVII.
"Haldimand Papers" in *Michigan Pioneer and Historical Collections*, Volume XIX.
Illinois Historical Collections, Volumes IX-XVI.
The Papers of Sir William Johnson, edited by Sullivan, Flick, and Lauber. Albany, 1921—. 9 volumes.
"James Kenny's Journal to Ye Westward, 1758-59" edited by John W. Jordan, in *Pennsylvania Magazine of History and Biography*, Volume XXXVII.
"Report that the Sieur Passerat de la Chapelle . . . made to M. de Kerlerec . . . 1761" edited by Louise Phelps Kellogg, in *Mississippi Valley Historical Review*, Volume XXII.
John Montresor's "Expedition to Detroit" edited by J. C. Webster, in *Transactions of the Royal Society of Canada*, Section II, Series III, Volume XXII.
Robert Navarre's *Journal of the Conspiracy of Pontiac*, 1763, translated by R. Clyde Ford. Detroit, 1910.
Documents Relating to the Colonial History of the State of New-York, edited by Edmund B. O'Callaghan. Albany, 1853-1887. 15 volumes.
"Rutherford's Narrative—An Episode in the Pontiac War, 1763," in *Transactions of the Canadian Institute*, Volume III.
"An Account of the Captivity of Charles Stuart . . ." edited by Beverley W. Bond, Jr., in *Mississippi Valley Historical Review*, Volume XIII.
Travels in New France by J. C. B., edited by S. K. Stevens, D. H. Kent, and E. E. Woods. Pennsylvania Historical Commission, 1941.
"William Trent's Journal at Fort Pitt, 1763" edited by A. T. Volwiler in *Mississippi Valley Historical Review*, Volume XI.

BIBLIOGRAPHY

"Journal of Robert Rogers . . . 1760 to 1761" edited by Victor H. Paltsits, in *Bulletin* of the New York Public Library, April, 1933.

SECONDARY SOURCES

Anburey, Thomas, *Travels Through the Interior Parts of America.* London, 1789.

Anthon, C. E., *Narrative of the Settlement of George Christian Anthon in America.* New York, 1872.

Bâby, William Lewis, *Souvenirs of the Past.* Windsor, 1896.

Blackbird, Andrew J., *History of the Ottawa and Chippewa Indians of Michigan.* Ypsilanti, 1887.

Burgoyne, John, *State of the Expedition from Canada. . . .* London, 1780.

Burton, Clarence M., *The City of Detroit, Michigan, 1701-1922.* Chicago, 1922. 2 volumes.

Burton Historical Collection Leaflets. Detroit, 1922-1930. 11 volumes.

Butler, Lewis, *The Annals of the King's Royal Rifle Corps.* London, 1913. Volume I.

Canadian Historical Review.

Carver, Jonathan, *Travels Through the Interior Parts of North-America. . . .* London, 1778.

Cass, Lewis, *Discourse Delivered Before the Historical Society of Michigan.* Detroit, 1830.

Charlevoix, Pierre F. X. de, *History and General Description of New France,* translated and edited by John G. Shea. New York, 1866-1872. 6 volumes.

————, *Journal of a Voyage to North-America. . . .* London, 1761. 2 volumes.

Collet, Oscar W., "Notes on Parkman's Conspiracy of Pontiac" in *United States Catholic Historical Magazine,* Volume II.

Colton, C., *Tour of the American Lakes. . . .* London, 1833. 2 volumes.

Day, Richard E., *Calendar of the Sir William Johnson Manuscripts.* Albany, 1909.

De Peyster, Arent S., *Miscellanies, by an Officer.* New York, 1888. 2 volumes.

Downes, Randolph C., *Council Fires on the Upper Ohio.* Pittsburgh, 1940.

Drake, Samuel G., *Indian Biography. . . .* Boston, 1832.

Eldredge, Robert F., *Past and Present of Macomb County, Michigan.* Chicago, 1905.

⟨ 328 ⟩

Ellis, Edward S., *The Life of Pontiac*. . . . Beadle's Dime Biographical Library No. 7, New York and London, 1861.

Essex Historical Society, *Papers and Addresses*. 3 volumes.

Farmer, Silas, *A History of Detroit and Michigan*. Detroit, 1884. 4 volumes.

Featherstonhaugh, George William, *A Canoe Voyage up the Minnay Sotor*. . . . London, 1847. 2 volumes.

Fenwick, Charles G., *International Law*. New York and London, 1924.

Franklin, Benjamin, *Narrative of the Late Massacres in Lancaster County*. Philadelphia, 1764.

The Gentleman's Magazine. London, 1763.

Gipson, Lawrence Henry, *Zones of International Friction: The Great Lakes Frontier, Canada, The West Indies, India, 1748-1754*. (*The British Empire Before the American Revolution*, Volume v.) New York, 1942.

Goodrich, Calvin, *The First Michigan Frontier*. Ann Arbor, 1940.

Goodrich, Samuel G., *Lives of Celebrated American Indians*. New York, 1844.

Heineman, David E., "The Startling Experience of a Jewish Trader During Pontiac's Siege of Detroit in 1763" in *Publications of the American Jewish Historical Society*, No. 23.

Henry, Alexander, *Travels and Adventures in Canada*. . . . New York, 1809.

Heriot, George, *Travels Through the Canadas*. . . . London, 1807.

Hinsdale, Wilbert B., *The First People of Michigan*. Ann Arbor, 1930.

————, *Historical Atlas of Michigan*.

Hodge, Frederick W., ed., *Handbook of American Indians North of Mexico*. Bureau of American Ethnology Bulletin 30. Smithsonian Institution, Washington, 1907, 1910. 2 volumes.

Hough, Franklin B., ed., *Diary of the Siege of Detroit*. . . . Albany, 1860.

Howe, Henry, *Historical Collections of Virginia*. . . . Charleston, 1845.

Humphrey, Helen, "The Identity of Major Gladwin's Informant" in *Mississippi Valley Historical Review*, Volume xxi.

Hunt, George T., *The Wars of the Iroquois*. . . . Madison, 1940.

Indiana Historical Society Publications, Volume ii.

Jacker, Edward, "The Mental Capacity of the American Indian" in *American Catholic Quarterly Review*, Volume iii.

Kellogg, Louise Phelps, *The British Régime in Wisconsin and the Northwest*. Madison, 1935.

Kellogg, Louise Phelps, *The French Régime in Wisconsin and the Northwest*. Madison, 1925.

Kinietz, W. Vernon, *The Indians of the Western Great Lakes, 1615-1760*. Ann Arbor, 1940.

————, "Our Prehistoric Predecessors" in *Michigan Alumnus Quarterly Review*, Volume XLVI.

Knapp, H. S., *History of the Maumee Valley*. . . . Toledo, 1872.

Knox, John, *An Historical Journal of the Campaigns in North America* . . . edited by Arthur G. Doughty. Toronto, 1914. Volume 1.

Lanman, James H., *History of Michigan*. New York, 1839.

Leacock, Stephen, *Canada, the Foundations of its Future*. Montreal, 1941.

Long, J. C., *Lord Jeffery Amherst*. New York, 1933.

Lossing, Benson J., *Harper's Popular Cyclopedia of United States History*. New York, 1893. Volume 2.

————, *The Pictorial Field-Book of the War of 1812*. New York, 1869.

Loudon, Archibald, *A Selection of Some of the Most Interesting Narratives of Outrages*. . . . Carlisle, 1808, 1811. 2 volumes.

McCoy, Raymond, *The Massacre of Old Fort Mackinac*. 2nd edition. Bay City, 1939.

McKenney, Thomas, *Sketches of a Tour to the Lakes*. Baltimore, 1827.

Mante, Thomas, *The History of the Late War in North-America*. London, 1772.

Michigan History Magazine.

Michigan Pioneer and Historical Collections.

Mississippi Provincial Archives. English Dominions, Volume 1.

Mississippi Valley Historical Review.

Moore, Charles, *The Northwest Under Three Flags, 1635-1796*. New York and London, 1900.

Morris, Thomas, *Miscellanies in Prose and Verse*. London, 1791.

Nevins, Allan, ed., *Ponteach, a Tragedy*. . . . Chicago, 1914.

The New-York Gazette for 1763.

Nicollet, J. N., *Report Intended to Illustrate a Map of the Hydrographical Basin of the Upper Mississippi River* . . . *1841*. Washington, 1843.

Palmer, Friend, *Early Days in Detroit*. Detroit, 1906.

Pargellis, Stanley, *Military Affairs in North America, 1748-1765*. New York, 1936.

————, "Braddock's Defeat" in *American Historical Review*, Volume XLI.

Parkman, Francis, *History of the Conspiracy of Pontiac*. . . . Boston, 1851; 4th edition, 1868; 6th edition, 1870.

Parkman, Francis, *Montcalm and Wolfe*. Boston, 1937. 2 volumes.

Patterson, A. W., *History of the Backwoods*. Pittsburgh, 1843.

Peckham, Howard H., ed., *George Croghan's Journal of His Trip to Detroit in 1767*. Ann Arbor and London, 1939.

Pennsylvania Colonial Records, Volume VI.

The Pennsylvania Gazette for 1763 and 1764.

Pittman, Philip, *The Present State of the European Settlements on the Mississippi*. . . . London, 1770.

Radisson, Pierre Esprit, *Voyages* . . . edited by Gideon D. Scull. Boston, 1885.

Randall, E. O., and D. J. Ryan, *History of Ohio*. New York, 1912. 5 volumes.

Rogers, Robert, *A Concise Account of North America*. London, 1765.

————, *Journals*. . . . London, 1765.

Sargent, Winthrop, *The History of an Expedition Against Fort DuQuesne, in 1755*. Philadelphia, 1855.

Savelle, Max, *George Morgan, Colony Builder*. New York, 1932.

Schoolcraft, Henry R., *Algic Researches*. . . . New York, 1839.

————, *Narrative Journal of Travels from Detroit Northwest*. . . . Albany, 1821.

————, *Personal Memoirs of a Residence of Thirty Years with the Indian Tribes on the American Frontiers*. Philadelphia, 1851.

Seaver, James E., *A Narrative of the Life of Mrs. Mary Jemison*. . . . Canandaigua, 1824.

Seeley, Thaddeus D., *History of Oakland County, Michigan*. Chicago and New York, 1912.

Severance, Frank H., *An Old Frontier of France*. New York, 1917. 2 volumes.

Sheldon, Electa M., *The Early History of Michigan*. New York, 1856.

Shetrone, H. C., "The Indian of Ohio" in *Ohio Archaeological and Historical Journal*, Volume XXVII.

Slocum, C. E., *History of the Maumee River Basin*. . . . Indianapolis and Toledo, 1905.

Smith, William, *An Historical Account of the Expedition Against the Ohio Indians, in the Year 1764, Under the Command of Henry Bouquet*. Philadelphia, 1765.

Stevens, Walter B., *St. Louis the Fourth City, 1764-1909*. St. Louis, 1909.

Stone, William L., *Life and Times of Sir William Johnson*. Albany, 1865. 2 volumes.

Thatcher, B. B., *Indian Biography*. . . . New York, 1832.

⟨ 331 ⟩

Thwaites, Reuben Gold, ed., *Early Western Travels*. Cleveland, 1904. Volume 1.
Villiers du Terrage, Marc, baron de, *Les Dernières Années de La Louisiane Française*. Paris, 1904.
Volwiler, A. T., *George Croghan and the Westward Movement, 1741-1782*. Cleveland, 1926.
Wallace, Paul A. W., *Conrad Weiser*. . . . University of Pennsylvania, 1945.
Wimer, James, *Events in Indian History*. Philadelphia, 1842.
Winsor, Justin, *The Pageant of Saint Lusson, Sault Ste. Marie, 1671*. Ann Arbor, 1892.
Wisconsin Historical Collections.
Wissler, Clark, *The American Indian*. 3rd edition. New York, 1938.
Wood, Edwin O., *Historic Mackinac*. New York, 1918. 2 volumes.

Bibliographical Note

The following volumes, published since the bibliography at the end of this book was compiled, include additional primary source material on Pontiac's War: Milton W. Hamilton, ed., *The Papers of Sir William Johnson*, vol. 13 (Albany, 1962), which is an addenda to the twelve-volume series published previously; Sylvester K. Stevens, Donald H. Kent, and Louis M. Waddell, eds., *The Papers of Henry Bouquet*, 7 vols. (Harrisburg, Pa., 1951–); Edward G. Williams, ed., *The Orderly of Colonel Henry Bouquet's Expedition against the Ohio Indians, 1764.* (Pittsburgh, 1960), and *Bouquet's March to Ohio: The Forbes Road* (Pittsburgh, 1975), "The Orderly Book of Colonel Henry Bouquet's Road, 1764: Samuel Finley's Field Notes," also in *Western Penna. Historical Magazine* (July 1983–April 1984).

Secondary sources referred to in the introduction include: John R. Cuneo, *Robert Rogers of the Rangers* (N.Y., 1959); Gregory Evans Dowd, *A Spirited Resistance, The North American Indian Struggle for Unity, 1745–1815* (Baltimore, 1992); Michael N. McConnell, *A Country Between, The Upper Ohio and Its Peoples, 1724–1774* (Lincoln, Neb., 1992); John Shy, *Toward Lexington, The Role of the British Army in the Coming of the American Revolution* (Princeton, 1965); Nicholas B. Wainwright, *George Croghan, Wilderness Diplomat* (Chapel Hill, 1959).

Index

d'Abbadie, Gov., quoted on Pontiac, 251; opposes him, 267; opposes Kaské, 268; dies, 268

Abbott, Edward, with Dalyell, 204, 207; on patrol, 232

Abenakies, 249

Abraham, Chapman, captured, 141; surrendered, 198

Alabama Mingo, Choctaw chief, 266

Allegheny River, 37, 38, 44, 50

Allerton, Ill., 281

Allouez, Claude, 7

Amherst, Sir Jeffery, 56, 58, 74; character, 57; Indian policy, 70, 71-72, 81, 88, 93, 177, 225, 226, 227; learns of Indian uprising, 171-175; learns of Bushy Run and Dalyell's defeat, 228; letter to Bouquet, 226, 227; to Egremont, 177; to Gladwin, 175, 226, 228; promotes Gladwin, 228; proposes using smallpox, 226; puts bounty on Pontiac, 227, 228; quoted, 81, 87, 88, 172-173, 173-174, 175, 177; returns to England, 242

Anaiasa, Huron chief, 82, 86

Anderson, Robert, 204

Anthon, Dr. George Christian, 66, 286n

Arkansaws, 267, 275, 298

Ashtabula Creek, 59

Askin, John, 124, 317

Atawang, Ottawa chief, at Maumee village, 252; entertains Morris, 257; sells him a Shakespeare, 259; goes to Detroit, 258; confers with Bradstreet, 261

Aubry, Charles Philippe, 268

Aughstaghregi, Huron chief, 290

Avoyelles, 245

Baby, Francis, 15n, 123

Baby, Jacques Duperon, 123, 140, 204

baggataway, see lacrosse

Balfour, Henry, 89, 90

Banks, Ens., 290

Barthe, Pierre, 193

Basset, Henry, quoted, 124-125

Baynton, Wharton, and Morgan, 310

Beaujeu, Daniel de, 41, 43

Beaujeu, Louis de, 89, 235

beaver trade, see fur trade

Belle Isle, see Isle au Cochon

Bellestre, François de, 62, 147, 248; surrenders Fort Pontchartrain, 63-64; sent to Fort Pitt, 65; related to Cuillerier, 79

Big Jaw, Huron chief, 107

Blackbird, Andrew J., 19

Black Boys, 279

Black Dog, see Makatachinga

Black Hawk, Sauk chief, 320

Blain, James, 204

Lower Shawnee Town, 304
Luke, John, 204, 207

Macatepilesis, Ottawa chief, at
  Detroit council, 82; collects
  powder, 140; messenger, 117;
  quoted, 83-84; visits Detroit,
  130n, 133
Macaulay, Lord, quoted, 40
McCormick, Caesar, see Cor-
  mick
McCullough, John, 98
MacDonald, James, 69, 204,
  208, 233
McDougall, George, 198; ac-
  companies Campbell, 138;
  held prisoner, 139; escapes,
  194; with Dalyell, 204, 207
Mackinac, Ottawa chief, 33,
  153
Mackinac Straits, 6, 7, 8, 9
McLeod, Norman, 91, 290,
  297
Mahiganne, an Ottawa, 123
Maiet, John, 301, 302
Maisonville, Mr., 307
Makatachinga, Peoria chief,
  310, 315
Manitou, Ottawa chief, 301;
  favors peace, 232; talks with
  Gladwin, 234; undermines
  Pontiac, 252
Maryland frontier raided, 216
Mascoutens, 86; capture Croghan, 280; help capture Fort
  Ouiatenon, 161; Pontiac
  visits, 244; settle at Detroit,
  8; submit to Croghan, 283;
  visit Fort de Chartres, 273
Matchekewis, Chippewa chief,
  164
Maumee River, 91, 160; Morris
  travels on, 257-259; Pontiac
  travels on, 244; two villages
  on, 252, 284

Mehemah, Ottawa chief, 54, 59
Meloche, Jean Baptiste, 135;
  his house used, 141, 144,
  190, 205
Menominees, 90, 165, 253
Messeaghage, Ottawa chief, 53
Meurin, Father, 311n, 313
Meyer, Elias, 91, 95
Miamies, 7, 16; location, 8, 30,
  35; attacked by Ottawas, 8;
  give up war belt, 106; go to
  Fort Pitt, 56; help take Fort
  Miamis, 160; kill Frenchmen, 8; Morris visits, 259-
  260; Pontiac visits, 244; submit to Croghan, 283
Michigameas, 269, 307
Michigan, 1, 35, 107
Michigan, sloop, 127; attacked,
  189; arrives at Niagara, 222;
  avoids fire rafts, 198; news of
  return, 188; sails to Niagara,
  157, 210; sent down river,
  149, 156; reaches Detroit,
  190; shells Pontiac's camp,
  196; wrecked by storm, 222;
  taken apart, 223
Minavavana, Chippewa chief,
  164, 265, 316
Mindoghquay, Chippewa chief,
  184
Mingoes, 39, 56; attack Clapham's, 166; yield to Bouquet, 263
Mississaughi-Chippewas, asked
  to council, 304; capture
  traders, 182; census, 30; included in Bradstreet's peace,
  262; join Pontiac, 149, 182
Missouri River, 10, 244, 310
Missouries, 269
Mohawk River, 51, 178
Mohawks, 81, 84, 229
Monckton, Robert, 58, 69
Moncrieffe, Thomas, 241

TITLES IN THE GREAT LAKES BOOKS SERIES

Detroit Images: Photographs of the Renaissance City, edited by John J. Bukowczyk and Douglas Aikenhead, with Peter Slavcheff, 1989

Hangdog Reef: Poems Sailing the Great Lakes, by Stephen Tudor, 1989

Detroit: City of Race and Class Violence, revised edition, by B. J. Widick, 1989

Deep Woods Frontier: A History of Logging in Northern Michigan, by Theodore J. Karamanski, 1989

Orvie, The Dictator of Dearborn, by David L. Good, 1989

Seasons of Grace: A History of the Catholic Archdiocese of Detroit, by Leslie Woodcock Tentler, 1990

The Pottery of John Foster: Form and Meaning, by Gordon and Elizabeth Orear, 1990

The Diary of Bishop Frederic Baraga: First Bishop of Marquette, Michigan, edited by Regis M. Walling and Rev. N. Daniel Rupp, 1990

Walnut Pickles and Watermelon Cake: A Century of Michigan Cooking, by Larry B. Massie and Priscilla Massie, 1990

The Making of Michigan, 1820–1860: A Pioneer Anthology, edited by Justin L. Kesten-baum, 1990

America's Favorite Homes: A Guide to Popular Early Twentieth-Century Homes, by Robert Schweitzer and Michael W. R. Davis, 1990

Beyond the Model T: The Other Ventures of Henry Ford, by Ford R. Bryan, 1990

Life after the Line, by Josie Kearns, 1990

Michigan Lumbertowns: Lumbermen and Laborers in Saginaw, Bay City, and Muskegon, 1870–1905, by Jeremy W. Kilar, 1990

Detroit Kids Catalog: The Hometown Tourist, by Ellyce Field, 1990

Waiting for the News, by Leo Litwak, 1990 (reprint)

Detroit Perspectives, edited by Wilma Wood Henrickson, 1991

Life on the Great Lakes: A Wheelsman's Story, by Fred W. Dutton, edited by William Donohue Ellis, 1991

Copper Country Journal: The Diary of Schoolmaster Henry Hobart, 1863–1864, by Henry Hobart, edited by Philip P. Mason, 1991

John Jacob Astor: Business and Finance in the Early Republic, by John Denis Haeger, 1991

Survival and Regeneration: Detroit's American Indian Community, by Edmund J. Danziger, Jr., 1991

Steamboats and Sailors of the Great Lakes, by Mark L. Thompson, 1991

Cobb Would Have Caught It: The Golden Age of Baseball in Detroit, by Richard Bak, 1991

Michigan in Literature, by Clarence Andrews, 1992

Under the Influence of Water: Poems, Essays, and Stories, by Michael Delp, 1992

The Country Kitchen, by Della T. Lutes, 1992 (reprint)

The Making of a Mining District: Keweenaw Native Copper 1500–1870, by David J. Krause, 1992

Kids Catalog of Michigan Adventures, by Ellyce Field, 1993

Henry's Lieutenants, by Ford R. Bryan, 1993

Historic Highway Bridges of Michigan, by Charles K. Hyde, 1993

Lake Erie and Lake St. Clair Handbook, by Stanley J. Bolsenga and Charles E. Herndendorf, 1993

Queen of the Lakes, by Mark Thompson, 1994

Iron Fleet: The Great Lakes in World War II, by George J. Joachim, 1994

Turkey Stearnes and the Detroit Stars: The Negro Leagues in Detroit, 1919–1933, by Richard Bak, 1994

Pontiac and the Indian Uprising, by Howard H. Peckham, 1994 (reprint)

Charting the Inland Seas: A History of the U.S. Lake Survey, by Arthur M. Woodford, 1994 (reprint)

Ojibwa Narratives of Charles and Charlotte Kawbawgam and Jacques LePique, 1893–1895. Recorded with Notes by Homer H. Kidder, edited by Arthur P. Bourgeois, 1994, co-published with the Marquette County Historical Society

Strangers and Sojourners: A History of Michigan's Keweenaw Peninsula, by Arthur W. Thurner, 1994

Win Some, Lose Some: G. Mennen Williams and the New Democrats, by Helen Washburn Berthelot, 1995

Sarkis, by Gordon and Elizabeth Orear, 1995

The Northern Lights: Lighthouses of the Upper Great Lakes, by Charles K. Hyde, 1995 (reprint)

Kids Catalog of Michigan Adventures, second edition, by Ellyce Field, 1995

Rumrunning and the Roaring Twenties: Prohibition on the Michigan-Ontario Waterway, by Philip P. Mason, 1995

In the Wilderness with the Red Indians, by E. R. Baierlein, translated by Anita Z. Boldt, edited by Harold W. Moll, 1996

Elmwood Endures: History of a Detroit Cemetery, by Michael Franck, 1996

Master of Precision: Henry M. Leland, by Mrs. Wilfred C. Leland with Minnie Dubbs Millbrook, 1996 (reprint)

Haul-Out: New and Selected Poems, by Stephen Tudor, 1996

Kids Catalog of Michigan Adventures, third edition, by Ellyce Field, 1997

Beyond the Model T: The Other Ventures of Henry Ford, revised edition, by Ford R. Bryan, 1997

Young Henry Ford: A Picture History of the First Forty Years, by Sidney Olson, 1997 (reprint)

The Coast of Nowhere: Meditations on Rivers, Lakes and Streams, by Michael Delp, 1997

From Saginaw Valley to Tin Pan Alley: Saginaw's Contribution to American Popular Music, 1890–1955, by R. Grant Smith, 1998

The Long Winter Ends, by Newton G. Thomas, 1998 (reprint)

Bridging the River of Hatred: The Pioneering Efforts of Detroit Police Commissioner George Edwards, by Mary M. Stolberg, 1998

Toast of the Town: The Life and Times of Sunnie Wilson, by Sunnie Wilson with John Cohassey, 1998

These Men Have Seen Hard Service: The First Michigan Sharpshooters in the Civil War, by Raymond J. Herek, 1998

A Place for Summer: One Hundred Years at Michigan and Trumbull, by Richard Bak, 1998

Early Midwestern Travel Narratives: An Annotated Bibliography, 1634–1850, by Robert R. Hubach, 1998 (reprint)

All-American Anarchist: Joseph A. Labadie and the Labor Movement, by Carlotta R. Anderson, 1998

Michigan in the Novel, 1816–1996: An Annotated Bibliography, by Robert Beasecker, 1998

"Time by Moments Steals Away": The 1848 Journal of Ruth Douglass, by Robert L. Root, Jr., 1998

The Detroit Tigers: A Pictorial Celebration of the Greatest Players and Moments in Tigers' History, updated edition, by William M. Anderson, 1999

Father Abraham's Children: Michigan Episodes in the Civil War, by Frank B. Woodford, 1999 (reprint)

Letter from Washington, 1863–1865, by Lois Bryan Adams, edited and with an introduction by Evelyn Leasher, 1999

Wonderful Power: The Story of Ancient Copper Working in the Lake Superior Basin, by Susan R. Martin, 1999

A Sailor's Logbook: A Season aboard Great Lakes Freighters, by Mark L. Thompson, 1999

Huron: The Seasons of a Great Lake, by Napier Shelton, 1999

Tin Stackers: The History of the Pittsburgh Steamship Company, by Al Miller, 1999

Art in Detroit Public Places, revised edition, text by Dennis Nawrocki, photographs by David Clements, 1999

Brewed in Detroit: Breweries and Beers Since 1830, by Peter H. Blum, 1999

Detroit Kids Catalog: A Family Guide for the 21st Century, by Ellyce Field, 2000

"Expanding the Frontiers of Civil Rights": Michigan, 1948–1968, by Sidney Fine, 2000

Graveyard of the Lakes, by Mark L. Thompson, 2000

Enterprising Images: The Goodridge Brothers, African American Photographers, 1847–1922, by John Vincent Jezierski, 2000

New Poems from the Third Coast: Contemporary Michigan Poetry, edited by Michael Delp, Conrad Hilberry, and Josie Kearns, 2000

Arab Detroit: From Margin to Mainstream, edited by Nabeel Abraham and Andrew Shryock, 2000

The Sandstone Architecture of the Lake Superior Region, by Kathryn Bishop Eckert, 2000